Adult ESL/Literacy

From the Community
to the Community

A Guidebook for Participatory Literacy Training

Oral English Proficiency Program
Purdue University

Adult ESL/Literacy

From the Community
to the Community

A Guidebook for Participatory Literacy Training

by Elsa Auerbach
University of Massachusetts at Boston

with
Byron Barahona, Julio Midy, Felipe Vaquerano, Ana Zambrano, & Joanne Arnaud

based on a collaboration between:
The University of Massachusetts at Boston
The Haitian Multi-Service Center
The Harborside Community Center
The Jackson-Mann Community Center
The Boston Adult Literacy Fund

LEA

LAWRENCE ERLBAUM ASSOCIATES, PUBLISHERS
1996   Mahwah, New Jersey

The contents of this book were partially developed under two grants, Grant No. X257A20021 from the National Institute for Literacy, and Grant No. D/ED T003V90080 from the U. S. Department of Education. However, those contents do not necessarily represent the policy of the National Institute for Literacy or the U.S. Department of Education and you should not assume endorsement by the Federal Government.

Correspondence regarding this book and the projects described in it can be directed to:

Elsa Auerbach
English Dept.
University of Massachusetts/Boston
Boston, MA 02125

Joanne Arnaud
Boston Adult Literacy Fund
666 Boylston St.
Boston, MA 02116

Correspondence regarding specific components can be directed as follows:

Haitian Creole literacy component:
Haitian Multi-Service Center
Adult Education Program
12 Bicknell St.
Dorchester, MA 02121

ESL component:
Jackson-Mann Community School
500 Cambridge St.
Allston, MA 02134

Spanish literacy component:
Harborside Community School
312 Border St.
East Boston, MA 02128

Lawrence Erlbaum Associates, Inc., Publishers
10 Industrial Avenue
Mahwah, New Jersey 07430

Library of Congress Cataloging-in-Publication Data

Adult ESL/literacy from the community to the community: a guidebook for participatory literacy training/ by Elsa Auerbach ... [et al.].
    p.   cm.
    Includes bibliographical references (p.   ).
    ISBN 0-8058-2267-4 (pbk. : alk. paper)
    1. English language--Study and teaching--Foreign speakers-
-Handbooks, manuals, etc. 2. English language--Adult education-
-Handbooks, manuals, etc. 3. Literacy programs--United States-
-Handbooks, manuals, etc. 4. Community life--United States-
-Handbooks, manuals, etc.   I. Auerbach, Elsa.
PE1128.A2A324 1996
428' .007--dc20

95-40919
CIP

Books published by Lawrence Erlbaum Associates are printed on acid-free paper and their bindings are chosen for strength and durability.

Printed in the United States of America

10 9 8 7 6 5 4 3 2 1

Foreword

Communities as sources of knowledge and producers of new knowledge are usually unrecognized, underestimated, and underutilized by educators. In the case of immigrant communities, their expertise is also lost under the misunderstanding of language and cultural barriers. *Adult ESL/Literacy From the Community to the Community: A Guidebook for Participatory Literacy Training* is an example of how, in a collaborative and participatory educational project, community needs are addressed by community resources, using the language(s) of the community and the expertise of its membership. The importance of this model is that, in addition to validating community knowledge, it contributes to community development.

The narrative of the book is easily accessible to practitioners, policymakers, and community members. It combines the personal experiences of community participants, Mentors and Interns with the theoretical and philosophical arguments that serve as the tenets of the model. The complex issues addressed—those of maintaining an authentic, unedited voice, of implementing a truly democratic, participatory curriculum for community participants and teachers-in-training, and of maintaining an equal collaborative model between a university and three community organizations—are of great value to those concerned with egalitarian and democratic practices in education.

At a time when immigrants are under attack and their communities are in danger of losing the few economic resources they have, inviting community residents to educate themselves and their communities is of paramount importance. Training community residents to further the education of their own communities not only helps meet community demands for services, but also contributes to community development by creating jobs in the community rather than draining it of its resources. In addition, when using a participatory curriculum that addresses the needs of adult participants, community teachers are of great value because they have a shared history; they live and face the same issues with other members of the community. This engenders a curriculum that truly addresses the needs of the community and its members.

From the Community to the Community also addresses the use of the linguistic and cultural resources of the community by implementing curriculum in the language(s) of the participants. It acknowledges the uses of literacy for real life— that literacy has purposes and meets goals, and that it plays a role in the everyday lives of the participants as family members, immigrants, community residents, and social agents.

The use of the native language in a participatory educational project not only facilitates the learning of English as a Second Language, but also opens the possibility for adults to serve as agents of change in public schools. At El Barrio Popular Education Program, for example, adult participants are critically analyzing and investigating how their participation in an adult literacy program is impacting their relationship to their children. Preliminary findings show that children are learning to appreciate their mothers' efforts to acquire an education and that this affects their own involvement with education. They also show that the mothers are getting more involved with their children's education, both at home by doing homework together, and in the community at large by exercising their rights to demand better education for their children. The adults are documenting these research findings in a video that will be available to the community at large and thus, making this knowledge immediately available to the community. This type of project can be viable when adult participants are able to voice their concerns and address their issues in the language they feel comfortable in and the language that is of predominant use in the community. In this way language is used to further education and promote change.

Finally, *From the Community to the Community* offers a new way of looking at teacher training; it reminds us that, in order not to replicate traditional educational models that fail to take into consideration the learners, it is important to design teacher training models that practice participatory education to allow teachers to learn by experiencing the model of action-reflection. By informing the readers of the experiences of the three programs in Boston, this book also validates and disseminates the work of small, participatory, native language literacy programs in ethnic and minority communities in the United States and in countries in Latin America, Africa, and Asia.

Klaudia M. Rivera
El Barrio Popular Education Program
New York City

Contents

Acknowledgments

This book is truly the product of a group effort. The projects that it describes were in many ways the brain child of the staff at participating adult education sites. Key administrative personnel at these sites contributed many hours to developing and implementing the projects as well as the model on which they are based. Special thanks go to Kathleen O'Connell and Paul Trunell of the Harborside Community Center (HCC), Mary Davies and Shelley Bourgeois of the Jackson-Mann Community School (JMCS), and Jean-Marc Jean-Baptiste and Carol Chandler of the Haitian Multi-Service Center (HMSC). Many other people at the sites also deserve thanks for their dedication and commitment to the projects. In particular, the Interns contributed many hours of their own time beyond the call of duty. Project Mentors, Julio Midy, Ana Zambrano, and Felipe Vaquerano played a key role in shaping the structure of the report and provided critical comments on each section as it was drafted. The work of Byron Barahona and Eugenie Ballering was also critical to the development of the model described in this book. We would also like to thank Klaudia Rivera, Cathy Walsh, Kathy Brucker, Loren McGrail, and Maria Gonzales for joining us to facilitate workshops.

Joanne Arnaud, the Executive Director of the Boston Adult Literacy Fund, deserves particular gratitude, not only for her insightful and timely assistance with the writing of the report, but also for her constant good cheer at every step in the implementation process. She was, in many ways, the midwife of this Guidebook, providing key support from its inception until its completion.

Several people at the University of Massachusetts at Boston provided invaluable support in implementing the projects. We are grateful to Dr. Donaldo Macedo, Director of the UMass Bilingual/ESL Graduate Studies Program (BES) for writing the proposal for the Bilingual Community Literacy Training Project through which the collaboration between the sites was initiated. Pam Price gave tireless and meticulous attention to the details of day-to-day work, as well as to transcription of the tapes. Fernando Colina provided critical technical assistance with computer matters, including rescuing project documents (and project staff!) at various points. Barbara Graceffa made space for our work in her busy schedule and busy office. We cannot thank them enough. Finally, Marc Prou, also on the BES faculty, deserves special mention for his key role in the supporting the development of Haitian Creole literacy instruction in the Boston area through a pioneering course in Creole linguistics that he taught at UMass/Boston in the early 1980s. One of his students, Jean-Marc Jean-Baptiste, originated the Creole literacy component at the HMSC.

Additional thanks go to Susan Lytle, Trudy Smoke, and James Tollefson for their thoughtful and timely reviews of the manuscript. Finally, we would like to thank our editor, Naomi Silverman, for enthusiastically embracing this project, editing the manuscript with sensitivity and respect for its intent, and moving the publication process quickly. It was a joy to work with her.

Preface: What is this Guidebook?

The need for adult literacy and ESL services within immigrant and refugee communities in the United States cannot be disputed. The National Adult Literacy Survey dramatically underscores the extent of this need with its finding that 25% of those performing in the lowest proficiency level were immigrants. At adult education centers across the U.S., these statistics translate into long waiting lists, large classes, inadequate resources, and pressure to move students through programs quickly. More and more of the students coming to the centers for ESL classes have had little chance to go to school in their own countries and are unable to read and write in their first languages. Teachers who are unfamiliar with the languages and cultures of these students often feel overwhelmed and underprepared. Clearly, the question facing policymakers, administrators, and teachers is not whether there is a need for adult ESL and literacy services, but how this need can best be met.

At the same time, however, resources within the communities of the learners often go unrecognized. Refugee and immigrant communities are rich with people who have strong educational backgrounds in their own languages and a desire to contribute to their communities. Because they have shared the experiences of coming to a new country, they are intimately familiar with the needs and concerns of literacy students, as well as with issues of cultural and linguistic transition. Yet they are often unable to make use of their strengths because of limitations in their English ability or lack of formal credentials; even as their English improves, it is difficult for them to find meaningful work or to access higher education. Thus, it is not uncommon for highly skilled, community-minded immigrants and refugees to find themselves working on assembly lines or cleaning offices.

This Guidebook describes a model for drawing on and enhancing the strengths of this latter group of immigrants and refugees in order to address the needs of those with minimal prior education, ESL, or literacy. It is a model based on the principle of *from the community to the community* in which community needs are addressed by community resources. The book documents a collaboration between three adult education programs that worked with the University of Massachusetts at Boston and the Boston Adult Literacy Fund to develop, implement, and evaluate a project designed to train immigrants and refugees as adult ESL and native language literacy instructors in their own communities.

What is the "from the community to the community" model?

The model described in this Guidebook has several key features:

community leadership development	Immigrants and refugees from the communities of the learners are trained to teach ESL and literacy in their own communities. Outstanding language minority adult literacy teachers are trained as Mentors; they, in turn, participate in training immigrant and refugee Interns who have demonstrated commitment to their communities as adult students, community activists, or tutors. Thus, the project develops leaders who come from the community and go back to the community.
participatory approach to literacy instruction	The approach to teaching literacy is participatory. Adult learners participate in setting goals, identifying needs, choosing learning activities, and evaluating progress. The curriculum content focuses on the learners' experiences and concerns. Because the teachers come from the learners' communities, they are able to understand the social problems learners face and work with them to address these problems.
participatory approach to instructor training	Likewise, the approach to training Interns is participatory: Interns identify their goals and needs, shape the direction of the training, and evaluate its usefulness. Training content is drawn from the interests, experiences, and concerns of participants.
native language adult literacy instruction	Adult immigrants and refugees who have little prior education and minimal literacy proficiency in their native language are taught basic literacy in their native language as a basis for ESL instruction. Once they have acquired this basic literacy proficiency, they make the transition to ESL through bilingual literacy instruction.
collaboration	Community-based organizations work with each other and with a university so that they can learn from each other's experiences, share expertise, and address common concerns collaboratively.

What was our project?

The model described in this Guidebook is based on a university-community collaboration designed to train literacy instructors from immigrant and refugee communities to teach in their own communities. Three community-based agencies in the Boston area were involved in the project:

- **the Harborside Community Center** (HCC) in East Boston,, which serves a large Central American population

- **the Haitian Multi-Service Center** (HMSC) in Dorchester, which serves Haitian immigrants and refugees

- **the Jackson-Mann Community School** (JMCS) in Allston, which serves over 26 different nationality and language groups.

The collaboration was funded from 1989 to 1992 by the Office of Bilingual Education and Minority Language Affairs (OBEMLA) of the U.S. Department of Education as the Bilingual Community Literacy Training Project (BCLTP) and then, from 1992 to 1993 by the National Institute for Literacy as the Community Training for Adult and Family Literacy (CTAFL) Project. The **Boston Adult Literacy Fund** (BALF), an organization that secures funding for the Boston adult literacy community, was the grant recipient and fiscal administrator for the CTAFL. The Project Coordinator was a faculty member at the **University of Massachusetts at Boston** (UMass/Boston), continuing a six-year history of collaboration between the university and local community-based literacy sites.

Through the project, Mentors from each of the agencies worked with Interns from the communities of the learners. Training took place both at the sites and at UMass/Boston. The site-based component consisted of on-going mentoring in the classrooms and weekly teacher-sharing meetings. The university-based component consisted of biweekly workshops for all of the Interns and Mentors.

The adult literacy instruction at each of the sites was designed to meet specific needs of the surrounding communities. Because there is a growing population of Haitians and Central Americans with little prior education or literacy background in Dorchester and East Boston, the project provided initial literacy instruction in Haitian Creole at the HMSC and in Spanish at the HCC. Because of the diversity of language and literacy backgrounds at the JMCS, instruction focused on beginning ESL there.

Who are we?

Before we tell more of the story of our project, we need to say a little about who we are and what we believe. The "we" in this book generally refers to the project staff, which included three Mentor Teachers (one from each of the sites) and the Project Coordinator. The Mentors are immigrants or refugees who come from the communities of the learners and share many experiences with them. Although the stories of the Mentors are told in more depth in Chapter Two, we'll introduce ourselves briefly here to give you a sense of our backgrounds:

•**Felipe Vaquerano,** the Mentor at Harborside, is Salvadoran. He began studying ESL at the JMCS in 1989 while working in a factory. In 1991, during the BCLTP, he became an ESL Intern at the JMCS, and went on to become the Mentor at Harborside in the CTAFL project.

•**Julio Midy,** the Mentor at the HMSC, is Haitian. Like Felipe, he started working in a factory; he has been an ESL teacher at the HMSC since 1985, and was the Master Teacher for the Creole literacy component of the BCLTP.

•**Ana Zambrano,** the Mentor at the JMCS, is Colombian. Before coming to the U.S. in 1984, she was an adult literacy worker in Colombia. She started studying ESL in a church in East Boston. She has taught ESL for 7 years, and was Master Teacher at the JMCS for the BCLTP.

•**Elsa Auerbach,** the Project Coordinator, is a North American whose parents were refugees from Germany. She too worked in a factory for several years before being hired as a part-time ESL teacher at UMass/Boston. She has coordinated several other university-community collaborative projects.

The "we" in this Guidebook also includes Joanne Arnaud, the Executive Director of BALF, who was very much a part of the project, as well as the Interns who were trained in the project. The Interns, like the Mentors, came from the communities of the learners and shared many of their background experiences. Most of them had been ESL students at the sites and/or at UMass. The Interns at HCC were Central American; those at the HMSC were Haitian; one of the Interns at the JMCS was Honduran, and the other was Peruvian of Japanese descent. Their histories are discussed further in Chapter Two.

What is our philosophy?

Although project staff had different backgrounds and experiences, through our work together, we came to share several basic beliefs about literacy education. These beliefs shaped the model and guided the training.

about the adult learners...	*We believe that the starting point for working with adult learners is respecting their knowledge and their experiences.* When adults come to ESL or literacy classes, it's already uncomfortable for them, at their age, not to know how to read and write, or not to be able to express themselves in English. We believe it is important to show them their own capacity to learn by drawing out what they already know and using their stories and experiences to teach them. The message they get should be, "You may not know how to read and write but that doesn't mean you don't have something to offer."
about the teacher's role...	*We believe that the relationship between teachers and students must be one of mutual respect in which they learn from each other.* This means breaking away from the traditional approach in which the teacher knows everything and it is his or her job to *give* this knowledge to the students. If the teacher is seen as the only one with something to offer, learners will feel less comfortable.
about literacy...	*We believe literacy practices vary according to cultures and social contexts.* Literacy is more than just a set of discrete, mechanical skills or functional competencies. Teaching must take into account culture-specific ways of using and understanding literacy; it must focus not on isolated skills but on socially significant literacy uses in learners' lives. Meaning is more important than form in literacy instruction.
about the goal of teaching...	*We believe that good literacy education means more than just teaching students to read and write.* What is important is how they can use what they learn to get involved in issues that affect their lives. Immigrants and refugees face many problems: being unable to find work, dealing with discrimination on the job, raising children in a new country, maintaining communication with their families at home, and more. We believe that education should enable participants to understand the social nature of these problems (rather than seeing them as personal problems or inadequacies) and to work together in finding ways to address them.
about the content of classes...	*We believe that students learn best when content is related to their own experiences.* They are able to do more when learning builds on what they know. This means that the curriculum comes from within the classroom. It draws on their own cultural and

personal histories: as such, the content doesn't have to be related only to life in the U.S.; it can also include telling, writing, and reading stories about their own countries and cultures.

about family literacy...

We believe that any literacy work that supports parents in their efforts to make a better life for their families is family literacy. Family literacy means much more than parents reading bedtime stories or helping children with homework; family literacy includes whatever strengthens communication within families and enables parents to advocate for family needs. Rather than imposing family literacy content through the instruction of particular practices or lessons, teachers should integrate family literacy concerns throughout the curriculum as they arise organically.

about the native language...

We believe that students' first language should be seen as a resource, not an obstacle, for literacy or ESL acquisition. Beginning literacy students can use their existing oral language as the basis for learning how to read and write. They can use first language (L1) literacy as a bridge to ESL. In ESL classes, students can decide when and how to use their first language to support learning English.

about methods and materials...

We believe that a variety of methods and materials should be used in classes. Because of past experiences, learners (and sometimes teachers) may expect teacher-centered and textbook-based classes focusing on mechanical and rote learning. However, relevant, engaging instruction entails interaction, meaning-based activities, and learner-generated materials. Thus, to reconcile students' expectations and teachers' styles in an effective approach, traditional and nontraditional methods should be integrated.

about teachers...

We believe that people who share the culture, language, and life experiences of the learners are uniquely qualified to teach them. A shared background can enable teachers to know what is relevant to students, how to make them feel comfortable, and how to draw out their concerns. We believe that these qualifications should be recognized and enhanced; committed immigrants and refugees who don't have credentials (or can't afford higher education) should be given the opportunity to utilize and develop their skills.

about training...

We believe that teacher training should be participatory. The knowledge and experience of trainees should be an integral part of training. As such, our view of training is similar to our view of teaching. Mentors and Interns should learn from each other so that everyone's expertise is valued. Training should emphasize dialogue, sharing, and investigation, rather than transmitting knowledge or prescribing teaching practices. The content of workshops should build on participants' classroom experience.

Why did we write this Guidebook and who is it for?

The first thing we should say about our model is that it is nothing new! The ideas of participatory literacy education and native language adult literacy are widely accepted in many parts of the world, especially in Asia, Africa, and Latin America. In particular, the idea that teachers should come from the communities of the learners is the basis for most literacy campaigns around the world. It is only in the U.S. (and other industrialized countries) that this practice is not the norm. Thus, one of our main goals is to make this model more accessible in the U.S.

to tell our story...

The first purpose of this Guidebook is to tell the story of how we adapted and implemented this model on a small scale in a North American context. In it, we have compiled and evaluated our own experiences in order to give other teachers and programs the chance to see what we did, what worked well, and what didn't. We were fortunate that our funding agency (the National Institute for Literacy) suggested that grant recipients write a final report that would be useful to practitioners. We see the Guidebook as a way to present our communities and our projects to the outside, especially to other education centers and people who are doing the same job we are doing.

to provide guidance...

Thus, in addition to presenting what we have done, we hope that it will be a reference for teachers, to help you serve your students better. We hope that others who are considering implementing a similar training project will use our experience as a guide. However, as Julio said, *"the Guidebook is not a Bible";* we don't assume you will agree with or follow what we've written. Each teaching context is different and no one can tell someone else what to do in his or her situation. The paradox of planning is that you can't actually know what to do until you listen—until you're in the situation with the people that you'll be working with, learning about their living situations, histories, and hopes. That's why much of the report is written in the past tense: we think it is more helpful to tell you what we *did* than what you *should do.*

to advocate for resources..

The Guidebook also has another purpose (maybe ultimately its most important one!) and that is to convince funders and policymakers that this is a powerful model for addressing the literacy needs of immigrant and refugee adults so that they will commit more resources to it. For this reason, we have not only evaluated our own particular work, but incorporated evidence from similar projects that indicate its potential.

How was this Guidebook written?

Although this Guidebook was originally written as the final report for the Community Training for Adult and Family Literacy Project (CTAFL), it incorporates experiences that go beyond the time frame of one project. All of the project staff had worked together in a prior collaboration, the Bilingual Community Literacy Training Project (BCLTP), which was founded on the same philosophy and principles. Because there were differences in the structure and scope of the two projects, we decided to include findings from both in order to incorporate the broadest possible base of knowledge and data. Although the one year time frame of the CTAFL limited what we could do, the wealth of experience from the prior project allowed us to compare what worked and what didn't in each. The lessons we learned in that project, and the lessons we learned in writing about it, are very much a part of this Guidebook.

the process

One of the principles of a participatory process is that everyone's voices and contributions are valued. In order for the voice in any documentation such as this to be truly authentic, each participant or participating agency would have to write about their own work. In fact, outsiders have often written about the work at participating sites, leaving site staff feeling that their voices were not represented. Although everyone on the staff of our project agreed in principle that it would be desirable for sites to write about their own practice, no one felt it was entirely feasible, given the constraints of time, funding, and experience. On the one hand, Mentors felt that any time spent writing should be paid; on the other, they felt that their priorities were teaching (and if money were available, it should be spent on services for students). In addition, the notion that only site representatives can write about the project obscures the collaborative nature of the project; much of what we did was done together, in joint work.

We addressed this dilemma about voice by trying to make the writing process as participatory as possible, even though one person (Elsa) did the actual writing. We started by looking at a range of models of final reports and literacy training guidebooks; each Mentor reported on features that he or she liked from the samples. Then, the Mentors generated a list of questions that practitioners and policymakers might ask about our project (these are the questions that form headings in each chapter). We then had a series of meetings in which we discussed each of the questions as a group, with everyone contributing what he or she thought should be included in that section. Elsa took minutes of those discussions, recording participants' actual words, and used what was said as the basis for each section. Elsa then wrote drafts that incorporated these discussions, as well as documentation that had been collected throughout the project. This documentation included:

•**minutes of meetings:** We had detailed minutes of core staff meetings, training workshops, and teacher-sharing meetings; these minutes recorded the actual words of Mentors and Interns.

•**samples of work**: We collected samples of Interns', Mentors', and students' work throughout the projects. These included lesson plans, writings, reports of discussions, and so on. Because many of the samples of learners' work that were collected include reflections on their own learning, their voices are also represented through these writings.

•**interviews**: Interns and Mentors interviewed each other at the beginning and end of the project. Interns also interviewed selected learners at the end of the project.

•**evaluation results**: We used a variety of evaluation tools (site surveys, anecdotes, student profiles, etc.), the results of which are included.

The drafts were then distributed to project staff, as well as to the BALF Director and interested Education Coordinators at the sites. Everyone gave feedback, which was discussed and incorporated into the final version. We struggled over various interpretations of the history or the project. The participatory nature of this process broke down to some extent as the deadline for submission of the report drew near: there wasn't enough time for the final chapters to be fully discussed by the group.

the language

In writing this report, we faced several challenges. The first was how to present findings in a way that adhered to the conventions of final research reports and, at the same time, present them in a way that is useful for practitioners. If an evaluation is technical and quantitative, or uses a very academic discourse style, it may exclude many potential readers. In our report of the first project (the BCLTP), we used somewhat academic language at times because we felt this would legitimate our findings to funders and policy makers. Because the purpose of this Guidebook is to popularize the model, we have chosen to use a colloquial and less academic style.

A related challenge was how to write this Guidebook in a clear and accessible way while at the same time capturing the richness and complexity of the issues we addressed. How could our writing be simple without being simplistic? How could it be usable without being prescriptive? How could it be straightforward without being mechanical? In addition to using a colloquial writing style, we have tried to address these concerns by including many examples from our practice. Whenever we suggest a particular tool, activity, or procedure, we try to include an account of our experience with it and reflections on how it went for us.

A third challenge was how to present our project in its most positive light (because our ultimate goal is to advocate for the expansion of this model) and, at the same time, present it in its full complexity. Like anyone involved in a demonstration project, we want to show how successful our work has been because we believe so strongly in the power of this model. But we also want to be honest because this is what will be most useful to others. How often, when we read about other projects, do we think, "It sounds wonderful, but I wonder what really happened?" We often feel constrained to write about the ideal, to make our work sound unproblematic even though, as any practitioner knows, there are always difficulties and limitations as well as contextual factors that shape the outcomes. This book tries to present both the power of our model and the challenges we faced implementing it.

the product

Another dilemma concerned the product of our work. Research studies often frame conclusions in terms of outcomes; training projects often frame them in terms of training packages or curricula. However, because our interest was in the complexity of the process, we didn't want to reduce our findings to a set of quantifiable outcomes. Likewise, because every teaching context is different, we didn't feel it would be appropriate to prescribe a single, predetermined training design that could be imposed or transposed regardless of the context. We did, however, arrive at generalizable conclusions and identify significant implications of our work. Thus, the findings presented in this Guidebook will be framed in terms of the processes of the development of our model; it will document why we did what we did, how our thinking and practice developed, and how we made sense of participants' reactions. Issues and contradictions we faced along the way will be integrated throughout the book, because it was the struggle with these issues that was the real motor force of the project, helping us to clarify our perspective and arrive at our conclusions.

How is this Guidebook organized?

Chapter One presents the background of the project, starting with **the context at participating sites**, explaining why and how they became involved with this model. It then presents **the rationale for the project design**, including a brief explanation of each of the key features of the project. It shows where the ideas for this design came from as well as how they are supported within a broader framework of theory, research, and practice. It ends by showing how we translated them into objectives.

Chapter Two, the overview of the **project structure and participants**, looks at how the collaboration was set up and administered, how the training was structured, who the participants were, and how they were selected. It introduces the Mentors and the Interns, giving a sense of their backgrounds and why they wanted to participate in the project.

Chapter Three presents a description of the Intern **training**, including our general approach, what we did within each training component (workshops, teacher-sharing meetings, mentoring), and issues that emerged in the process. It explores the meaning of participatory training, as well as the challenges that arise in implementing it.

Chapter Four presents a brief overview of the relationship between the training and what actually happened in the **ESL and literacy classes.** It includes key literacy teaching tools and gives examples of how they were used. It also addresses teaching issues that emerged from practice.

Chapter Five focuses on project **evaluation**—our approach, plan, and evaluation tools. It outlines the process of evaluation and how the design changed. It goes on to present results of the evaluation, discussing the **impact of the project** on Mentors, Interns, learners, and sites.

The Conclusion summarizes our **findings** regarding each of the key characteristics of the "from the community to the community" model. In addition, it examines **dilemmas and challenges** we faced and includes **recommendations** for the field of adult literacy, discussing the broader potential of this model and what is necessary to realize it.

The Appendices include an article about the **Spanish Literacy Component** at the Harborside Community Center (written by Byron Barahona, the original Spanish literacy Master Teacher at that site) and an analysis of how Creole literacy was promoted at the HMSC. The third appendix presents **descriptions of workshops** held at UMass during the BCLTP, as well as reflections on those workshops.

Some notes on terminology

native language

We use the term *native language* to refer to learners' first language or mother tongue (the language that is primary for them). The terms *native language, first language,* and *mother tongue* have different connotations in various parts of the world and to different people. In this book, we use them interchangeably. In the context of our work, some Haitian Creole speakers and some Spanish speakers were placed in native language literacy classes because they had minimal prior education and did not have a basis of first or native language literacy; the rationale for this model is explained in Chapter One.

L1 and L2

L1 is used to refer to someone's first or native language; L2 is used to refer to someone's second language (which, in the case of our project, was usually English).

Creole
Kreyol

Although there are many kinds of Creole used in the Boston area (Cape Verdean Creole, Jamaican Creole, etc.), Haitian Creole was the only one used in our project; for this reason, when we use the term *Creole* in this report (e.g., the Creole literacy classes), we are referring to Haitian Creole. We have not used the Haitian spelling, *Kreyol*, because the report is in English.

training

We called our projects *training projects* because this is the commonly accepted way of describing short-term programs for teaching specific vocationally oriented content. However, we are uncomfortable with this term because it often connotes transmitting specific skills or techniques; our approach focused much more on drawing out group knowledge and sharing experience than on transmitting a particular method or technique. Our goal was not that participants would "master" a predetermined body of knowledge or teaching competencies, but that they would develop a stance or approach to teaching. We use the term *training* because we haven't found a better one, but don't view it in a mechanical way.

Master Teacher and Mentor

In both the BCLTP and the CTAFL, each site had one experienced teacher who was responsible for supervising and mentoring the Interns at that site; these teachers were part of the core staff of both projects. In the BCLTP, we called these teachers *Master Teachers,* but we decided to change the title to *Mentor* for the CTAFL because the term seems to imply less of a hierarchical relationship with Interns.

Chapter One: The Context and Rationale

*The idea for the Community Training for Adult and Family Literacy Project did not fall from the sky or emerge from an ivory tower: it was a response to realities confronting the communities of the participating sites and was based on a history of practice at the sites. Its impetus and rationale came from the sites' specific needs and built on initiatives that they had already undertaken to address those needs. This chapter looks at the contexts at the sites, the history of the project, and the reasons for its design. The **so what?** sections highlight implications of our particular experience for others undertaking similar projects.*

the contexts at the sites

The collaborating sites have many commonalities. Each has deep and long-standing roots in the community where it is situated; all are well known among local immigrants and refugees and have long waiting lists for classes. Each has had an adult education program for at least 10 years and has participated actively in the adult literacy community in the Greater Boston area. They provide a range of services in addition to ESL classes, from counseling to childcare, and, in some cases, health care, and legal services.

In addition, the sites share a commitment to developing the leadership of people from the communities of the learners and to expanding services for learners with minimal prior education and literacy backgrounds. Before we began working together, each had begun developing this model, but had not had sufficient financial or structural support to sustain these efforts independently. The collaboration, thus, became a vehicle for continuing initiatives already under way at the sites.

At the same time, however, the conditions at the sites are quite different in terms of the backgrounds of students they serve, the kinds of services they offer, the internal structures of the sites, and the relations of the sites to the learners' communities. The project component at each site was tailored to fit the needs of students within its community. This background information is included here because, in any project, the context is critical in shaping the content, direction, and outcomes.

so what?

Thus, our experience suggests that collaborations need to both provide a common framework for participating sites (based on their shared needs and vision for training and instruction) and, at the same time, respond to site-specific conditions. Balancing the tension between common purposes and particular conditions is precisely the challenge of collaboration—the challenge of adapting commonly held principles and processes to differing contexts.

1

East Boston Harborside Community Center Adult Literacy Program

The most striking characteristic of the context of the Harborside Program is the rapidly changing demographic situation in East Boston, where it is located. According to the Hispanic Office of Planning and Evaluation, the growth rate for Hispanics in the state of Massachusetts between 1970 and l980 was 11 times faster than that of Whites and 5 times faster than that of Blacks; Hispanics accounted for 67% of the total population growth in the state during that period; 22% of the population in East Boston are refugees and immigrants, many of them recent arrivals from Central America with limited English language abilities and few economic resources. Hispanic families have the highest poverty rate of any group in the area. An estimated 20% of the Hispanic adults who seek educational services have less than a fourth grade education and are minimally literate in Spanish.

The Harborside Community Center (HCC) offers the only free ESL classes in East Boston. Its Adult Literacy Program has been offering basic education services since l983. It provides four levels of ESL classes, as well as reading, writing, and math for native English speakers, from basic literacy levels through high school equivalency. Over 300 adult literacy students from many ethnic, linguistic, racial, and class backgrounds enroll in it annually; of these, 34% are Hispanic. Thus, although the learner population at Harborside is a mixed one, and the agency serves many different ethnic groups, it is clearly the central place in East Boston that Hispanics go for educational services. The HCC also offers a range of other programs including After School Day Care, After School Reading, Community Counseling, Peer Leadership, summer camps, and, most recently, a program aimed at giving East Boston youth a safe place to go after school where they can study, meet other teens, and work on projects that give something back to the community.

In addition, in l989, the HCC initiated Khmer literacy classes to meet the increasingly apparent needs of the Cambodian community. This project supported the HCC Adult Learning Program's commitment to multicultural, participatory adult education in which the content of classes is driven by the interests, experiences, and community concerns of learners. Part of the HCC's mission is to "utilize participatory classroom activities and curricula which encourage our students to use their personal experiences and goals as the basis for a meaningful learning experience." The HCC has a history of training, hiring, and promoting staff from the communities of the learners. The staff has included several language minority ESL teachers; in addition, bilingual aides (like the Cambodian aide in the Khmer class) and bilingual volunteer tutors have assisted in classrooms for many years.

The Haitian Multi-Service Center

Over the past decade there has been exceptionally rapid growth in the number of Haitians living in the greater Boston area, making it presently one of the largest Haitian population centers in the U.S. (following Miami and New York). Current estimates place the Haitian population in the state at over 60,000; the majority of Haitians – up to 25,000 – live in the Dorchester and Mattapan areas of Boston. Despite this continuing increase, the HMSC is the only agency that provides educational and social services specifically targeted for the Haitian community in Boston. It is located geographically in the heart of this community. It is the largest human service agency serving Haitians in Massachusetts.

The mission of the HMSC is based on a "Haitians serving Haitians" model; it provides human and educational services as well as promoting community development and leadership in a culturally and linguistically familiar context. It has a broad range of services; in addition to adult education, it provides pre-school, pre-natal care, AIDS outreach and education, refugee resettlement, legal services, family counseling, and translation services. Adult education is its largest component, serving over 300 students daily in 18 classes. The waiting period for regular classes is up to 3 years, and the waiting list numbers over 400 students.

The Adult Education Program provides morning, afternoon, and evening classes. It includes two levels of Kreyol (Creole) literacy, four levels of ESL, and a high school diploma program. Through the Massachusetts English Literacy Demonstration Project (MELD), the HMSC has provided advanced reading and writing classes to students transitioning from ESL to high school diploma classes and college credit reading, writing and math classes through Roxbury Community College. The HMSC Study Center provides a computer lab available for all classes, elective classes in math, as well as conversation and program development support for teachers to explore ways to integrate math, science, and technology in the curriculum.

The HMSC has been committed to the hiring of bilingual/bicultural staff since its inception. In the mid-1980's, the Adult Education Program established a 2 year Bilingual Teacher Training Project to address the need for increased recruitment, training, and hiring of bilingual Haitian teachers in adult education. In addition, the HMSC has worked extensively with local colleges and universities to recruit Haitian undergraduates for internship and work-study positions; it was instrumental in establishing the Student Literacy Corps at UMass/Boston. Students at the HMSC are also encouraged to take on responsibilities within the program and are often hired to teach or administer Study Center activities.

The Jackson-Mann Community School

The primary difference between the Jackson-Mann Community School in Allston-Brighton and the other project sites is the incredible diversity of ethnic and linguistic groups represented in its classes. According to the Boston Redevelopment Authority (BRA) Boston Household Survey for 1985, 20% of households in Allston-Brighton identify a language other than English as their primary language; early indications from the 1990 Census suggest that this percentage is growing. Allston-Brighton is home to 28% of all Hispanics living in Boston, 43% of the city's Russian residents, 26% of the people from other Eastern European countries, 30% of Boston's Asian community, and 15% of its Brazilian population. The population served in Allston-Brighton is predominantly low income, including local public housing residents, AFDC recipients, and the working poor. Although many of the students in the program hold jobs (and some hold more than one job at a time), most are low-wage, entry-level jobs: housekeeping, janitorial, fastfood cooking and counter positions, and assembly line jobs.

The classes at the JMCS reflect the diversity of the area's population: the program serves 450 students per year from 25 to 30 different ethnic groups. An estimated 5% of the adults in the ESL classes have less than a fourth grade education in their home countries. Thus, at this site, the need is more for beginning ESL than for first language literacy; further, because classes are so linguistically mixed, ESL is the only viable option for the immigrant and refugee learners. The program has four components: ESL, ABE, GED (General Education Development), and EDP (an External Degree Program for high school equivalency). Because many of the students are employed, most of the classes are held at night at the JMCS.

There are over 400 adults on the waiting list to get into ESL classes. The JMCS has never had to actively recruit students because it is well-known among immigrant and refugee communities as a center that offers free quality ESL classes. In addition, the issue of waiting list length has been addressed by having class sizes of up to 30 and involving students as much as possible in assisting teachers and working with other students.

The JMCS has a long history of promoting leadership from within the learners' communities. It has had advocacy training projects to develop students as community activists. It has hired language minority teachers and teaching assistants. Students have produced a magazine and been involved in various aspects of program governance (including a student council).

4

What is the history of the project?

These were the conditions at the sites that gave rise to the ideas underlying the CTAFL project. As the following account indicates, the basis for the project was already in place long before it actually began.

needs identified

In the mid-1980s, a group of community-based agencies in the Boston area had identified the need to diversify the adult education workforce (which until then was predominantly made up of White, Anglo North Americans with undergraduate and/or graduate degrees) and to train instructors from the learners' communities. With resources limited, many programs were seeking additional ways to continue providing services for incoming students while at the same time, increasing opportunities for advanced students who had completed existing courses. The idea of training exceptional students to become instructors for lower levels was seen as a way of providing a "step up" for them as well as addressing the demand for increased services and a multicultural workforce.

In addition, a growing need for first language literacy had been identified. At Harborside, a Khmer literacy program was initiated in 1989; further, a previously hidden population of immigrants with limited educational backgrounds (many of whom were Central American) began to enroll in classes in order to meet requirements for amnesty. These were students who had been too intimidated to come to a school setting until they needed to do so for legalization purposes. Once enrolled, students who didn't know how to read and write in their first language were struggling (and often failing) in ESL classes. The existing ESL classes were unable to meet their needs and the few places that taught literacy in Spanish required students to pay for these services. Thus, Harborside saw the need to start a Spanish literacy component for the growing numbers of learners who might otherwise have been relegated to the waiting lists or never come for classes at all.

The Haitian Multi-Service Center (HMSC) had been providing Creole (Kreyol) literacy instruction since 1984 to serve the needs of a growing number of refugees coming to Boston as a result of political and economic instability in Haiti; many of them had had no access to education in Haiti and needed basic literacy instruction. Attitudes toward Creole were changing since it had become the official language in Haiti after the fall of Duvalier. Further, a Creole linguistics course at UMass/Boston taught by Marc Prou fostered this interest. In the mid-1980s, through a collaboration with Roxbury Community College, the HMSC provided workshops in Creole linguistics for teachers and college interns.

As a result of all of these conditions, a number of projects were initiated by community-based organizations during the 1980s:

• **The Boston Adult Literacy Fund** secured funding for a city-wide pilot project to train people from the communities of the learners as teaching and administrative assistants.

• **The Haitian Multi-Service Center** had decided to recruit, hire, and train bilingual teachers in the early years of its program development and actively pursued funding for this purpose. It secured funding from several sources to establish a Bilingual Teacher Training Project, which was successful in providing a pool of trained Haitian teachers for the HMSC's educational program. At the same time, the HMSC actively recruited bilingual interns and work-study students from local colleges and universities as tutors and teaching assistants. As a result of this work, an increasing percentage of the staff was Haitian and included college interns and program graduates. In addition, the HMSC initiated Creole literacy instruction in the mid 1980s.

• **The Jackson-Mann Community School** had received a grant to train advanced students to become community educators for employment and housing issues. It also worked with two other community-based agencies (the Community Learning Center and El Centro del Cardenal) and UMass/Boston in the English Family Literacy Project which included a Spanish literacy component.

• **The Harborside Community Center** received funding to initiate a bilingual Khmer ESL class; in the spirit of commitment to community leadership, it hired a bilingual North American ESL teacher and a Cambodian teaching assistant for this project.

Despite the great need for programs like these and their many successes, there was generally inadequate financial or structural support for them. Although funding agencies and policymakers often paid lip service to the importance of diversifying the field and promoting leadership from within minority communities, they did little to concretely follow up on these goals. Other L1 classes around the city were taught by volunteers, who, in many cases, had no training; funding and logistical support for these classes was minimal. As a result, despite their successes, these initiatives were often unstable, lasting a few months, with frequent teacher and student turnover. However, the HMSC, JMCS, and HCC were exceptions, and their endeavors inspired the projects described in this Guidebook; for example, the particular structure of the HMSC's Bilingual Teacher Training Project became a basis for the project model described here.

6

Given this proliferation of community-based initiatives, it was clear that the historical moment was ripe for training community literacy instructors. It was at this point that the idea for a university-community collaboration arose. The proposal to train community literacy instructors was submitted to and funded by the Office of Bilingual Education and Minority Language Affairs. This project, the Bilingual Community Literacy Training Project (BCLTP), focused on three kinds of literacy classes in accordance with the conditions at the sites: Haitian Creole at the HMSC (as well as ESL), Spanish literacy at the HCC, and ESL at the JMCS. It was a 3-year project that involved monthly training workshops, weekly site-based teacher sharing meetings, and mentoring. Up to 16 Interns were trained each year.

The HMSC played a key role in this process, both in terms of developing a model for the training of community literacy instructors and in terms of bringing it to the university. Because the HMSC was founded on a "Haitians serving Haitians" model, the primary goal of its Adult Education Program had been, from its inception in the early 1980s, to actively recruit and train bilingual Haitian teachers. As mentioned earlier, the HMSC developed a Bilingual Teacher Training Project which recruited and trained teachers for its Adult Education Program. This HMSC model was then shared with the Bilingual/ESL Graduate Studies Program at UMass/Boston. Several aspects of the HMSC model informed the subsequent collaborative projects (including recruitment of participants from the community, site-based and on-the-job training, co-teaching and mentoring). In addition, the HMSC played a key role in the inclusion of native language literacy instruction in the projects' design. During the first year of the BCLTP (in which the HMSC was the only participating site) the HMSC educational staff made the decision to focus its training on native language literacy instruction in order to expand its Creole literacy component; as such, it was the first site in the collaboration to specifically gear instruction to native language literacy.

It was with this history of joint work that the sites embarked on the Community Training for Adult and Family Literacy (CTAFL) project. The new project was similar to the BCLTP in terms of the overall model, approach, and rationale; however, it differed in terms of time frame, scope, and training design. These differences are discussed in more detail in Chapter Three. We have included information about both projects because our experience with each enriches the knowledge base about the "from the community to the community" model.

What were the objectives and key features of the project?

Based on the needs identified by the sites and the priorities of the funders, we identified the following objectives and key features in our CTAFL proposal:

objectives

- to recruit and provide opportunities for professional development for teachers and Interns from underserved ethnic minority groups

- to develop a multifaceted, practice-oriented model for training community Interns to teach adult and family literacy based on recent adult literacy research and theory

- to train a core group of bilingual Mentors to supervise on-site training and model teaching to community Interns

- to train a core group of bilingual community Interns to become instructors of adult and family literacy

- to facilitate the development of the literacy proficiency of non-English speaking adults, including parents of bilingual students, increasing their educational attainment, their ability to function in ESL classes, and their ability to support the literacy development of their children

- to build the capacity of community-based literacy programs serving the needs of adult ESL and literacy students

- to disseminate the model so that it can be replicated and implemented on a nation-wide basis

key features

Underlying these objectives were four key features of the model:

- **a meaning-based, culturally variable view of literacy**

- **a participatory approach** to literacy instruction and teacher training

- **native language literacy** for adult learners with little prior schooling

- **training and leadership development** of community instructors

How is this model supported by theory and research?

Although the rationale for our model arose directly from the concrete conditions, needs, and initiatives at the sites, we were by no means alone in arriving at these conclusions. There is substantial justification for each of the key features of the model from a wide range of other sources. This support comes from language acquisition and literacy theory and research, as well as from the work of other practitioners and projects both nationally and internationally. The next sections briefly examine some of the research, theory, and practice, indicating why each of these project's key features is educationally sound.

Why a meaning-based, culturally variable view of literacy?

cultural variability in literacy practices

The past decade has seen advances in the theoretical understanding of the nature of literacy, and, in particular, of the ways it varies according to culture and context. Studies of literacy practices in a range of cultures indicate variation in types of texts, participant interactions around texts, purposes for creating and using texts, social meanings/values attached to texts, ways of producing texts, and ways of socializing children through interactions with texts. A new paradigm has emerged in which literacy is viewed not just as a set of isolated decoding skills to be acquired in an essentially similar universal process, but rather as a set of social practices that vary according to cultures, contexts, purposes, and participants. This means that culture-specific aspects of language and literacy use must be taken into account in literacy programming and curriculum development; wherever possible, teachers must be aware of culture-specific discourse practices, literacy uses and forms of learners' cultures (Heath, 1983; Reder, 1987; Street, 1984; Taylor and Dorsey-Gaines, 1988).

connections between oral and written language

Another aspect of this emerging paradigm is that, increasingly, the divide between oral and written language has come to be questioned. Older views claimed that literacy was unique in that it allowed meaning to be represented autonomously, without reference to context; recent studies show that, in fact, there are many features of what has traditionally been thought of as oral discourse in written language and vice versa. A new conception of *literacies* has emerged in which a variety of discourse forms are seen to encompass a range of features of both oral and written language. Culture-specific uses of oral language shape the way that learners take and make meaning through texts. Teachers must draw on learners' oral language practices in developing their reading and writing (Gee, 1990; Tannen, 1982; Street, 1984).

9

literacy acquisition as a meaning-making process

Further, this paradigm claims that literacy acquisition involves not just mechanically connecting sounds and symbols, but making meaning by interacting with texts. Reading and learning to read are active, constructive processes, as are writing and learning to write: learners bring their own knowledge to texts in order to make sense of them. Culture plays a role in learning: learners' cultural familiarity with the content and forms of texts shape their reading processes. Learners become proficient to the extent that instruction is connected to their background knowledge, life experiences, and communicative purposes. Traditional approaches that focus on the individual's acquisition of skills without consideration of social context disconnect literacy acquisition from learners' knowledge and lived experience. Thus, it is critical that instruction be meaning-centered, rather than mechanical, and that content be relevant to the life experiences of learners (Carrell and Eisterhold, 1983; Street, 1984).

connections between the word and the world

Current literacy theory suggests that literacy is meaningful for learners to the extent that it enables them to better understand and shape their world. Brazilian educator Paulo Freire says that there must be a connection between the **word** and the **world** (Freire and Macedo, 1987). Mechanical approaches that focus on the acquisition of isolated skills without consideration of the social conditions of learners' lives disconnect literacy acquisition from their knowledge, concerns, and experiences. As literacy educator Susan Lytle (1991) says, "Being and becoming literate means using knowledge and experience to make sense of and act on the world" (p. 8). In the approach proposed by Freire (1970), instruction starts with learners' social reality, providing a context for analyzing it and taking action on it. If literacy acquisition is linked with this kind of critical analysis, it can enable learners to challenge the social conditions that disempower them. Thus, literacy instruction should involve exploration of the social issues and concerns of learners' lives.

so what?

Findings from this theoretical and practical work suggest that:

•Training must explore various conceptions of literacy; participants views of literacy acquisition must be made explicit. Training should also explore ways of connecting literacy instruction to issues of importance in learners' lives.

•Similarly, work with students should involve dialogue about their conceptions of literacy and their prior learning experiences; literacy instruction should incorporate culturally familiar literacy forms and practices, building on learners' oral language resources.

10

Why a participatory approach?

adult learning theory

The view of literacy just outlined is congruent with recent perspectives from adult learning theory which suggest that adults learn best when instruction is contextualized in their life experiences, related to their real needs, and when they are involved in determining instructional goals and content. Their purposes for reading and writing can be expected to vary according to social contexts. Thus, adult learning theory, like literacy theory, suggests that the content of instruction should be linked to meaningful, authentic language and literacy use (rather than focusing on abstract, decontextualized decoding skills or generic topics). It must reflect students' everyday reality so that literacy becomes a tool that can enable learners to understand and change their lives (Kazemek, 1988; Knowles, 1984; Lytle, 1991; Nunan, 1988).

curriculum theory

In order to implement this goal, the traditional concept of curriculum development must be changed; in the traditional model, the teacher identifies what to be covered in a course (e.g., skills, grammar, competencies) before coming in contact with students; instruction then is a process of finding the most efficient way of transmitting this information from teacher to students. In place of this model, the concept of learner-centered and emergent curriculum development is becoming increasingly widespread. The new model involves collaborative discovery of learners' goals and concerns, involving constant dialogue and negotiation at every step of the way (Nunan, 1988). Chris Candlin (1984), a curriculum theorist, describes this as an interactive syllabus model

> which is social and problem-solving in orientation rather than one which transmits preselected and often predigested knowledge. The model thus becomes one in which participants, both teachers and learners, are encouraged to ask questions from the outset about syllabus objectives, content, methodology and experiences. (p. 34)

adult ESL educators' practice

North American adult ESL educators have extended this learner-centered model to include content specifically focused on the social context of learners' lives, combining Freire's approach to literacy pedagogy with the emergent approach to ESL curriculum development (Auerbach, 1992; Barndt, 1987; Wallerstein, 1983). This participatory model for adult ESL literacy offers a systematic process for building curriculum around learners' lived experiences and social realities. As one of the Interns in our project said, in this model, *"The students' lives are the curriculum."*

11

This participatory curriculum development process developed through this practice involves moving toward a model with the following components:

•**Investigation and identification of themes:** Teachers investigate the social conditions of learners' lives with them in order to identify their concerns and goals.

•**Re-presentation and dialogue:** As teachers discover what is important in learners' lives, they create or select materials to present the themes back to students as lesson content. Participants then discuss these issues in terms of how they have experienced them, their root or social causes, and possible strategies for addressing them.

•**Extension:** A range of tools are utilized to extend language and literacy proficiency, exploring these issues as the content of instruction. Materials and learning activities (language experience stories, grammar and vocabulary work, reading and writing, role plays, etc.) focus on the issues.

•**Action:** Students apply what they have learned inside the classroom to address concerns outside the classroom.

•**Evaluation:** The class evaluates the learning process and the actions they have taken.

Of course, the challenge is adapting this model to particular groups of students. When the social context of learners' lives is incorporated in instruction, relevance is ensured. As students participate in identifying themes that are important to them, in developing learning tools they will use, and in evaluating what they have learned, they gain a measure of control over their own learning which extends to their lives outside the classroom.

so what?

Findings from this theoretical and practical work indicate that:

•Adult learners should be involved in curriculum development at every stage of the process, from deciding the content, methods, and processes of instruction to participating in evaluation.

•Curriculum content for adults (whether in a training or literacy instruction context) must incorporate the realities, concerns, and goals of participants.

12

Why native language literacy and bilingual transitional ESL?

The theoretical framework outlined previously suggests that oral language should be used as much as possible as a bridge to literacy. This means that teachers must be able to draw on learners' linguistic resources in a culturally appropriate way, to the extent possible, and teach literacy through oral language usage. Further, research on ESL literacy acquisition indicates that strong first language literacy and schooling are key factors in second language/literacy acquisition (Cummins, 1981). Although this is a widely accepted finding for children's literacy acquisition (and, in fact, has been the basis for the bilingual education movement), it has been less widely accepted for adult literacy acquisition. Adult ESL literacy research, however, indicates that it is equally relevant for low-literate, non-English speaking adults. It is relevant first because of the difficulties that adult learners face when they try to learn English without being literate in their first language, and, second, because of the positive consequences for literacy and ESL acquisition when they start with L1 literacy classes (Gillespie and Ballering, 1992; Klassen, 1991; Rivera, 1990; Robson, 1982).

A number of studies document the difficulties of adult ESL students with minimal first language literacy proficiency. They indicate that people who are not literate in their first language are at a double disadvantage: on the one hand, ESL literacy programs often turn them away because their oral English is not adequate and, on the other hand, they often have difficulty functioning in or benefitting from ESL classes because these classes assume L1 literacy.

•Klassen (1991) found that, without first language literacy, ESL classes were virtually inaccessible to Spanish-speaking adult learners. Students in monolingual ESL classes reported that they had no idea what was going on in their classes; they responded by becoming completely silenced, making virtually no progress, or dropping out. The lack of English, in turn, affected their ability to find jobs, to support their children's schooling, and had important negative implications for their self-esteem.

•Strei (1992) found that those with little L1 literacy background and schooling (whether from Spanish-speaking or another linguistic background) are often caught in a "revolving door syndrome" in which learners start a course, fail, start again, and eventually give up.

Likewise, there is strong evidence showing that first language literacy is critical to economic and political participation, as well as to the acquisition of English literacy.

•Studies by Vargas (1986) and Wiley (1990-1991) indicate that those who are literate in their first language (even if they are not literate in English) have advantages over those who are not functionally literate in either language in terms of economic success, political participation, and employment.

For these reasons, adult educators are increasingly advocating L1 literacy instruction as a basis for ESL acquisition for adult learners with little prior education and bilingual ESL instruction for those with slightly more L1 literacy. Although these L1 literacy programs are still few and far between in the U.S., practitioners, researchers, and learners involved in them report positive results (Collingham, 1988; Gillespie and Ballering, 1992; Rivera, 1988).

The first benefit of such programs at the beginning levels is that they attract and retain previously unserved students. These include students who had been unable to participate in ESL classes because of limited first language literacy and schooling: students who report having dropped out of ESL classes come back to classes when first language literacy is offered.

•Strei (1992) reports that a pilot native language literacy program for Haitians in Palm Beach County, Florida dramatically increased their retention rate once they enrolled in ESOL classes: the drop-out rate decreased from 85% prior to the program to only 10% after it was started.

•Teachers at Centro Presente, a program in Cambridge offering bilingual ESL, report that many of their current students had previously dropped out of monolingual ESL classes.

A second benefit of using the L1 is that it reduces affective barriers to English acquisition, and thus allows for more rapid progress.

•Hemmindinger (1987) found that a bilingual approach to ESL for nonliterate Hmong refugees was more effective than monolingual ESL; students who had made almost no progress in 2 to 3 years of monolingual survival ESL classes, made rapid progress once a Freirean bilingual approach was introduced. She attributes this in part to the fact that the latter approach allowed language and culture shock to be reduced.

14

•D'Annunzio (1991) reports that nonliterate Cambodians made rapid gains in ESL in a program involving "pedagogically unsophisticated" bilingual tutors. Despite a relatively short total instructional time, highly significant results were attained in speaking, reading, and vocabulary, as indicated by pre- and post-test scores on a number of standardized tests, portfolio analysis, and ongoing informal assessment.

•Teachers at Centro Presente report that use of the L1 naturally gives way to increasing use of English. They claim that because students don't just start by thinking in the L2, allowing for the exploration of ideas in the L1 supports a gradual, developmental process in which use of the L1 drops off naturally as it becomes less necessary.

•Garcia's (1991) research on effective instructional practices found that academically successful students made the transition from Spanish to English without any pressure from teachers and were able to progress systematically from writing in the native language initially to writing in English later.

A third benefit of native language literacy instruction is that it promotes a meaning-based conception of literacy among learners. Starting with the L1 reduces anxiety and enhances the affective environment for learning, takes into account sociocultural factors, facilitates incorporation of learners' life experiences, and allows for learner-centered curriculum development. Most importantly, it allows for language to be used as a meaning-making tool and for language learning to become a means of communicating ideas rather than an end in itself. As such, it is congruent with current theories of language acquisition, literacy and adult learning.

so what? Findings from this theoretical and practical work indicate that:

•Literacy in the first language is an essential resource for the transition to second language literacy for low-literate adults.

•Where possible and as needed, native language literacy classes and bilingual transitional ESL classes should be offered for these adults.

•Knowledge of the learners' first languages should be considered an important teaching qualification.

15

Why literacy teachers from the communities of the learners?

The final feature of our project which fits with a social-contextual view of literacy and a participatory approach to adult education is its focus on training people from the communities of the learners as teachers. Although the idea of hiring teachers who do not have either traditional higher education or teaching credentials may seem unusual in the U.S. context, it is not uncommon in other parts of the world.

•In the early 1960s, a classic study of Spanish literacy acquisition among Mexican Indians found that learners taught by Indians from their own community with little pedagogical training learned to read in both the vernacular and in Spanish better than did those taught by native Spanish speakers from the dominant culture with more training (Modiano, 1968).

•Many of the mass literacy campaigns of third world countries are based on the principle that people who know a little more can teach people who know a little less. International organizations like UNESCO promote the strategy of relying on these nontraditional teachers as the main way of addressing widespread illiteracy.

•In Nicaragua, for example, it was the shortage of teachers that initially prompted the campaign to train people who had themselves just learned to read and write to become literacy workers. According to Fernando Cardenal (1990), the director of the literacy campaign and a poet, this decision

> came really out of the pressure of not knowing at that point exactly what to do. But we put our trust in the people and the extraordinary result was that it was incredibly successful and most of these people became very good teachers. In fact, the literacy workers' lack of traditional background was an advantage: they had shared the experiences of the learners and could say, "Look, I learned... so can you." The literacy workers' insecurity, lack of professionalism, and inexperience enabled them to be part of the students, helping them to overcome their fear of learning. (p. 45).

In the U.S., we would call this peer teaching; its power comes from the fact that barriers between teacher and learner are broken down.

Preliminary work in the United States suggests that this model is highly relevant for this context as well, and is particularly promising for adult native language literacy instruction. Beyond the fact that traditionally credentialed teachers may not be available (Anglo teachers may not be able to teach the L1 because they don't know it, whereas language minority teachers may opt for elementary or secondary positions because the pay is better), there are a number of reasons why community teachers are particularly suitable.

•In addition to sharing a linguistic background with learners, their shared cultural background can be a resource, enabling them to draw on culturally familiar discourse forms (e.g., fables, proverbs, rules for interaction).

•Their common cultural, political, and historical knowledge base can be integrated into learning.

•People from the communities of the learners are in a particularly good position to elicit and facilitate learning around learners' life experiences because they have shared them and can understand them. Their experience as immigrants or refugees, struggling with issues of transition to the new culture, can be a powerful tool for participatory curriculum development. Further, their own experience facing linguistic and cultural challenges enables them to act as role models for students and resources for colleagues trying to understand the issues facing language minority communities.

Several recent literacy programs and research projects provide evidence of the effectiveness of teachers from the learners' communities:

•D'Annunzio (1991) reports on a project in which Cambodians were trained to tutor ESL; he attributes much of its success to "the use of bilingual tutors who shared the students' experiences" and argues that, with brief training, bilinguals (who, in the case of this program, were "only high school graduates") can become effective tutors and trainers of other tutors. He concludes that this model "may break the chain of reliance on heavy professional intervention" (p. 52).

•Hornberger and Hardman's (1994) study of instructional practices in a Cambodian adult ESL class and a Puerto Rican GED class corroborates the importance of shared background between teachers and learners. In the case of the Cambodian class, they found that because the teacher herself was Cambodian, 1) the students had the option of using Khmer to respond to her questions and to help each other, 2) the teacher and students shared assumptions about the learning paradigm, and 3) classroom activities were intimately connected with learners' other life activities and cultural practices. Likewise, in the GED class, instructional activities were embedded in a cultural and institutional context that integrated and validated learners' Puerto Rican identity. Their study suggests that the reinforcement of cultural identity, made possible by the shared cultural background of learners and teachers, is critical not just for L1 literacy acquisition, but for ESL acquisition as well.

•Describing a project at the Quincy School Community Council in Boston's Chinatown, Hooper (1992) makes a powerful case for recruiting and training advanced ESL students as tutors for beginning learners. In his article, "Breaking the waiting list logjam: Training peer tutors for ESL," he reports that the project (called the Take and Give or TAG project) was designed in response to the fact that the program has over 1000 people on its waiting list who have to wait up to 4 years for a slot in the program. Students who have completed the highest level of ESL, but want to continue in the program and expand their ESL proficiency, are trained to provide home-based tutoring for students on the waiting list, utilizing a beginning ESL video series. According to Hooper, the fact that the tutor and the learner share a common first language and a common immigrant experience enhanced the model. Hooper claims TAG is working not only as an innovative solution to the waiting list logjam, but as a strategy for eradicating barriers to "empowerment, to personal and community resource development, and to self-direction and self-fulfillment...and to communication in English" (p. 4).

But what about the appropriateness of this model for ESL instruction? The notion that native speakers of English are the most qualified to teach ESL is almost axiomatic in TESOL circles. This notion rests on the assumption that linguistic competence is the single most important criteria for teaching and goes hand in hand with the assumption that English should be taught entirely monolingually. Increasingly, however, both of these assumptions are being challenged by researchers and practitioners.

18

•Phillipson (1992) claims that those qualities which are seen to make native speakers intrinsically better qualified as English teachers are, in fact, learned and can only be instilled through training. Moreover, he argues, nonnative speakers possess certain qualifications which native speakers may not: they have gone through "the laborious process of acquiring English as a second language and...have insight into the linguistic and cultural needs of their learners" (p. 195).

•Thonis (1990) argues that anyone who teaches language minority students should possess the following qualities:

  •awareness of cultural differences
  •recognition of language diversity
  •understanding of the students' realities
  •sensitivity to the values of families
  •knowledge of the history and heritage of the group
  •recognition of the potential of all students
  •knowledge of second language acquisition theory
  •willingness to modify instruction as needed
  •solid understanding of curriculum imperatives students
      learning a second language (p. 19)

Significantly, the first six of these qualities may be more readily attributable to people from the learners' cultures than to native speakers of English. The last three are, as Phillipson says, acquired through training or education regardless of one's language background.

These arguments are presented not to discredit the skills and strengths of monolingual ESL teachers, but rather to show that bilingual teachers have qualifications which, until recently, have been virtually ignored and excluded from consideration. Being a non-native speaker of English has often been seen more as a disadvantage than as an advantage in ESL circles.

so what?

Findings from this research and practice indicates that:

•Because of their linguistic, cultural, and experiential backgrounds, people from the communities of the learners may be particularly suited to implementing a culturally sensitive, learner-centered curriculum.

•With adequate training in curriculum development and literacy pedagogy, people from the learners' communities can be effective native language literacy and ESL instructors.

19

Why is this kind of project important?

What is its significance for the field?

Although there is ample theoretical and research justification for a "from the community to the community" model for adult literacy instruction, the strongest justification for this model comes from project participants themselves. Perhaps the best way to end this chapter is by summarizing their views on why this model is significant. Here is what the Mentors said about why this model is important for them as well as for Interns, learners, the sites, and the field of adult education as a whole.

for Interns and Mentors...

•It gives opportunities to immigrants and refugees who cannot afford the traditional route to getting a degree; it gives us access to training and jobs that wouldn't otherwise be available.

•It gives us the chance to do meaningful, rather than menial, work.

•It gives us the opportunity to serve our own people while earning money at the same time.

•It gives us a sense of community with peers.

•It enables us to see people like ourselves as co-workers and to learn from our peers. It enables us to learn how to work with other people.

•It affirms our strengths and allows us to learn about ourselves.

•It demystifies the process of training and teaching others.

•It gives us a chance to learn about people from other cultures, to understand similarities and realize the extent of differences.

•It helps us build a work history and becomes a network for jobs.

•It gives us a chance to meet people and to extend acquaintances with others in the field.

for learners...

•It enables them to obtain services that would not otherwise be available, services which they thought they would not be able to get in this country.

•It gives them the chance to see people like themselves in teaching positions, as well as learning with them. It provides motivation for them.

•It enables them to change their lives for the better: they gain self-esteem and independence; they become more productive in society. It gives them a place to talk about and work on problems that they face.

•It enables them to accomplish specific goals like writing to their families, taking care of their own accounts, and so on.

for the sites...

•It enables the sites to expand services.

•It enables the sites to provide greater support to students.

•It enables the sites to provide leadership opportunities for learners.

•It increases the diversity of the teaching staff.

•It allows for greater rapport with various student populations.

•The collaboration allows for cultural sharing between sites. It enables sites to share their experiences and problems, seeing their own work in a broader context.

for the field as a whole...

•It provides a concrete process for diversifying the workforce.

•It expands the resources available to meet the need for literacy services.

•It enriches the base of cultural understanding within the field.

21

Chapter Two: Project Structure and Participants

The "from the community to the community" model aims to provide opportunities for community-based organizations to work together, guided by a shared vision, while at the same time taking into account the differing conditions and needs of each individual site. This chapter examines how we attempted to achieve a balance between collaboration and independence in our work. It looks at how the project was set up (project design), how decisions were made (project administration), who the participants were, and how they were selected.

How was the project set up?

As a collaboration, the project was set up to enable participating agencies to work together in some ways and separately in others. Thus, although there was a common approach to training and literacy instruction (participatory and learner-centered), the language of instruction varied from site to site: instruction focused on Haitian Creole at HMSC, Spanish at HCC, and ESL at JMCS. The project design involved the following features:

- **three sites**, one focusing on Haitian Creole literacy (HMSC), one on Spanish literacy (HCC), and one on ESL (JMCS)
- **three Mentors** (one at each site) and a **Project Coordinator** (UMass/Boston faculty member), each of whom worked half-time for the project
- **two Interns** at each site
- **fiscal management** by the Boston Adult Literacy Fund (BALF)
- **site administration** (project design, fund-raising, hiring, liaison) by Site Adult Education Coordinators

The following diagram represents the project structure:

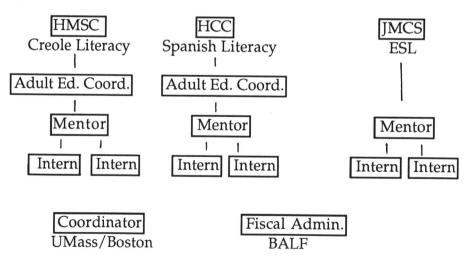

How was the project administered?

*We tried to follow a participatory process in the way the project was administered. This meant that, rather than hierarchical project administration, there was **collective decision-making** and a **division of labor** among participants. Some tasks were undertaken by the group while others were undertaken by the individual sites. In general, the joint work involved fund-raising, planning, university-based training, evaluation, and documentation. The separate work included selecting Mentors and Interns, and recruiting students. Administration and implementation of the instructional component was entirely in the hands of the sites.*

collective decision-making	Planning and decisions about collaborative aspects of project administration took place at bi-weekly two-hour meetings; the Mentors, Coordinator, and usually the BALF Director took part in these meetings. The Education Coordinators of the sites attended meetings related to fund-raising and project design. Meetings focused on planning and evaluating workshops, reporting classroom, site, and Mentoring concerns, designing project evaluation and documentation, as well as dissemination.
individual roles	The **Mentors** wore two hats as staff of both the project and their respective sites. Each Mentor was responsible for:

- administering the instructional components
- recruiting Interns
- teaching at least one literacy/ESL class
- coordinating and supervising the work of the site's Interns
- facilitating site teacher-sharing meetings
- carrying out site evaluation and documentation activities
- acting as liaison between the project and the site

The **Project Coordinator** was responsible for facilitating the collaboration as well as coordinating the university-based component, for the documentation of project work, and for its dissemination. This meant:

- taking minutes of staff meetings
- preparing materials for and facilitating the workshops
- coordinating documentation and evaluation
- writing reports for the funders
- helping with fund-raising

The **BALF Executive Director** was responsible for fiscal management of the project, assistance in fund-raising, and liaison with the funders regarding matters of funding.

What was the training design?

*The training included both **university-based** and **site-based** components. Chapter Three will focus on the approach to training and its content, describing what actually happened in workshops, mentoring, and teacher-sharing. The following summarizes the overall design of training.*

university-based training

The university-based training consisted of **workshops** which all project participants attended. Workshops took place once a month on Saturday mornings for 3 hours in the BCLTP and twice a month on Friday afternoons for 2 hours in the CTAFL. These workshops were contexts for exploring topics related to participatory literacy instruction, as well as sharing experiences and concerns among sites. Topics for these workshops are outlined in Chapter Three; they included:

- Participatory curriculum development
- Assessing learners' needs, concerns, and goals
- Processes, tools, and activities for teaching literacy
- The transition from native language literacy to ESL
- Assessing student progress

site-based training

The site-based training consisted of **in-class mentoring** as well as **teacher-sharing meetings.**

- **Mentoring**: Each Intern worked with the Mentor at his or her site. The original plan was a 45 week training program, divided into three 15 week cycles for observation, co-teaching, and independent teaching, respectively. Interns were to begin by observing the Mentor, working with individual students or small groups, and assisting the teacher. They would gradually assume more responsibility, teaching under the Mentor's guidance until they were ready to teach on their own.

- **The teacher-sharing meetings** were designed to provide time to share ideas, resources, materials, and concerns.

- **Schedules**: Interns were to work a total of 8 to 10 hours per week. Two hours a week were designated for meetings and the rest for in-class work. The weekly meetings alternated between university-based workshops and teacher-sharing meetings at the sites. Schedules for in-class teaching/mentoring time varied in accordance with the sites' instructional schedules. In some cases, Mentors and Interns taught twice a week for 3 hours; in others, classes met four times a week for 2 hours. At some sites, classes were held during the day and at others, in the evening.

Who were the Mentors?

Probably the most critical aspect of implementation of this project is the selection of the Mentors. Their role is key in the day-to-day implementation of the project. They provide role models for students and Interns, oversee teaching at the sites, guide the work of the Interns, facilitate interactions between Interns, and address any tensions that arise. They are the link between the university-based and site-based training, guiding the process of translating what has been done in the workshops into practice. This section looks at the process for selecting Mentors, their backgrounds, and their reasons for participating in the project.

the selection process

In order to ensure that the project would be as fully integrated into the work of each site as possible, the selection of Mentors was left to the sites. They were chosen because they were outstanding individuals, usually already working at the sites, who seemed 'natural' for the position. Most had been at the site for several years, and thus were already deeply familiar with the student population and were an integral part of the agency's staff. Each had experience teaching beginning-level ESL literacy students and strong ties to the communities of the learners. At the beginning of the CTAFL, when the Mentor's position became open at the HCC, a formal search was conducted and one of the Interns at the JMCS (who had been trained in the BCLTP) was hired.

criteria for selection

Because the process for selecting Mentors in our work was somewhat informal, we came up with a list of criteria for the selection of Mentors retroactively, based on our experience of what is important for effective Mentoring. The following criteria should be seen, however, not as a blueprint, but as a general framework for Mentor selection. It is quite possible, even likely, that someone who is highly qualified to be a Mentor may not fulfill all of these criteria.

- background as immigrant or refugee; bilingual
- intimate knowledge of the community of the learners
- various kinds of involvement in the community (e.g., through church activities, sports clubs, radio shows, volunteer work, as well as educational activities)
- strong commitment to and love of his or her community; a desire to serve the community
- experience with and commitment to participatory, community-based education
- experience teaching beginning ESL/literacy
- love of teaching and a nonhierarchical stance toward learners
- familiarity with and relationship to the site

25

Issues in selecting Mentors...

As the following discussion suggests, the process of Mentor selection is more complex than a formal list implies.

As we thought about criteria for selecting Mentors, we debated whether to include "political stance" because the notion of literacy as a tool for social change is so central to a participatory approach. We decided not to make this a criterion in itself because, in fact, the notion of politics can be interpreted and applied in so many ways. At one point in a prior project, for example, someone with an explicit social change agenda totally alienated students by attempting to impose his politics in the classroom. Thus, we decided that we needed to break down the concept of being political into component parts:

•The person should be someone who has the trust of the community and can provide guidance to others.

•The person should be able to lead the community to an understanding of the social and political nature of community issues (regardless of whether he or she seems "revolutionary" or soft-spoken and mild-mannered).

•The person must be able to draw out students' experiences so that they can reflect on them (asking questions like, "Did you choose not to learn to read and write? Why do you have to come to class now, at your age?" in order to invite reflection on the political causes of illiteracy).

•The person should be comfortable enough (have enough self-confidence) to guide and share knowledge with people like him or herself without being threatened.

•The person must be willing to explore Interns' perspectives without feeling the need to impose a particular point of view.

Another issue in the selection process revolved around sites vs. project hiring criteria. A particular site, for example, may put high priority on hiring from within. It may want to give preference to people who have been Interns at that site. However, there may be an external candidate who has stronger leadership qualifications or otherwise fits the profile for a Mentor more appropriately. There are no simple solutions to this dilemma; each site has to balance the factors in terms of the particular applicants and the implications of the choice for both the site and the project.

possible interview questions

In our project, the Harborside Community Center used the following interview questions to determine the teaching and Mentoring qualifications of applicants for the Mentor's position:

- Why are you interested in doing this job?
- Describe one of your best classes.
- What approach do you use in your teaching?
- Can you describe an activity you might do with the class?
- How do you become aware of and mediate sensitive issues?
- How would you provide guidance for Interns? How do you see yourself as a supervisor?
- What would you do if you felt an Intern was not doing a good job?
- What are your goals for this class?
- What are your goals in your own life?

so what?

As the list of criteria for Mentor selection indicates, we saw formal teaching or higher education credentials as less important than Mentors' ability to serve as role models to the Interns (because they themselves had overcome obstacles to become effective teachers). Of course, it's not enough to be from the community of the learners or to have a work history at the site. Mentors must also have very specific qualifications in terms of teaching and working with others in a leadership capacity. However, as a field, we have to let go of the notion that the only qualifications that count are formal ones, framed in terms of higher education or credentialing.

The following accounts of the histories of the Mentors in our project provide a sense of what we mean by 'non-traditional' backgrounds. Although the particular paths leading each of them to the project were different, they shared many underlying motivations. They each had a strong sense of love for and commitment to their communities and saw the project as a way of giving back what they had gained through their own education. For each, the project was a way of doing something that they felt was deeply meaningful and getting paid for it at the same time; even more, they saw it as a way to extend their own education while contributing to that of others. In addition, all of them situated their work in the context of a larger process of social change. The power of their life experiences was not just that they could empathize with students' situations because they had been there, but that they were living examples of moving beyond this kind of exploitation.

27

What were the Mentors' backgrounds and why did they join the project?

This is my dream...

Julio Midy (below), the Mentor at the HMSC, has been living in the U.S., "unfortunately", as he says, for 11 years. It is unfortunate, he says, because:

Julio Midy

When you come from a country where 88% of the people do not know how to read and write, and if you had the privilege in your childhood to go to school, then that's the place you should be in order to help those who don't know how to read and write. And believe me, if I had the choice, my place would be in Haiti, doing just that.

Julio had studied anthropology at a university in Haiti, but left because "when you get through all your studies, you still cannot see the light at the end of the tunnel." Like many of his students, Julio started out his work life in the U.S. in a minimum-wage factory job, boxing pillows for $3.00 an hour (the same pillows he then saw for sale at $21.00 apiece at fancy department stores). In 1985, he enrolled as an undergraduate at UMass/Boston; his first UMass teacher was also the Adult Education Coordinator at the HMSC; she invited him to work at the Center and he has been an ESL teacher there since 1985. He also worked for many years in the Haitian Bilingual Program of the Boston Public Schools. Julio's ties in the Haitian community go beyond his work at the Center: he has his own Creole radio show in Boston and is a leading Haitian soccer organizer and player in the Northeast.

Julio sees his work as a Creole teacher as a concrete way to contribute to his community. For him, teaching is a way both to prove his commitment and to work for his people. It's a way for him to make money and be useful at the same time.

I have to tell you that I love Haiti, but saying that doesn't mean anything if you don't do anything concrete to prove your love. I love education for two reasons. First, even though I don't make much money – I don't make the money I'd like to make – I get paid for doing what I love. And also, teaching gives me a chance to help my own people. It gives me the opportunity to kill two birds with one stone– that's the reason why I really do love it. I'm working with my people and I'm doing it as my job. So I'm doing what I did not have a chance to do in my country, which is educate my own people. I have the privilege to do it in the United States. That's why I love teaching.

Julio sees his teaching as laying the groundwork for some day going back to Haiti and making a contribution there.

My goal is to learn more and more every day. I think you can learn from each student. Every day you'll have to learn something new. And you learn from people from different countries, you learn from different teachers. My goal is to learn as much as possible. One day we'll have to build a new Haiti. And I will be there using what I'm learning in the United States now.

Julio sees his teaching as part of the process of challenging exploitation and working for a better world.

The reason why [I chose to do education work] is that we have this unequal world, this world where people are exploiting other people. Just because some people don't really have the knowledge, some people don't really have any education, it's easy to exploit them. So, I think, as a teacher... I reduce the rate of illiteracy; therefore the lawyer will have less to do. If you want to talk about change, you have to educate your people...

Finally, Julio sees literacy education as intimately tied to the struggle for social justice.

The last thing I would like to say is that I hope one day we'll not have to talk about literacy in the world. Because, like I always say, illiteracy is the result of exploitation. So I think everybody has a right to know how to read and write. If you know how to read and how to write, if everybody knows how to read and write, definitely we would have a better world. This is my dream.

People are misunderstood and abused...

Ana Zambrano (below), the Mentor at the Jackson-Mann Community School, came to the U.S. from Colombia in 1984.

Ana Zambrano

Ana has dealt with issues relating to literacy throughout her life, and for her, this project was a natural extension of prior work as a learner and a teacher. She started learning English at a church program in East Boston and just a year later got a teaching position at the JMCS. Her background as an adult educator in Colombia had laid the groundwork for this quick transition to teaching.

Ana spent her childhood on a farm, in a family where her grandmother didn't know how to read and write, but her father read a lot; theirs was the only family in a 50 or 60 mile radius that owned books. She learned how to read at age 7 and her reading took her out of "reality as a child of a farm family with so much poverty and misfortune around." As a teenager, she worked in a literacy campaign that trained community people to teach basic skills. Ana then moved to Bogota and worked in a mothers' cooperative for 3 years. Her experiences in these two settings influenced her approach to teaching:

> *When I taught farmers, we used farmers' tools which were right around us. The [literacy] part only came in when you knew the tool... People could relate it immediately with what they were doing. It was very real, very relevant. In Bogota, the curriculum we developed was around children, and taking care of the children. The women were all working mothers who had children and basically nothing to live on. So the curriculum was that. So it was their reality.*

But when Ana first started learning English in the U.S., she was confronted with a completely different approach to education:

> *I learned English in a place where the teachers were all North American college students. So there was a kind of confusion for me*

when I came in because the people who had taught me English were people who had nothing to do with me or with my reality as an immigrant working at a warehouse. I had taught literacy and so all the values I had gotten from that, all the pride I had gotten, was somehow shaken or vanished to some extent by being taught by this group of young North Americans from the most expensive universities here, with completely different socioeconomic backgrounds than mine.

At the same time, however, Ana had brought a sense of community activism with her to the U.S. From her earliest days as an ESL student, she had taken on the role of assisting people to get what they needed. From this, the transition to becoming a teacher was a natural one. When asked what made her continue in education, she said:

It's as simple as this: by the time I was learning English, I was already going places with people to request services and helping them with translations. I knew tons of people and kept meeting more people who were misunderstood, abused, because they don't speak the language. I thought if I had learned, everybody else could learn to defend and advocate for themselves.

When Ana became a teacher, her first instinct was to follow the text- and teacher-centered approach that her own ESL teachers had used:

So I was in the middle of trying to weigh if what I had done in the past had anything to do with learning. I valued so much what [my ESL teachers] did because I had learned a lot. They gave me this book to read and I read. In the beginning it was hard to make sense of both worlds. In the beginning I tried to dismiss what I had done in the past and I tried not to relate it to my teaching at that moment. I tried just to follow "the rules."

At the same time that Ana was teaching, she was working as a counselor and advocate. This work, along with her participation in a critical thinking project, prompted her to re-examine her teaching:

But after a few years of confusion, I started to listen better and to look at people's realities in a more humane way. My own assumptions about people who came to this country were being completely challenged by people's realities in my advocacy and counseling job. I could see that reality right with my own eyes every single day. If I saw these realities, what was so different in the classroom? Why did I address those things in the classroom in such a different way? This started me in the process of thinking. I think I started to be much more myself again. I had to go through this cultural clash.... In Colombia, I was called a community leader.... After that I started really looking at what the community needs, what they want... And that has been a switch in my teaching for a few years. And it becomes clearer every cycle, and it changes according to the group, and it changes according to the make-up of the class. This doesn't necessarily mean that everybody is happy with this approach, but I feel it is more effective.

Ana's motivation for becoming involved in Intern training stemmed from her desire to teach people to advocate for themselves, to defend themselves and to be less dependent on others. Like Julio, she saw this work as very much tied to the fight for social justice.

Somebody did the work of teaching me. Now I could teach somebody else not to depend on somebody. I know for me [knowing the language] made the difference so it should make a difference for other people. That kept me in teaching. And it is basically an instinct in me to fight against injustice.

Being in a position to train others (most of whom had been her own ESL students) gave Ana a special sense of purpose in this project.

Now, by having the Interns, I see the efforts multiply by five. And there is much more of an impact on people's lives with five people directly involved. It will help them in the future to teach or guide their lives. It makes me feel that my work is much more important.

In addition, being a trainer gave her a new sense of pride in herself and enabled her to see her own teaching in a new light:

I have learned and see much better what I know.... Before I didn't think that I knew that much. I know now that I really know a lot about this stuff.... When I see the Interns teaching, I'm observing myself. The new teachers have made me reflect a lot on what I do and how I do it. Who did she/he learn this from? Where did he or she learn this? There are times you feel so proud! Other times you see your own mistakes so clearly you want to hide! ...So I know I can be a good trainer. But it is a continuous reflecting exercise.

In the daytime I was a robot; at night I was a human being...

Felipe Vaquerano (below) came to the U.S. from El Salvador in 1988 at the age of 19. Much of his life in El Salvador had been shaped by the war there.

Felipe Vaquerano

Felipe grew up in the countryside, helping his father on the farm, but the war forced him to move to the city at age 11. There he lived with his sister while he continued his education. Because of the political situation, he left El Salvador to join a brother in the U.S. 3 days after he finished high school.

Like Ana, Felipe got his start doing literacy work in his own country. In El Salvador, high school students were required to teach Spanish literacy to adults for 6 months in order to get their diploma.

It was good experience for us. I had always wanted to be a teacher but I had never thought about teaching adults. It was so nice to see people who were 25 years old and you were helping them. It was nice to help people who were always saying "I'm too old to learn."

The approach to teaching that was used there prepared Felipe for his work in the U.S. in some ways, and, in others, was quite different.

In El Salvador, we tried to use the students' experiences to motivate them to go back to school. But we didn't have methods like using stories or codes. We didn't deal with issues. We started with the alphabet, then put the consonants and vowels together. With writing, we had to teach them how to hold a pencil. The teacher did hand over hand.

Coming to the U.S. was difficult for Felipe at first. He had to work two jobs, one at Burger King and the other in a plastics factory, making $5.75 per hour. He spoke no English and this presented problems for him at work.

33

I remember one time they wanted me to clean the parking lot at work, but they didn't know how to tell me and I couldn't understand. So they pointed at me to get the phone. They had to call somebody who spoke Spanish on the phone to tell me what to do. When I got to the phone somebody said to be sure to clean the parking lot. I asked her who she was and she said a friend of the boss. I felt so frustrated. At that time I had to work two jobs; it was difficult and I said "I'm not going to have this kind of life. I'm going back to school."

Felipe enrolled as a beginning ESL student in night classes at the JMCS in 1989. At the JMCS, Felipe immediately excelled as a student; he learned English quickly and volunteered to work on the student magazine. After only five semesters at the JMCS, he had moved to the advanced ESL class, and began to take courses at the Harvard University extension school. He also enrolled for Human Services training at a local agency serving Spanish-speaking people and volunteered as a translator at Children's Hospital.

In 1991, Felipe was selected as an Intern in the BCLTP because he had become a leader among students so quickly. At the same time, he continued to work at the factory during the day. Felipe had several reasons for wanting to become an Intern. He saw it as a chance to try something new, to get to know other cultures, and to become a role model for his peers:

After working in a factory, it was like a whole different world for me. When I first began, I was curious about how people taught English here, and I just wanted to be a teacher. I always admired my teacher, you know, and I wanted to work in a classroom with people from different countries, to get to know their culture. At the same time, I wanted to try to show people that even though we didn't go to the university, we have skills that we can use to teach, to help others. And on the other hand, it was an opportunity for me to get into a better job.

For Felipe, teaching represented doing work that was meaningful. He often said, *"In the daytime, I felt like a robot, but at night I was a human being."* The importance of this work was reinforced for Felipe when, as his English became more proficient, he started having difficulty at the plastics factory. After a few months with the project, he was laid off because, he says:

I was learning English and I knew about my rights as a worker, and I knew they were not complying with them. I had been there without a raise for 2 years and I had asked for one. I had one week vacation and when I came back, they said, "We have bad news for you. You are going to be laid off." Just like that. I didn't know what to think.

This experience reinforced for Felipe the need to get into a different kind of work. Becoming part of this project was a chance to move ahead; he saw it as opening doors that otherwise would have been closed. In spite of the fact that he was such a good student, there was no way that he could afford to go on to the university for higher education. This project gave him the chance to gain experience and skills, to learn something concrete that he could use for future employment, and to move out of a dead-end job. As he said, through this project, he could develop a job network, a resume, and a base of experience. In his words, *"Now when I have to look for another job, I can say I have done this. I have this certificate and experience which is more important than a certificate."*

As an Intern, Felipe distinguished himself: he took great initiative and quickly gained confidence in teaching. He worked well with other Interns, and volunteered to present his work at project-wide workshops. He grasped the concepts of participatory education and was able to put them into practice in his own ESL classrooms. He was the only Intern in the BCLTP who prepared and facilitated a workshop for the whole group; his workshop focused on using games to teach ESL and literacy.

In fact, Felipe's motivation and outstanding performance as an Intern did result in his using the project as a stepping stone to better jobs. After being laid off at the plastics factory, he was hired as a Teaching Assistant in a special needs school, largely, he believes, because of the training and experience he acquired in the BCLTP. He was one of several candidates for the position of Mentor at the HCC (including a certified bilingual teacher and some internal candidates); he made such a good impression in the interview that he was hired as the Spanish Literacy Mentor.

Thus, the project was concretely important for Felipe. For him, being able to earn a higher salary was not something to be laughed at: a friend of his who has been in the U.S. for 18 years is not yet making the salary that Felipe makes as a Mentor. In addition, the work gives Felipe the chance to do something meaningful:

> *I have my own desk, and I have my paper here, my notebook, my dictionary. I had never thought about working in a classroom in this country. It's good because it gives you the chance to express who you are, how you feel, and to show people that even though you are not American or you haven't been here for a long time, you can do something for yourself and for other people.*

Who were the Interns?

Over the course of the 4 years of both the BCLTP and the CTAFL projects, a total of 36 Interns participated in the training. The next section on Interns incorporates our cumulative experience with both projects because this experience yields the greatest knowledge base from which to generalize.

general Intern profiles

In conceptualizing the model, we envisioned four kinds of people who might be recruited as Interns:

1) **Former teachers or literacy workers** from communities surrounding the participating sites who have strong first language educational backgrounds, but may have weak ESL proficiency or lack U.S. professional credentials, and are therefore unable to secure jobs in their fields of expertise. In training them to teach L1 literacy, the project would provide an opportunity to utilize their previous background in the process of developing ESL proficiency and upgrading skills relevant for employment in the U.S.

2) **Advanced ESL students** currently enrolled in collaborating sites who have excelled in their own language learning, are interested in helping lower level learners, and want to further their own education while contributing to their own community. The project would enable them to gain professional skills and lead to higher education for some participants.

3) **Bilingual undergraduate students** from UMass or other local universities who are eager for opportunities to "give back" what they have gained in the form of community service. For these students, the training program would offer the chance to develop skills that draw on their cultural, linguistic, and educational strengths, and, in some cases might lead to education majors and careers in bilingual education or ESL. This category included undergraduates who had received literacy training, and tutoring experience through the Student Literacy Corps project at UMass.

4) **Community and parent leaders** who have expressed a strong commitment to the educational development of their communities. These might be individuals who have emerged as parent, housing, or health advocates in their own communities and express a desire to serve in these communities. The project would enable them to access professional development to supplement or enhance their current roles.

As with the Mentors, the actual selection of the Interns was done by the sites through their own networks of contacts. This process varied from site to site. In some cases, Interns were selected from people already in contact with the sites; in others, they were recruited. At the HMSC, for example, there is an ongoing stream of people from the community who come to volunteer or work at the site. Some of those who became Interns were UMass/Boston Student Literacy Corps tutors, former literacy workers in Haiti's literacy campaign, school administrators, active church members, students in the ESL program, and non-teaching site staff (the receptionist and the in-take worker). At the JMCS, all but one of the Interns were former ESL students in the program who showed exceptional promise and had been leaders in student activities at the site. At the HCC, Interns were recruited through personal and community networks in the local Central American community.

criteria for selection of Interns

The following factors were considered in selecting Interns:

- strong motivation to teach (desire to become an Intern for substantive rather than financial reasons)
- commitment to community (prior service/volunteering)
- demonstrated leadership potential (through prior work at site or in community)
- L1 literacy proficiency and high school education
- learner-centered, non-authoritarian views on teaching
- willingness to learn from peers and students
- prior experience in literacy education (participation in literacy campaigns, training as teachers, or work in public education)
- appropriate time availability (no scheduling conflicts)

Again, we did not expect that each Intern would meet all of these qualifications; they served as guidelines in the selection process. The process for assessing Intern qualifications varied from site to site. Usually, once a potential Intern was identified, the Mentor informally explained the requirements, schedule, and objectives of the project, as well as getting a general sense of the Intern's potential. Then an interview took place which, in some cases, involved formal interview questions and in others, an informal discussion. The JMCS developed a set of scenarios and invited potential Interns to explain how they would respond to them. For example, Interns were asked how they would respond to someone who said, "I don't want you as a teacher because you're not an American." In one case, a potential Intern said she would invite the student to stay in the class for a little while and see how it went before deciding; in another, a candidate said he would tell the student, "You have no place here"; the latter was not hired. Selection was based on responses to questions such as these.

One of the things that we learned through the interview process is that recruitment is a two-way process: what we say to Interns is just as important as what they say to us in the initial interview. The more open and informative we are about the expectations and approach, the more we will get a sense of the Intern's interest and potential. Being open at the beginning prevents difficulties later and sets the tone for a relationship of mutual learning. In the BCLTP, we relied on interviews and initial meetings to introduce Interns to the project. However, in the CTAFL project, we decided to be more formal about what participating in the project meant, both in terms of logistical expectations and in terms of the approach to training. We sent each Intern a letter outlining exactly what the project was before the first workshop. The letter addressed the following questions:

- What is the project?
- Who is involved in it?
- Why are we doing this project? What are its goals?
- How is the project funded?
- How long will the training last?
- What will we do in the project?
- How many hours will we work and how will they be divided?
- What will happen in the site meetings?
- When and where will the workshops take place?
- What will happen in the workshops?
- What will happen at the end of the project?

We also included the following sentence, which set the tone for the trainings, and gave Interns a sense of our approach to teaching:

We believe that teaching is an art, not a science: we will provide the paint and brushes, but you must paint the pictures!

As the training proceeded, Interns often referred back to this idea of teaching as an art, and mentioned this sentence in the letter.

Issues in selecting Interns...

As with the selection of Mentors, the process of selecting Interns is more complex than a simple list of criteria suggests; we found that our initial assessments of an Intern's potential from interviews were not always accurate. We have had many discussions retroactively about which criteria were in fact most important in determining the success of candidates.

One issue we have discussed is whether it is an advantage or a disadvantage for an Intern to have had **prior teaching experience.** Some Interns who had been teachers before focused on books and had the attitude, "I'm the teacher—I'm the authority." These Interns had to unlearn traditional ways of relating to students and teaching literacy. In other cases, however, having a teaching background allowed Interns to jump into teaching with ease and confidence, contributing their experience to the group's knowledge.

Another issue which applied to Interns as well as Mentors was the question of the Intern's **political stance or world view:** because the project was participatory in its orientation, and instruction was aimed toward connecting literacy with the social context of students' lives, did this mean that Interns needed to share, at least to some extent, a social change perspective when they came into the project? We found it wasn't always an advantage to have a social change perspective and it wasn't necessarily a disadvantage not to have one. As with Mentors, what seemed most important was the Intern's general stance in regard to learners, that they have a respectful attitude rather than a paternalistic one. It was important, as Ana said, that Interns present themselves as fighters, as people willing to take on struggle and advocate on behalf of themselves and students. Within this framework, we were able to problematize the issue of social change as part of the content of workshops, making it a subject of inquiry and dialogue rather than a prerequisite for participation. In fact, differences in opinion helped push forward everyone's thinking.

A related issue concerned the role of the Intern's **religious beliefs**. In a number of cases, either people wanted to become Interns to fulfill a sense of mission, or their religion was so central to their thinking that it permeated their view of how to teach literacy. We were concerned that these beliefs might shape their teaching processes (attitudes toward students) or even its content (imposition of religious ideas). Actually, however, these fears were realized to a very limited extent in only one case (where the Intern seemed to view her students more as poor victims needing to be "saved"). In most cases, Interns treated their beliefs as personal matters which they chose to share or not share like any other ideas. In no cases did they impose their beliefs; rather, these beliefs seemed to strengthen their commitment to working with students.

Likewise, the role of **motivation for being an Intern** was less than clear cut. In general, our view was that Interns needed to be motivated by a real commitment to their communities and a desire to contribute. Nevertheless, because Interns were paid a stipend for participation, a potential motivation was the additional income. Although we tried to screen out anyone who was participating primarily for the sake of the money, it became clear that a few of the Interns saw the project as an interesting way to make some extra money. However, at least in one case, an Intern who began with this attitude became so involved and committed through the course of the project that she volunteered to continue teaching after the funding ran out.

Even **knowledge of the target language** turned out not to be a bottom-line requirement for the Creole component. Because French has traditionally been the medium of instruction in Haiti, many highly literate Haitian adults have not had the opportunity to study Creole. Thus, two of the Interns who were qualified in other ways had to learn to read and write in Creole themselves (through Creole workshops and intensive independent study) to prepare for teaching.

so what?

Thus, our experience has been that many factors interact to determine an Intern's effectiveness, including attitude, prior experience, openness to learning, and flexibility. People who have weaknesses in one area often have strengths in another, and are able overcome weaknesses through the work of the project itself. A few generalizations can be made about recruiting Interns:

•Risks can be minimized by recruiting candidates who are known to the site, who have a strong track record as a student, staff member, or volunteer.

•Interns' attitudes are key in determining effectiveness: they must show respect for students and openness toward a participatory approach, and be motivated by a desire to strengthen their community and fight the injustices it faces.

•Complete agreement about perspectives is not necessary, but willingness to exchange ideas and learn from peers is.

•Full participation in training activities should be mandatory. Scheduling expectations should be clearly stated at the outset.

What were the Interns' backgrounds?

age and education

The hallmark of the group of Interns trained in both projects was its diversity. Participants came from Haiti, Brazil, Guatemala, Honduras, El Salvador, Peru, and Colombia. They ranged in age from their early 20s to retirement age. Their educational backgrounds varied: some had university degrees from their home countries, others had not completed high school there; one had been a pre-med student. Many had come as recently as 1989 and had enrolled in beginning ESL classes at the participating sites upon arrival. Some were in the process of receiving their GEDs while they were Interns; others were enrolled in community colleges or universities.

occupation in homeland and in the U.S.

In terms of occupations, many had been professionals in their homelands (engineers, computer programmers, educators). In addition to those who had been teachers in their home countries, some had worked in literacy campaigns; others had been involved in related aspects of literacy work (e.g., as radio broadcaster for a literacy campaign, director of an adult education school). Once they arrived in the U.S., almost all of them had to work in unskilled entry-level jobs (in factories, hotels, restaurants, or as housecleaners). Others had office jobs–as computer operators or receptionists–which they found mechanical or unchallenging.

Laudize and Kerline, two of the Interns from the BCLTP

41

TABLE 1: Intern Profiles

Countries of origin	Backgrounds in home country	Occupations in the U.S.	Connection to site

Haiti
 	
Honduras
 	
El Salvador
 	
Brazil
 	
Guatemala
 	
Colombia
 	
Peru
	students:
	   high school
	   medical school
	   college
	   computer science
	   dentistry
	
	teachers:
	   day care
	   elementary
	   secondary
	   adult education
	
	literacy campaign
	   worker
	
	radio show host
	
	computer
	   programmer
	
	director of school
		security guard
		
		car mechanic
		
		factory worker
		
		student
		   GED
		   ESL
		   college,
		   comm. college
		
		housecleaner
		
		hotel room service
		   worker
		
		dishwasher
		
		bookkeeper
		
		pizza deliverer
		
		adult ed center:
		   receptionist
		   in-take worker
		   childcare worker
		
		women's shelter
		   worker
		
		computer
		programmer
		
		office worker
			community
			   volunteer
			
			UMass tutor
			
			receptionist at
			   site
			
			GED student at
			   site
			
			former ESL
			   student at site
			
			family contact of
			   Mentor
			
			church choir
			   leader
			
			church activist
			
			daughter of ESL
			   student
			
			in-take worker at
			   the site

Why did the Interns want to participate in the project?

In both projects, Interns were interviewed about their backgrounds and reasons for wanting to teach. The following discussion includes excerpts from these interviews.

"It happened to me..."

Many of the Interns talked about joining the project as a way to help others who were going through the struggles they had gone through. Some used the term "we" in the interviews, referring to themselves not as individuals, but as members of a community that includes both people who are literate and people who aren't. Because they had faced the same problems as learners when they first came to the U.S., the Interns felt they could help others get through difficulties with the language:

When I didn't speak English, I knew how it feels not to understand when people open their mouths so big, saying "Do you understand?" It happened to me. Then I said to myself, "You will have to speak English and to help the other people who are in the same condition." The language barrier is so restricting that people think you are out of your mind if you don't speak the language, not everyone, but some people. That's the reason I wanted to do this work with Latinos.

"There was a lot of discrimination..."

For some Interns, it wasn't just the general struggles with the language, but specific experiences dealing with discrimination that motivated them to want to teach. One Intern, for example, describes what happened when she was placed in a regular English course at a community college:

I had some problems there because the teacher didn't want to give extra attention to the four foreigners and told them that they wouldn't pass the class. We complained to the Dean but they didn't do anything about it.... I did face a lot of discrimination down there. And it really hurts me. I think that was one of the main reasons for deciding to help my people. I don't think that it is fair that if you come from another country, you have to put up with people, the way they treat you like you are a stranger, you don't know how to write. They put you down. They don't realize that you have an education too, that you are a person...they have to see the people the way they are. It's hard, they don't see you. They only think that because you are Spanish, you are automatically no good.

She went on to say that part of her reason for wanting to teach was to help others defend themselves against the kind of discrimination she experienced:

They don't know their rights and they suffer. I already went through that and I don't want them to go through what I went through. Because when I came to this country, there was a lot of discrimination.

Another reason the Interns wanted to teach L1 literacy related to their understanding of the special challenges (beyond the language barrier and discrimination) people face in the U.S. when they are not literate. It is the differences in the social context that make illiteracy even more of a problem here. One Intern, for example, talked about the problems of never having learned to read and write being exacerbated in the U.S:

In my country not everybody is literate. Most are illiterate.... When I came here, [literacy] was more necessary than in my country: you had to sign a check. In my country you didn't need it; poor people don't have to sign checks.

Several of the Interns had had experiences in their own countries that had inspired them to want to learn more about teaching literacy. For them, the project was a way to follow through on something they had started earlier in their lives and, perhaps, to learn something they could eventually bring back to their countries. One, for example, had taught literacy to about 50 students every night for 2 years when she was a teenager.

I did that because I always like to be active in the community. I like to help people because you know they need it. It is also a good way to get to know people and to help them with their lives over here.

Many Interns had worked in literacy campaigns in their countries and had been inspired by that experience to continue teaching:

When I was there, I did 5 months in literacy work with adults. And when I loved it, I saw at the same time that the people loved me too. I love to teach adults because I think I have something to give them.

Another Intern told the story of an experience that influenced his later desire to teach:

When I was much younger and in Haiti and failed the state exam, there was a beach where I used to go very often. Since I wasn't doing anything, there was plenty of time to do what I wanted to do. The beach was 5 kilometers from where I lived and I liked to walk up the hill to the beach and keep healthy. I met a fisherman there, about my age, named Joba. Joba had a girlfriend who knew how to read and write and he couldn't. I told him not to worry about it; it wasn't a big deal. I told him, "Listen, I have plenty of time, we are going to work on this. I'll teach you at least to sign your name." I kept going to the beach to meet Joba... and before I left the country Joba could sign his name. If I could make this impact, this progress, a new life for someone–that had a very strong impact on me. That's one of my biggest achievements... Because of me, Joba could write his name. That was very significant for me.

One Intern was inspired by teaching a maid how to read as a child:

When I was a little girl in Haiti, we had maids.... So there was one of the maids who didn't know how to read and write. I taught her how to read and write at that time. She was so grateful and when I came here it had sunk in my mind.

"I can't fix the world, but at least I can do a little bit..."

The project gave many of the Interns the feeling that they could make a difference. It satisfied their need to do something socially useful while at the same time doing something for themselves: by meeting the learners' needs, they would, in various ways, be meeting their own needs. The project provided a framework for learning how to utilize their own background in a constructive way. One Intern expressed this as follows:

I thought that I can't fix the world, but at least I can do a little bit. With a little help, I can make other people happy, maybe.

Another saw the project as a way of using his own education for the community while at the same time doing something personally and intellectually challenging:

I feel like someone who has an ability should do something; this is my commitment. As far as I'm concerned, I don't really see education like something for the future to make money. I like it and it's a kind of intellectual work that I find myself into.

Several Interns saw the project as something that humanized them, giving meaning to their lives. Although they used their hands during the day, they were able to use their heads and their hearts at night:

I love it.... After working as a housekeeper all day, working with cleaners and mops and things like that, it's like a refreshment to go to the school and teach and be with the students and offer something from myself, something that is not my strength, my legs.... For me, this is a refreshment.

For Interns who came to the project with a more explicit social change perspective, the project offered the opportunity to go beyond the rhetoric of politics. A Haitian Intern, for example, sees teaching as a way to "put his money where his mouth is," to take a kind of action which may make a real difference:

The Haitian community has a lot of problems in terms of education and needs a lot of help. As a Haitian myself, I feel like I should help instead of talking about the problem. What do I do as a Haitian for the community? I was interested in politics in Haiti, to be on a radio station to talk very abstractly or tell where I stand. There is a huge amount of people in Haiti who cannot write, who cannot read. Now, if I go back to Haiti, I would like to work with those people. This is the kind of politics in which I would like to be involved. It is a concrete way of helping people.

An Intern who had been a teacher in Haiti saw his teaching more globally in terms of making the world a better place, a goal he has had since his childhood:

When I was young, my father said to me all the time, "You can help better the world when you teach someone." All the time I think about that. After my studies, I thought about helping. I also like the thought that someone said, "When you open a school you close a prison."

If there is one theme that can be said to represent all the Interns' reasons for participating in the project, it is the theme of commitment to their communities. In every case, it was a deeply felt desire to contribute to the well-being of people who were in situations similar to their own that moved people to join the project and pushed forward their work. One Intern summed up this feeling when she said, *"I'm not a professional teacher, but I know that I have something inside to offer."*

Who were the students?

Because this project focused primarily on training Interns to teach literacy and ESL, rather than on the teaching itself, we focused less on documentation of the literacy students' backgrounds than on that of the Interns. However, the following brief profile will provide a sense of who the students were; Chapter Four will describe how their backgrounds and experiences shaped instruction.

How were students recruited?

JMCS

Recruitment varied from site to site, depending on the language of instruction and relation of the site to the community of the learners. Because Interns worked in ongoing classes at the Jackson-Mann, recruitment was not an issue: students were assigned to classes from the long waiting list, and Interns were placed in these classes; when Interns were ready to teach independently, additional classes were formed from people on the waiting lists. Special recruitment for project classes was unnecessary.

HCC

The Harborside school was the only site where an entirely new component was set up through the project. Although many students who were not literate in Spanish had been identified through the amnesty ESL classes (students who came to the HCC for the first time because they needed the required number of hours of ESL instruction to become documented), at that time there had been no financial or structural support for Spanish literacy. The Master Teacher of the BCLTP undertook a concerted outreach effort which included calling and writing personal notes to former amnesty students, making announcements at churches, having house parties at former and current students' homes, and inviting potential students, making announcements in ESL classes at Harborside, posting flyers, making announcements in local newspapers and newsletters, and contacting other ESL, adult education, and Hispanic community agencies.

Because potential students were often hesitant about coming to classes, and were not always clear about why they should learn to read and write in Spanish (as opposed to English), they were told that they would be in a special class designed for people with similar backgrounds and that it would make it easier for them to learn English in the long run. The key in convincing the Spanish literacy students seemed to be personally meeting the teacher or Interns and discussing their fears and questions before coming to the Center. Students were also told that they could decide when they felt ready to begin learning English.

Once classes began, it was the students themselves who were the primary resources for recruitment of new students: they brought friends and relatives, conducted an informational open house in which they displayed their work, and even produced a video about the classes which was aired on neighborhood cable TV. In addition, when Felipe became the Mentor, he used his own personal network of contacts in the Central American community to recruit students; one of the students he recruited was his roommate, whom he had been trying to convince to go back to school for some time. His aunt, who sells *pupusas* (a Central American food), also helped by trying to convince her customers who didn't know how to read and write to go to literacy classes.

HMSC

At the Haitian Multi-Service Center, when this project started, there was a long waiting list for ESL classes which included many people (an estimated 20%-30%) who were not literate in their first language. The HMSC offers a variety of services (including health, legal, job training, etc.) and has a largely Haitian staff; for these reasons, the site attracted many Haitians with little schooling who might not have gone to a mixed-language ESL site (because of being intimidated either by the school context or by the fact that the sites are not bilingual). Further, since the HMSC is the only agency in Boston that exclusively serves Haitians, it is a central contact point for newly arrived Haitians in the Boston area. Although their original reason for going to the HMSC may not be educational, these students often sign up for classes once they see it is a safe bilingual setting. Thus, there was a significant population of students already in contact with the Center who were prime candidates for the classes.

Creole literacy classes had been offered at the HMSC since the early 1980s. These classes were always popular and in demand by students who recognized their benefit. In fact, it was a group of women in a Creole Literacy class taught by Marjorie Delsoin that led to the decision of the HMSC to focus on training Native Language Literacy as well as ESL teachers in the BCLTP. This group of students had organized an event to celebrate their work; their enthusiasm for learning in their native language inspired the program to expand the Creole literacy component and train additional teachers. Once new classes were set up, however, not all the prospective students were convinced of the value of learning to read and write in Creole. To some extent, this was the same issue that faces any native language literacy program: students question the usefulness of learning to read and write in their first language when they are in the U.S. However, the situation at the HMSC was compounded by the fact that, unlike Spanish, Haitian Creole was,

48

until recently, rarely the language of initial literacy acquisition; further, because, historically, French was imposed as the official language and the language of education (in order to ensure the domination of the elite and exclude the masses from political and economic power), Creole has traditionally been stigmatized and seen as an impediment to improving one's life. For these reasons, the challenge at the HMSC at the beginning of the BCLTP was not so much one of finding students, as one of encouraging all who could benefit to enroll. A centerwide process of dialogue and discussion resulted in a substantial change in attitudes toward Creole literacy among those who were initially reluctant; see Appendix B for an account of this process.

strategies for promoting L1 literacy

Strategies for validating and promoting L1 literacy instruction at both the HCC and the HMSC included the following:

- discussing the relationship between L1 literacy and ESL acquisition with students

- situating the issue in its broader sociopolitical and historical context (why people were unable to go to school in their home countries, why their L1 was devalued, how illiteracy was used as a tool for stratification)

- inviting students to express and explore their resistance to L1 literacy

- giving students choice: inviting them to try L1 literacy class for a limited time or to try a beginning ESL class and then decide; negotiating the ratio of L1 literacy and ESL with them

- integrating dialogue about the issue of L1 literacy into the curriculum itself; linking specific literacy activities with reflection on students' literacy histories

- discussing the issue of L1 literacy with the whole center (not just literacy students) in order to legitimate it, prevent marginalization of the L1 literacy component, and create understanding between various groups of students

- enhancing teachers' understanding of the history, linguistics and approaches to L1 literacy through workshops and training

- incorporating specific and limited time for ESL instruction into literacy classes to demonstrate how L1 literacy can facilitate learning English

What were the students' backgrounds?

JMCS

There was a great deal of variation in the student populations both within and between sites. At the JMCS, for example, students in the beginning ESL classes came from 26 different nationality groups, a variety of educational histories (from finishing only a few years of school to graduating from college), and both urban and rural backgrounds. They ranged in age from late teens to pensioners. There was a relatively even split between men and women. They were both refugees and immigrants, here for political, personal and/or economic reasons. Regardless of their educational backgrounds, many were employed in low-wage manufacturing or service sector jobs (in factories, restaurants, hotels, hospitals, or housecleaning).

HMSC

At the HMSC, most of the literacy students had either never gone to school or had gone only for a few years. Many were older people (mainly women) who had come to the U.S. years ago, and lived in a virtually all-Haitian community in Boston (perhaps staying home to care for family). Often they had worked in the markets or other kinds of self-employment in Haiti and were unemployed in the U.S. Others had come more recently and, of these, some were quite young (in their late teens or 20s). After the coup against Aristide, the HMSC became a resettlement site for refugees, and this brought a new group of Creole literacy students. These students were primarily men, from a range of educational backgrounds, separated from their families and living in groups.

HCC students

The student population at Harborside went through various phases. The first group of students in the BCLTP was quite homogeneous: they were peasants and fishermen from El Salvador. As the project developed, new students from other Central American countries (Guatemala and Costa Rica) enrolled; they, too, were primarily from rural environments, although some of them came from urban backgrounds; a few students from Puerto Rico started classes near the end of the project. Students ranged in age from their 20s to 40s. At the beginning, most of the students in the classes were men, but by the end of the project, classes were evenly divided between men and women. Many of them had experienced war and political repression as well as economic struggles in their homelands. They often worked in the most marginalized jobs when they could find work (washing dishes, cleaning offices, working in the lowest paid factory jobs).

Getting a sense of students' histories and reasons for learning English was also very much a part of the learning process itself. Interns often explored students backgrounds as a preliminary step in curriculum development (see Chapter Four). Table 2 (which was done as the basis for a class activity) gives a sense of who the students were in one ESL class.

TABLE 2: Student profile chart, Jackson-Mann Community Center (ESL II Class)

Name	Country	Job in Your Country	Do in U.S.A.	Don't like in U.S.
Leya fuksman	Russia	Engineer	Retired student	cold winds
thant thuy	vietnan	student	student	cold wheater
Ramiro Abello	Colombia	Supervisor	Bus boy cleaning person	cold weather
Gildete Rocha	Brazil	student	Housecleaner	cold weather
Aleksandr Gombert	Russia	worker	Retired student	the MBTA slow.
Cuong	vietnan	potographer	worker	cold weather
francisco Escobar	Guatemala	Farmer	Factory worker	cold weather
Oscar ventura	Honduras	self employed	Cashier	the weather
Angela Araujo	Brazil	Secretary	Babysitter	cold weather
Douglas Mature	Honduras	Dental asistant	Factory worker	cold
Patricia Villagran	el salvador	student	cashier	cold
* I did it with 28 students it took me 2 hour: class	⟶	⟶	⟶	⟶

What brought the students to literacy and ESL classes?

In order to get a sense of students' reasons for coming to class, and to assess the significance of the classes in their lives, we interviewed students from each site at the end of the project. We asked them to talk about what their lives were like before joining the project and why it was important for them to learn to read and write or to learn English (depending on the context). In addition, we asked them how their lives had changed since they had begun the classes (their responses to this question are included in Chapter Five).

I never thought it would make a difference...

Literacy students often said that they had lived here for years without considering going to school; they didn't have confidence that they would be able to learn, or understand what a difference being able to read and write might make.

I wasn't aware of many things I didn't know. I have been in this country for 9 years but I never thought that learning to read and write could make a difference in my life. If I had known that, I could have started before and I could have gotten a better job already. I hadn't known how beautiful learning to read and write was, and how important it is. I was a little scared because I thought that learning was for children or young people, but I found that there are many opportunities for adults also.

At the same time, however, they often said that they endured many difficulties because of their lack of literacy. They often talked about the desire for independence as a motivation for learning.

One of the most common things that students said is that, before learning to read and write, they were vulnerable to being taken advantage of by others. One student, for example, told the story of paying his utility bills through a friend; he noticed that he had to give more and more money each month because the bill kept getting bigger. He finally went to the utility office and asked why the bill was so large only to discover that his friend had been keeping half of the money for himself each month. He pulled a knife on the man and might have ended in prison except for the fact that, when they went to court, it was discovered that the other person had a criminal record.

Now I can do it myself...

Both literacy and ESL students talked about the desire to overcome this kind of dependence as a reason for wanting to learn. A Spanish literacy student, for example, said:

When I came to this country, I needed to find somebody to write a letter for me and now I can write it. I feel good about it because I can write anything I want. You are not able to express your real feelings when somebody is writing for you. You can only say the most important things. I can go to a bank and try to fill out papers. I can try to find out where I am by reading. I can communicate more with my family.

An ESL student expressed a similar motivation:

I was in the hospital 7 months pregnant, not able to say a word in English. And later on, when he was born, my son was giving me trouble because his life was in danger. I felt lost, isolated, with a newborn baby and with the problem of having to depend on an interpreter for everything. Whenever I had to take him to the hospital for a check-up or just for anything else, I used to see White people, and I felt they were colder; maybe it was my insecurity at being in this country without knowing the language.

I have walked a good distance...

The same student talked about intangible reasons for learning—not only becoming independent, but also, gaining a sense of confidence:

It was important to me to learn English so that I could be independent from my family. I used to need my family's help even to go shopping. Now I feel I have walked a good distance. I am not afraid anymore. I have a lot more self-confidence. I can read English. I can understand when people talk to me and overall, I don't feel isolated.

It was often these intangible reasons that were the first reason for coming to class, rather than an immediate desire to get a job. Literacy students especially saw work-related goals as less immediate than being able to communicate better with family members. When asked what his hopes were, one student said:

I want to learn more Spanish: I need to improve my writing because I can read more than write. I want to write more to my family. After that, I want to learn English and look for a better job.

These excerpts give a sense of the range of student motivations for coming to class. What was striking about their responses is that they focused as much on affective and family-related reasons for participating as on narrowly functional reasons.

Chapter Three: The Training Component

Although the underlying approach to training was the same for both the BCLTP and the CTAFL projects, the design of the training was different. Because we had experience with two different training designs, we were able to compare their effectiveness. This chapter looks at the common underlying approach to training, the differences between the two projects, the ways that each training component was structured, and the issues that emerged in training Interns.

What was the approach to training?

the guiding principle

The guiding principle for our approach to training was the belief that the way that we conducted the training should be consistent with our approach to teaching: we wanted to practice (in training) what we were preaching (about teaching). Because our approach to literacy education was a participatory one, our goal was to make the training itself participatory. The Mentors characterized some of the ways we did this as follows:

- *We started by trying to make people feel comfortable in the training.*

- *We didn't tell people what to do. We tried to challenge their idea that training meant learning techniques.*

- *We tried to let the Interns participate or talk more than us.*

- *Most of what happened in the workshops came from the Interns. We used Interns' experiences as examples.*

- *We tried to demystify the belief that we as "trainers" were experts who had all the answers.*

- *We didn't give solutions to problems, but created a context for figuring them out.*

Embedded in these comments are three key aspects of a participatory approach that we modeled in the training: 1) the notion of transforming teacher–learner relations, 2) the notion of the negotiated or emergent curriculum, and 3) the notion of inquiry and experience-based learning. These notions constitute the theoretical framework that informed our approach to training. The next section will explore each of these notions and their implications for training.

**teacher–
learner
relations**

According to Freire (1970), both the content and the processes of education can either reinforce or challenge the powerlessness of marginalized people. Traditionally, the teacher is seen as the expert whose task is to transmit knowledge, filling learners with new information or skills which they passively receive. Learners' own knowledge and realities are excluded from the classroom. This teacher-centered process, Freire says, leaves learners silenced and powerless to act on the conditions that marginalize them.

In participatory education, transforming teacher–learner roles is central to enabling learners to assume more control of the direction of their lives. Education becomes a context for understanding and challenging the forces that maintain their powerlessness. Thus, the educational process should both model changes in power relations inside the classroom and allow learners to rehearse for changes in their roles outside it. The learners' experience and knowledge are seen to be the starting point of participatory curriculum development. The teacher's task is to draw out this knowledge and involve learners in determining the goals and content of education. Thus, learners are not seen as passive consumers, but as active contributors. This new role inside the classroom lays the groundwork for challenging inequalities outside the classroom: through sharing and comparing experiences, reflecting critically on them, and developing joint strategies for change, learners move toward changing the conditions that have left them powerless. In this process, the acquisition of skills is contextualized in critical reflection. The following principles, derived from participatory education theory, informed our approach to training:

**implica-
tions for
training**

- *The goal is not just a transfer of skills or techniques: it is to address real problems and take action for change.*

- *The starting point is the experience of the participants; their needs and concerns should be incorporated in training.*

- *There are no experts. Everyone teaches, everyone learns.*

- *The collective knowledge of participants develops through dialogue and sharing.*

- *Skills and techniques should not be presented in isolation; they should be related to reflection and analysis.*

the emergent curriculum

Because the content in a participatory approach centers around issues and experiences of learners, the curriculum emerges through interaction with them. It is based not on needs assessment done before instruction begins, but on collaborative investigation of critical issues affecting learners; this investigation is integrated with the instruction itself. Thus, rather than having a prespecified syllabus, its content emerges. The particular steps of this process depend to some extent on the context. Regardless of the particular formulation, the general sequence is a cyclical process of investigation, identification of themes, dialogue, critical reflection, acquisition of skills, action, and further reflection (evaluation).

implications for training

We adapted the following processes from this framework in developing the training curriculum:

- *Investigation:* Needs assessment is based on the lived experience of participants, not on the analysis of outside 'experts'; investigation is part of the learning process.

- *Dialogue and reflection:* Participants share experiences and relate these experiences to an analysis of the broader social context; this process validates everyone's knowledge and becomes the basis for creating new knowledge. As participants situate their own knowledge in the context of others' experience and look for connections or generalizations, they gain a more critical understanding of their own experience.

- *Problem-posing:* Participants address problems or concerns from their day-to-day reality through a collective sharing of strategies; solutions come not from experts, but from group resources; by exchanging ideas and experiences, participants work together to develop ways of addressing problems.

- *Action:* Participants act to change some aspect of their social context based on strategies developed through dialogue, reflection, and problem-posing. They try something new in order to resolve or address a problem they have identified.

- *Evaluation:* Participants assess the effectiveness of their work, reflecting on what happened, why it happened, what they learned and might do differently. Thus, evaluation itself is participatory, and part of the learning process itself; it informs subsequent curriculum development.

inquiry-based learning

  The notions of learning through observation, investigation, reflection, and dialogue are integral to the process just described. If information is not transmitted, participants must become actively involved in constructing it. In participatory education, this process is started through the carefully structured elicitation of participants' experience; participants learn how to gather information, name or identify issues, and analyze them. They address problems by sharing experiences and strategizing together in a problem-posing process, rather than seeking solutions from outside experts.

implications for training

  These principles and processes are very much congruent with the current emphasis on practitioner research, inquiry-based staff development, and experiential, problem-oriented learning in teacher education (Lytle, 1992). A central notion of current teacher education theory is that effective teaching is not achieved through the implementation of a teaching technology, but rather through critical responsiveness to learners. Training in specific classroom methods, behaviors, or techniques in itself doesn't prepare teachers for the complex reality of the classroom; it is the ability to discover needs and decide how to act on them that makes good teachers. Thus, what teachers need is not a prescription for what to do and how to do it, but rather investigative skills and a conceptual framework for making decisions (Gebhard, 1990). This frame-work can best be developed through observation, practice, and reflection in the context of dialogue and analysis with a community of experienced teachers and knowledgeable peers. We applied this theory to our own work through the following processes:

- *modeling:* learning new instructional techniques and processes by actively participating in trying them out and/or observing someone else try them

- *teacher-sharing:* dialogue about plans, issues, and concerns in which peers share ideas and approaches, reflecting together on practice

- *problem-posing:* a specific structured process for addressing problems of classroom practice in which peers share experiences, analyze causes of problems, and collaboratively develop strategies for addressing them

training compo- nents

As Chapter Two states, the training design had three components:

- *classroom-based mentoring* during which Interns observed and worked alongside experienced Mentors

- *site-based teacher sharing meetings* during which the Mentor and Interns at each site shared planning, issues, and concerns

- *university-based workshops* during which project participants developed a conceptual framework for teaching, explored classroom tools and shared experiences with participants from other sites, and invited outside facilitators.

These components were closely related, starting with and going back to what was happening in the classrooms. The teacher-sharing meetings focused on what the Interns and Mentors were doing with students; the issues and concerns that arose in the teacher-sharing meetings were, in turn, brought into the training workshops. As Julio said, *"Training was a chain: We saw things that happened in the classrooms and we talked about them in the training meetings."*

implemen- tation of the compo- nents

The ways that each component was implemented differed in the first and second projects (the BCLTP and the CTAFL). Several structural differences including the time frame, funding, and number of participating Interns shaped implementation of the model in each project. First, the BCLTP was a 3-year project with three 10-month training sequences whereas the CTAFL was a 1-year project of which, in fact, only 7 months could actually be devoted to training. As with any project, the first few months of the CTAFL were devoted to start-up activities (securing and accessing funding, setting up budgetary mechanisms, hiring, consolidating the staff, selecting Interns, setting up a training plan, and developing the evaluation plan). Because the grant did not include funding for Intern stipends (unlike the BCLTP), the sites had to devote considerable time and energy to fund-raising for this aspect of the project. We were able to piece together funding for only 6 Interns in the CTAFL (compared with at least 12 per year in the BCLTP). Because we had less time for the workshops, we compressed two into each month. As the Conclusion indicates, the BCLTP model was considerably more effective because it allowed for a longer training cycle, more time between workshops, a larger group of Interns, and longer workshop sessions.

Table 3: Structural Differences between the BCLTP and the CTAFL

Component	BCLTP	CTAFL
mentoring	•each Mentor worked with at least four Interns •ten month Mentoring period •variable cycles of observing, co-teaching, and independent teaching •Curriculum Specialist rotated between sites to act as Mentor	•each Mentor worked with two Interns •seven month Mentoring period •variable cycles of observing, co-teaching, and independent teaching •no Curriculum Specialist
teacher-sharing meetings	•regular weekly meetings •documented through minutes	•bi-weekly meetings; less regular •no minutes
workshops	•monthly •three hours •Saturday mornings •several outside speakers •planned in a participatory way •up to twenty participants at each workshop	•bi-weekly •two hours •Friday afternoons •one outside speaker •planned primarily by Coordinator •eleven participants at each workshop

BCLTP project participants

What happened in the mentoring component?

The descriptions of each component on the following pages draw on features of both projects. They present the more elaborated process which was possible with adequate time and funding, as well as the process we implemented when time and funding were more constrained. The advantages and disadvantages of each model are examined in the Conclusion.

mentoring cycles

Our original conception when we designed the BCLTP proposal was that there would be a formal sequence of 3 month training cycles moving from observation to co-teaching to independent teaching for Interns; however, the reality was that different Interns were ready for increased responsibility at different rates. In general, Interns with little teaching experience spent a longer time working alongside an experienced teacher and Interns with more experience transitioned into independent teaching more quickly. Some Interns, however, were uncomfortable teaching on their own even after two cycles; they didn't want to let go of the Mentor. Others were anxious to begin with their own groups after only one cycle; they wanted to let go of the Mentor as quickly as possible. In addition, the sites needed to have a Mentor teach specific classes or hours in order to cover their course offerings.

Thus, we tried to set up mentoring in a flexible, context-specific way in order to meet the needs of individual Interns and to accommodate the schedules of the sites. In practice this meant that there was a range of models:

•Interns at one of the sites followed the prespecified three-cycle plan quite closely; they worked in the classroom of the Mentor for two cycles and then taught independently.

•In another, some of the experienced Interns began teaching right away while others worked side-by-side in the Mentor's classroom for two cycles; in one case, an Intern worked first in the Mentor's class for one cycle and then in the class of a more experienced Intern before going on to take his own class.

•In the third site, the Mentor moved between two classes, spending 2 days a week with each of the Interns, so that they taught independently part of the week and with him the rest.

mentoring principles

The guiding principle for mentoring was always that its purpose was mutual learning among peers rather than evaluation or prescription. We tried to establish an atmosphere in which Interns and Mentors would observe and learn from each other, rather than having Mentors observe or model for Interns in a hierarchical or didactic way. We started this process with a training workshop that explored the following principles for observation:

- *Everybody learns; nobody evaluates.*

- *Describe, don't prescribe.*

- *Separate out what is happening from how you feel about it.*

- *Leave control in the hands of the person being observed. Let him or her decide what to focus on; the observer acts like a mirror so the person being observed can see him or herself differently.*

- *Don't tell the person being observed what to do or do better. Let him or her generate strategies and alternatives.*

Mentors' responsibilities

Thus, it was largely up to the Interns to determine how they wanted to interact with the Mentors, depending on what they were comfortable with. In practice, this meant that the Mentors were called upon to carry out the following kinds of responsibilities:

- modeling or demonstrating a particular kind of activity or task
- observing Interns and giving feedback or making suggestions
- designing activities for the Interns to do
- relegating specific responsibilities to Interns
- planning lessons with the Interns
- assisting with materials development (e.g. typing up a language experience story and suggesting how it might be used)
- facilitating the resolution of tensions between Interns

In addition, Mentors might identify an issue or positive practice to share with the others at the weekly meeting, or a more general issue to be dealt with at a training workshop. For example, if Interns seemed to have difficulty knowing how to respond to students' errors, he or she might bring this to the attention of the rest of the staff so that it could be addressed in a training workshop. In addition to more formal mentoring, there was a great deal of informal peer-observation and sharing.

61

What happened in the teacher-sharing component?

Each site had periodic site-based meetings in which Mentors and Interns discussed their practice. For certain periods, these meetings took place each week, and were carefully documented with minutes. At others, the meetings took place less regularly and were less structured because of scheduling conflicts and funding constraints; sometimes the sites deemed it more important to utilize the Interns' limited hours in direct teaching rather than in meeting time. Thus, what follows describes the most elaborated version of teacher-sharing (its most "ideal" form).

Teacher-sharing meetings were a place for Mentors and Interns to discuss classroom practice (both past and future). In keeping with a participatory approach, they were intended to support Interns' development in a non-directive way, with Mentors and Interns learning from each other (rather than Mentors telling Interns what to do). The particular content and format of these meetings varied from site to site and within a given site. They were generally a time for Interns and Mentors:

functions of teacher-sharing

- to reflect on what they did during the past week
- to plan for the subsequent week
- to share positive teaching strategies, experiences, and activities
- to pose and discuss problems emerging from teaching
- to discuss materials and to share resources
- to develop materials
- to evaluate training workshops
- to figure out whether/how training content could be adapted for use at the site
- to identify topics for future training workshops
- to address tensions among Interns or between the Mentor and Interns
- to discuss logistical matters (scheduling, pay, recruitment, etc.)

One of the most important functions of the teacher-sharing meetings in this model is to link the training workshops and the work at the sites. Sometimes this occurred most effectively when one Intern had missed a workshop and others had to report back about it. These site-based discussions of the trainings helped the Interns explore issues and ideas more openly, take ownership of the ideas, and concretely evaluate whether/how to apply them in their own work. Similarly, issues arose at the teacher-sharing meetings which suggested topics for further exploration at the training workshops.

A possible process for teacher-sharing...

The following skeletal format represents a possible problem-posing process for structuring teacher-sharing meetings:

1. *Report back:* Participants quickly go around the table reporting what they did in class during the past week, noting particular problem areas or successes.

2. *Identify an issue/theme/topic for exploration:* The facilitator tries to identify some significant teaching issue, concern, or theme. It can be a common issue (that recurs in several Interns' accounts of their practice), a particularly pressing concern of one person, or an example which others might learn from. The facilitator either reflects back what he or she sees as a theme for further exploration or asks participants what they would like to focus on. Alternatively, the facilitator can bring in an issue that he or she has noted by observing Interns' practice. In any case, the issue is re-presented as a question/description, rather than as a criticism or solution.

3. *Reflect on the issue through structured dialogue:* The group collectively reflects on the theme, addressing questions like: What was the problem here? Why did this happen? What are the roots of this problem? Have you experienced anything like this? What did you or might you do in a situation like this? Why? In discussing positive examples of practice, we explore questions like: What were the steps in the process? Why was it so successful? How would you change it next time?

4. *Propose alternatives and strategies:* Each participant (including the facilitator/Mentor) suggests how he or she might follow up on the issue with learners. At this point the facilitator can present new information, ideas, activities or theory to deepen the discussion. After a range of possibilities is generated, the group discusses possible plans of action each Intern feels comfortable with, giving the choice back to Interns with questions like: What might you like to try from this discussion? What ideas did you get from this discussion for your class? No one is told that they should do anything; rather, each Intern takes what they want from the discussion.

benefits of teacher-sharing

Teacher-sharing has several benefits. It is a nonjudgmental way of dealing with unevenness or weaknesses in Interns' practice; for example, when one Mentor felt uncomfortable about the way an Intern was handling corrections, rather than telling her she was doing it incorrectly, the issue was brought back to the group as a neutral topic. The group generated a range of strategies; everyone was invited to look over the alternatives, choose a new strategy to try, and evaluate its effectiveness (and eventually the topic was brought to the monthly workshops for further exploration). This process depersonalizes the issue, allowing for mutual learning and development through inquiry rather than prescription.

In another case, a Mentor noted that at one point Interns didn't seem to be doing much planning for classes, usually followed a mechanical approach to instruction, and didn't try to implement the tools we had been exploring in the training workshops. Rather than reprimanding them or telling them to change, he suggested that they evaluate the workshops and classes. He started by asking for feedback about the workshops and then asked questions like the following to facilitate dialogue:

• What do you think we are doing well in the classes?
• What can we do better?
• How are you using the workshops?
• What have you brought into the classroom from workshops?
• What are your goals for the rest of the cycle?

After this discussion, the Interns began changing their practice; the Mentor reported that one Intern stopped using the book to drive lessons and stopped focusing on syllables in isolation; instead she began using information elicited from students to teach them.

Teacher sharing is also particularly effective in validating Interns' knowledge: when Mentors observe a particularly effective lesson, they can invite the Intern to share it at the meeting so others can learn from it. As Interns share their practice among knowledgeable peers, they gain ideas but also begin to reflect more critically on their own practice. In addition, if careful minutes are taken of teacher-sharing meetings, this documentation can become a tool for the evaluation of training and teaching.

challenges of teacher-sharing

Of course, there are also challenges in teacher-sharing. The three most common problems we had were scheduling meetings, balancing concrete planning with open-ended dialogue/reflection, and addressing tensions between Interns. There never seemed to be enough time for everything!

What happened in the training workshops?

Although the workshops are presented last here, in some ways they provided the unifying framework for the other components. They brought together all of the participants from each site and provided a context for working through concerns about practice. In this section, the process for planning the workshops, their structure, and the sequence of topics are presented. The Appendices contain some examples of the actual content of the workshops and reflections on how they went.

our approach to designing workshops

We developed training workshops through interaction with Interns, rather than predetermining a training curriculum which specified skills, competencies, or topics. Of course, we started with an overall sense of the direction, content, and processes for the workshops. By the end of the workshops, we hoped that Interns would have a grasp of a **conceptual framework for participatory literacy/ESL instruction** as well as a sense of how to develop curricula based on themes from learners' lives. We hoped they would be comfortable with each of the following steps of this **participatory curriculum development process**:

1. **Listening** to find important concerns and themes in students' lives

   •Using **catalysts** and **conscious listening** to discover what is important to learners

2. **Re-presenting themes as lesson content**

   •Utilizing a range of **tools** to present and develop themes

   •Facilitating **dialogue** about the themes

   •Introducing **language/literacy work** related to the themes (key words, readings, grammar, writing, etc.)

3. **Taking action** outside the classroom based on new understanding and proficiencies

4. **Evaluating** learning and action

What were the process and format of each workshop?

process goals

We had several process goals for the workshops:

- to incorporate the Interns' concerns and experiences
- to trigger active participation
- to promote dialogue
- to create space for participants to learn from each other
- to model activities; to teach by showing rather than telling
- to involve participants in determining workshop content

general format

For these reasons, we tried to always start with participants' experiences, eliciting what they had done in the intervening weeks since we had seen each other. We then introduced new information or concepts through a presentation, creating space for participants to relate it to their own experiences. We went on to do some kind of hands-on, participatory activity to demonstrate a tool which Interns could use with students. We then discussed how the Interns might use what they had learned at their sites (an action plan). Finally, we elicited feedback and suggestions for future workshops. The following diagram illustrates the general pattern that our workshops followed. Our model also included evaluation of the workshop itself.

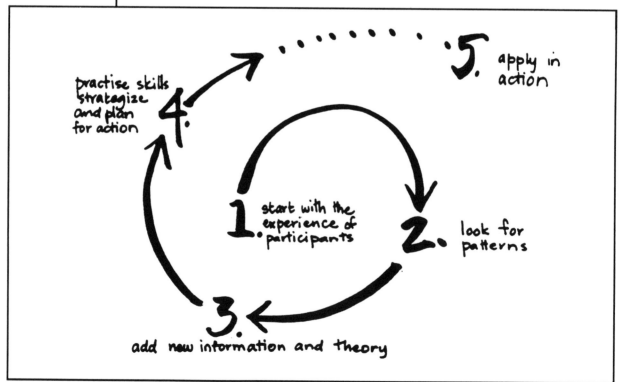

From Arnold, Burke, James, Martin, & Thomas, <u>Educating for a Change</u>, the Doris Marshall Institute, Toronto, Canada.

How did we plan workshops?

In the first project (BCLTP), when we had monthly workshops, the entire staff spent several hours planning each workshop in the time between workshops. We were able to elicit feedback from the previous workshop before planning the subsequent one. In the second project (CTAFL), there was less time for collaborative planning because workshops were held every 2 weeks and staff meetings took place on the day of the workshop itself. Thus, the planning was much less participatory, with consequences which will be discussed in the Chapter Five on evaluation. The following section describes the process we followed in the BCLTP because it was closer to our ideal of participatory training.

identifying needs and topics

Possible topics were determined in a number of ways. At the beginning, we identified topics based on our own objectives for setting the tone of the training. Right from the start, though, we tried to get Interns' input about their own needs and goals by asking them why they were participating in the project and what they hoped to get out of it. As we proceeded, we also listened for specific issues, requests, or problem areas that came up during the course of workshops and follow-up evaluations. In some cases, Interns themselves identified problems (e.g., they wanted to focus on finding materials for native language literacy); in others, we identified issues through our own observations of their practice. For example, Mentors noted at one point that Interns needed to refine their approach to responding to errors; at another point, an Intern cut off a heated dialogue because he didn't know how to integrate it with literacy work; subsequent workshops focused on responding to errors and facilitating dialogue, respectively.

We also structured specific activities during workshops to elicit topics for subsequent sessions. Midway through the CTAFL, for example, Interns identified the following issues as topics for workshops: multilevel classes, the teacher's role, assessment, and student participation. Thus, overall, our own process for determining training topics modeled the participatory approach in that the training curriculum was emergent and negotiated. We ourselves practiced **active listening** and **structured elicitation** to identify Interns' needs.

determining objectives

Once the topic had been selected, we discussed objectives in greater detail. The bottom line questions were, "Why is this workshop important? What do we hope that Interns will come away with in this session?" The answers to these questions then helped us determine activities.

67

choosing activities

After developing some objectives, we brainstormed activities that would allow us to get at the topic interactively and to model the process or tool being presented. If we weren't sure how to begin planning, we sometimes started just by talking about our own practice as teachers in dealing with the topic at hand. We then tried to generalize and identify aspects of the topic that we should explore in the workshop. At this point, we didn't try to put activities into a sequence.

doing our homework

Once the group had fleshed out a general set of objectives and possible activities for a session, we did some further research to find activities or information that might supplement our preliminary ideas. We looked at a variety of participatory education/literacy/ ESL guides (see Resources), at ESL texts, and at resources we had developed ourselves in other projects. From these, we got ideas for activities, as well as articles and examples to use as handouts. Mentors brought in examples of how they addressed a particular issue in their own practice. In addition, we consulted colleagues about how they designed workshops on specified topics.

developing a plan

The next step was to pull together the ideas and information into a sequence of activities. Although we did not consciously follow a predetermined format or schema for the workshops, we tried to keep in mind the overall goals for the workshops (starting with participants' experiences, reflecting on the individual experiences as a group, presenting new material, doing an activity to model the tool, coming back together for more reflection and evaluation). We planned a variety of participant structures or groupings so that Interns could work in pairs, in small groups with people from their own sites, in small groups with people from other sites, and in a large group.

fine-tuning logistics

The final step in the planning process was working out logistical details: who would facilitate which parts of the workshop, how long each segment would take, who would be responsible for bringing materials and props. We tried to divide the responsibilities so that each staff member would have some role in facilitating or presenting, depending on what he or she felt comfortable doing. In addition, as the project developed, we increasingly invited Interns to take some role in the training. Timing was a persistent and inevitable problem: we always planned too much and what we planned always took longer than expected. Thus, one of our final jobs was to think realistically about how long each part might take and what to do in case something took longer than expected.

What was the sequence of workshop topics?

Although the sequence of topics roughly corresponded to the steps of participatory curriculum development outlined earlier, the actual order of presentation, types of activities, and particular content were determined according to the process just described. The following pages present the two sequences of workshop topics developed in the BCLTP and the CTAFL. Most sessions focused on a general concept or topic and modeled specific tools for use with learners. Specific workshop activities are described in the Appendices.

Sequence I (BCLTP)

Session #1: Conceptual framework: *What is a participatory approach?*

    Tool: Using photographs to explore learning experiences

Session #2: Listening to find important concerns in learners' lives: *What's an issue or a theme? How do you find issues?*

    Tools: "Ways In" to student issues/themes (photos, grammar exercises, conscious listening)

Sessions #3-7: Exploring themes through dialogue, language, and literacy work

What do you do with an issue once you find it? How do you use an issue to extend analysis and literacy? What is problem-posing and what forms can it take?

    Session #3 Tool: Language Experience Approach
    Session #4 Tool: Making and using codes
    Session #5 Tool: Theater and socio-drama
    Session #6 Tool: Problem-posing trees
    Session #7 Tool: Photostories

Session #8: Action to address problems and make changes in practice: *How do you make the transition from theory to practice in teaching literacy/ESL?*

    Tool: Problem-posing trees (using problem-posing to address classroom concerns)

Session #9: Evaluation to determine where we've been and where we want to go

Sessions #10 - 15: Issues of practice for further exploration (identified through evaluation):

    Session #10: *What is the relationship between politics and literacy? How does politics relate to literacy work?*
    Session #11: *How do we work with students just making the transition into beginning ESL?*
    Session #12: *How can we use games to teach literacy and ESL?*
    Session #13: *What can we learn from literacy campaigns in other countries?*
    Session #14: *How can we assess student progress?*
    Session #15: *How can we assess our own learning?*

Sequence II (CTAFL)

Session #1: <u>Group profile and goals</u>: *Who are we and what do we hope to get out of this training?*

    Tools: Interviews, Profile Charts, Lifelines

Session #2: <u>Overview of adult learning</u>; <u>finding learners' needs, strengths and goals</u>: *How do adults learn best? How can we find out what they can already do, need, and want to learn?*

    Tools: "Ways In" to student issues/themes (photos, charts and maps)

Session #3: <u>Classroom observation</u>: *How can we learn from each other and our own classrooms?*

    Tools: Observation formats and techniques

Session #4: <u>Overview of participatory curriculum development</u>: *How can we find "hot spots" in our classrooms? How can we use themes to develop curriculum? What are our own "hot spots" or teaching issues that we want to explore further?*

    Tools: Conscious listening; worry circles

Session #5: <u>Using student issues for ESL and literacy development</u>: *What can we do with themes once we find them?*

    Tools: Codes

Session #6: <u>Using codes to promote dialogue and student participation</u>: *How can we engage students in dialogue once themes have been identified?*

    Tools: Dialogue questions

Session #7: <u>From dialogue to literacy/ESL work</u>: *How do we connect dialogue and discussion with specific learning activities to develop learners' ESL/literacy proficiency?*

    Tools: Language Experience Approach

Session #8: <u>Linking literacy with action</u>: *How do you develop curriculum around a loaded theme? How do you link what happens in class with action outside the class?*

    Tools: Breast cancer curriculum units

Session #9: <u>Using and developing materials</u>: *How can you use, adapt, and develop materials for native language literacy classes?*

Session #10: <u>Finding and evaluating materials</u>: *Visit to the Adult Literacy Resource Institute*

Session #11: <u>Assessing student progress</u>: *How do you know if students are learning?*

    Tools: Student assessment tool kit

Session #12: <u>Assessing student progress</u> (cont.); <u>Dialogue journals</u>

So what ever happened to Family Literacy?

*You may have been wondering, as you read, where the "family literacy" was in the Community Training for Adult and **Family Literacy** project. There are a number of reasons that none of the workshop sessions are called "family literacy:"*

what counts as family literacy?

Much of what we did with students really was family literacy, even though it wasn't labeled as such: enabling parents to advocate for services for their children, to send a letter to family members, to become less dependent on children, to fill out a money order, to look for a job, and to discuss sexually transmitted diseases with teenagers certainly counts as developing family literacy in its truest sense. As Ana said, ***"If family literacy means reading bedtime stories, we, as educators, are sunk."*** We worked on the assumption that family literacy is more than a label or a lesson: it is using literacy in a socially significant way to address family concerns and to strengthen adults' ability to care for their families. Based on this concept, we chose not to limit our exploration of family literacy to a particular session or to define it as a particular set of behaviors, activities, and family interactions.

participatory topic selection

A second reason that family literacy was not a workshop topic related to the participatory nature of our approach to training: we were committed to involving Interns in topic selection and gearing sessions to their needs. Whenever we elicited their input about topics for subsequent sessions, there were always more ideas than weeks left, but family literacy was never one of them. When we suggested it, Interns resisted. Family literacy was clearly not their priority and we did not feel that we could impose it. However, at various points, issues related to family literacy arose organically: for example, during the session on codes, the issue of children acting as interpreters for their parents emerged. Thus, while Interns were uninterested in exploring family literacy if we introduced it, they were open to it if the issues came from them.

learner population

Finally, the nature of the learner population may have shaped participants' priorities. None of the sites limited enrollment in project classes to parents because they wanted to serve the broadest possible number of students in need of services. At the JMCS, a class funded through another grant restricted enrollment to the parents of children in public schools; only eight students signed up for that class whereas there was a waiting list of several hundred for the other classes. Thus, students in our classes came from a variety of family situations and not all saw family literacy as a priority.

Training issues...

A cyclical recurrence of issues emerged in the workshops. Some of these issues pertain to the general approach to teaching adult literacy, some to the workshops themselves, and some to the relationship between training and teaching (site-based practice). This section will summarize key training issues and explain our processes for addressing them, ending with guidelines for training which came out of our cumulative experience struggling with them. For each of the issues listed here, there were different perspectives among Interns and changes in perspective within any given Intern through the course of the project. These changes are discussed further in Chapter Five.

"What method are we supposed to use?"   In the first project, many Interns started out wanting us to provide recipes for practice and to tell them what to do in the classroom: they were looking for a method or techniques that could be applied directly from the trainings to teaching. In part, this may have been due to the fact that the project was called a "training" project – the name itself suggested that they would be taught skills. The initial focus on exploring a conceptual framework and a process for generating context-specific curricula seemed frustrating or confusing for some. While they expected us to tell them the "right way" to teach, we wanted them to experiment, discover, reflect, adapt, and figure out for themselves what would make sense in their own contexts. We had to find a balance between establishing a guiding conceptual framework and providing practical, hands-on content that they could use immediately. This was less of an issue during the second project, in part because we had stated in our letter to Interns that we see teaching as an art, and would not be focusing on techniques; in addition, from the very first workshop, we explicitly named those activities that could be used with students and included time to plan for classroom applications.

"Where's the curriculum?"   Similarly, some of the Interns felt strongly that the project or the sites should give them a curriculum or a list of what is to be covered at each level. At the same time, their accounts of successful lessons often involved not following a preplanned sequence of activities but responding to student issues that arose spontaneously or as a result of a trigger activity. Thus, there was a tension between the legitimate need of new teachers for a guiding curriculum and the notion that the most effective curricula are those that integrate ongoing student issues and emerge through negotiation with students. In the native language literacy classes, the dearth of published materials suitable for adult learners in the respective languages intensified the problem.

"What do the experts say?" A related issue was the sense, among some Interns, that outside experts had the "answer," that there was some external body of knowledge about how to teach literacy the right way. At times, some felt that the information of an outside expert was more valuable than their own knowledge or that constructed by the group through sharing, dialogue, and reflection. Yet, very often the workshops that the Interns responded most positively to and were most engaged in were the ones in which they shared their own experiences and practice with each other. Thus, one of our tasks became the demystification of the "everybody else knows better" view.

"Why are we talking about unemployment? This is not a job agency." Because many of the Interns had experienced only a very traditional, teacher-centered and skills-based approach in their own education and had learned to read using a decontextualized, bottom-up phonics method, there was some resistance to a meaning-centered approach, particularly for teaching initial literacy. It was a struggle for some Interns to see dialogue about student concerns as relevant to literacy education or as a possible context within which to teach skills. A central issue about the content of the training, thus, was whether we should be following a mechanical (skills-based, teacher-centered) approach, a participatory (meaning-based, learner-centered) approach to literacy, or somehow integrate the two approaches.

"That doesn't apply to my students." The diversity among and within sites challenged us to ensure that we were addressing the particular needs of everyone while not excluding anyone. Because participants were teaching in three different languages, with some ESL and some native language literacy, and with students at a variety of levels both within and between classes, the challenge was great. What might work for ESL contexts might seem irrelevant for L1 literacy. In this sense, our group mirrored the situation of many ESL classes in its multiplicity of levels and needs. As trainers, we faced the same question that teachers face: how could we find common areas for training when the particular needs were so different?

"I didn't have time to do that." At almost every workshop, we invited Interns to try something that we had modeled; sometimes we handed out short readings including background information, examples of lessons, or teachers' accounts of practice utilizing the tools we were focusing on in the session. Frequently, however, Interns came back to the next session and reported that they had not had time to implement the activity or read the handouts. In many cases, the activity did not fit organically with whatever was going on in class. Because the readings were in English, they may have been difficult for some of the Interns to read.

One of the great challenges in responding to training issues was to balance the Interns' expectations with our perceptions of what would benefit them. This, of course, is precisely the challenge that teachers face in working with adult learners; very often learners have internalized the traditional model of education which has been least productive for them. Similarly, when Interns came into the sessions during the first project, they expected and asked to be taught techniques; they wanted to be told exactly what to do in class, and they especially liked the idea of outside experts coming in to do this. We had to figure out how, on the one hand, to address these desires, and on the other, to be true to our own philosophy of literacy education. We negotiated differences between Interns' expectations and the project agenda in a variety of ways:

- *by including concrete classroom-related activities which incorporated learners' realities in each workshop*

- *by posing training issues back to participants for dialogue*
  For example, the issue of expertise was addressed by creating multiple opportunities for Interns to compare the knowledge they constructed themselves with that provided by experts.

- *by involving Interns in the selection of topics for workshops*

- *by using training issues as content in the modeling of tools*
  For example, we made codes about tensions between different needs in order to demonstrate the use of codes.

- *by making our own rationale for designing a workshop explicit*
  We talked about our own process of identifying issues and incorporating them into training.

- *by including many opportunities for peer learning*
  For example, the issue of corrections was addressed by presenting it back to Interns and eliciting alternatives from the group.

The Interns' changing notions of what was important and how they wanted the sessions to be structured was one of the indicators of the development of their conceptions of education. Whereas at the beginning of the first project, many wanted to be told what to do, one of their criticisms in the second project was that they didn't have enough time to talk to each other!

Guidelines for workshops

The following guidelines reflect what we learned through our practice, including both what was effective and what was problematic.

•Involve Interns in the selection of topics.

•Link presentations to work at the sites, using examples from Interns' practice or from the shared experience of the group.

•Link content to participants' life experience as immigrants and learners as well as their experience as teachers.

•Use the content of workshops themselves and issues that emerge from training to illustrate ways of developing curriculum.

•Keep it simple; don't overwhelm Interns with too much new material or information. Don't plan too many activities. Allow time for the unexpected.

•Let go of the plan mid-stream if it isn't working; talk about why you're making this decision. Don't get stuck on the agenda.

•Bring in something external for people to react to: videos, outside speakers, skits; allow time for participants to evaluate them critically.

•Don't count on participants doing their homework (e.g., coming prepared with examples of their practice, doing readings, or trying suggested activities in their classes).

•Combine practical, hands-on techniques and activities with theory and reflection; combine the presentation of new information with interaction around participants' experiences and ideas. *Elicit* rather than just *transmitting.*

•Make the workshop active and experiential, modeling activities, not just describing them. Be concrete. Don't present abstract concepts in isolation: give examples that you can see, touch, feel, interact with. Show, don't tell.

•Structure ways for Interns to learn from each other and validate the knowledge they've gained from practice; don't leave all the presenting in the hands of a few trainers. Allow plenty of time for discussion and sharing between sites.

•Invite Interns to explore various aspects of a debate in the field (e.g., whether to correct while doing language experience stories) rather than presenting only the "correct" side of the debate; present the debate itself.

•Make it clear that you're presenting options and alternatives, not prescriptions - that you're sharing, not telling people what to do; ask Interns if there's anything they might like to try. Invite them to experiment and investigate.

•Resist the temptation to be problem solvers. Give Interns tools for trying to resolve their own problems rather than trying to solve them for Interns.

•Allow time for participants to figure things out for themselves; don't jump in to provide answers if they're struggling.

•Include space for people to talk about their fears and failures; don't focus just on successes and models of "good" practice. Reinforce the notion of learning through mistakes – that everyone has times when things flop.

•Talk about the process and reflect on what's happening as you go; if something turns out to be inappropriate, discuss reasons why and the parallels with what happens in class.

•Explain things in clear, understandable language; avoid jargon or academic terms.

•Gradually increase Interns' roles and responsibilities in conducting the workshops.

•Situate what you're doing in a broader context; talk about what others are doing in various parts of the country or the world so that Interns get a sense of how their work fits into a bigger picture.

•Build in time for evaluation both at the workshop and at the sites.

•Include action planning as a regular part of workshops.

•Follow up on workshop ideas at the sites with discussion of ideas/activities and planning for implementation.

Chapter Four: From Training to Teaching

Because this project focused primarily on training rather than teaching, we did much less documentation of what actually went on in the classes than on what happened in the workshops. Most of the information about the Interns' and Mentors' practice comes from what they reported in the workshops. In this chapter, we look at the approach to teaching that informed the training, the relationship between what happened in the workshops and the classes, some examples of specific tools and themes explored in the classes, and some recurring teaching issues.

What was the approach to teaching?

guiding principles

One of the central aspects of a participatory approach to adult literacy instruction is that teaching is context specific: curriculum content arises from the needs and interests of each group of participating learners as much as possible. Because the language of instruction, learner populations, and community contexts differed at each project site, what happened in the classes varied as well. Thus, although there were some common underlying principles that guided the teaching, the ways that these principles were applied varied from class to class, teacher to teacher, and site to site. The guiding principles for participatory literacy instruction were explored in Chapter One. Briefly, they include the following:

- *Start with learners' needs and interests.*
- *Involve learners in determining the content of instruction.*
- *Focus on meaning, not mechanics.*
- *Contextualize work on form (connect form to function and meaning).*
- *Center instruction around themes drawn from learners' social reality.*
- *Encourage dialogue and critical analysis of social realities.*
- *Use a variety of participatory tools to explore themes.*
- *Move toward action outside the classroom.*
- *Involve students in evaluation.*

As we said in the last chapter, the sequence of training workshops paralleled the participatory curriculum development process, moving from finding out about students' histories, needs, and goals, to exploring their social realities and concerns, to developing language and literacy through the use of participatory tools, to generating strategies for addressing problems collectively, to evaluating learning with them.

What was the relationship between training and teaching?

Having said all this, we now have to admit that all of these principles and processes for participatory curriculum development really did not correspond in any one-to-one way with what actually happened in classes. There was great variation in terms of the activities that Interns did, the ways in which they combined mechanical and meaningful work, and their stance toward learners. There was also a considerable amount of change among individual Interns from the beginning to the end of the project: some Interns who adhered strictly to a mechanical approach early on began to incorporate more meaningful activities as they proceeded. Interns increasingly took risks in terms of addressing social issues with their students; they became more and more creative and confident about introducing their own ideas–ideas that had never been discussed in workshops (these Intern changes are discussed in Chapter 5). Thus, to imply that there was a single, uniform process of curriculum development based on these guiding principles would be misleading.

Similarly, although each workshop focused on a particular aspect of curriculum development and incorporated specific tools for classroom application, there was often no direct relationship between what we did in the workshops and what the Interns did in their classes. Early on in the training cycle, when we asked Interns to report back on what had happened in their classes between workshops, we noticed that often what they reported had nothing to do with what we had done in the training: they may not have tried any of the activities we had suggested in the workshop. At first, as coordinator, I was concerned about this, wondering if this meant that the training was ineffective, not meeting participants' needs, or somehow irrelevant. However, the Mentors were less concerned; they saw it as natural and inevitable.

"The transition has to be gradual..."

•Felipe said that even if Interns don't use what is presented immediately, they may use it in the future. When they use it depends on the context of the class. In his case, for example, the beginning students had strong expectations about learning; they were not used to a participatory approach, and he felt that the teachers could not bombard them with innovative activities until they were more comfortable. The transition from expectations of a traditional, more mechanical approach to a participatory approach had to be gradual.

78

•Ana said that each group adapts what is presented in the training to their own particular situations: what Interns get from the workshops varies according to what they are ready for and they will use it as the site needs dictate it. As the trainers, we can't expect that each class will follow our plan.

•Julio said that we need to think of workshop activities as tools that can be used on an appropriate occasion: "I don't expect to go to class and make a photocopy of it." He said, "I never ask: did you use what we did at the workshop? The time will come." Part of the reason for this stance is that some of the Interns look to him as the expert, expecting him to tell them exactly how to teach. If he fulfills this expectation, the Interns won't develop their own creativity. Thus, he feels it is important not to pressure Interns to follow up on the workshop. He also noted that they had already used some of the ideas presented in the workshop *before* the workshop.

Looking back, there seem to be several general patterns to how Interns connected the training and teaching:

•*resisting exploration of workshop activities in their classes:* For a period of time at the beginning of the project, a few Interns at one site seemed to completely ignore what we were doing in workshops, using a mechanical, decontextualized, skills-oriented approach to teaching. They spent a great deal of time working on syllables and words with no connection to themes or vocabulary related to students' lives. In this case, the Mentor designed a self-evaluation activity for the Interns in order to prompt more reflection of the connection between workshops and teaching. Shortly thereafter, the Interns began to draw material from students' lives, using pictures, stories, and contextualized texts. Thus, site-based follow-up to workshops was key.

•*attempting to directly apply what we demonstrated in the workshops to their teaching:* Sometimes Interns would introduce an activity but because they did not fully understand it, or feel comfortable with it themselves, it would lead to frustration. For example, after a session about making space for students to explore loaded social issues, an Intern elicited a heated discussion about jails, but when he felt at a loss about how to follow up on it, he suddenly cut off the discussion to "get back to work." We used this incident as a trigger for discussion in a subsequent workshop.

•*adapting workshop tools to their own contexts:* Many of the Interns were very creative in modifying an activity which we had demonstrated to fit what was already going on in their classes. For example, after our session on doing group profiles (in which we interviewed each other in pairs and then wrote the composite group information onto a chart), one Intern adapted the activity by incorporating a specific grammar focus *(used to)* for her ESL students. Another Intern had his students write their own information on small pieces of paper which they later stuck onto a large cardboard chart with blank spaces on it.

•*choosing not to use the tools:* In some cases, Interns made conscious choices not to do certain activities that we had demonstrated because they felt they were inappropriate. For example, one Intern decided not to do a group profile chart because his students had worked together for a considerable period of time and already knew each other; he felt that it would be artificial to do the profile under those conditions. In other cases, the Interns didn't try a workshop suggestions because it would have interrupted an ongoing unit. Classes had a momentum of their own which they did not want to derail for the sake of training needs.

•*being creative in ways that went beyond what we did in workshops:* At times, Interns' choices to introduce activities unrelated to what we had done in workshops indicated that they had attained a new level of self-confidence and independence. For example, one Intern, who had started out feeling a strong need to be told what to do at every step, got to the point where she requested to be left alone to create her own curriculum. At the Harborside, the teachers worked with students on creating a video to use in recruiting new students. Often Interns introduced their own ideas and brought them to the workshops to share with others, who, in turn, tried them in their own classes (e.g., JMCS Interns did a health-related unit which inspired HCC Interns to do one too).

In summary, we learned that the fact that Interns didn't always apply workshop tools directly in their teaching wasn't necessarily a sign of the workshop's failure or the Interns' inadequacy. Instead, it was often a positive sign, a sign that they were being sensitive to the dynamics of their classrooms and developing a critical capacity to see what was or was not relevant for a particular group at a particular time. What was important was the Interns' application of participatory principles, a process that developed unevenly over time, rather than the linear application of a particular tool or activity from each session to a subsequent class.

How did the context of students' lives shape teaching?

Teaching was shaped not just by what we did in the workshops and Interns' development, but by what was happening in the students' lives and in the life of their communities. Because a participatory approach is responsive to the social context, these factors were particularly important in shaping teaching.

Because the essence of a participatory approach to literacy/ESL education is allowing the issues and concerns that preoccupy students to become the motor force of instruction, the starting point for curriculum development has to be an understanding of students' lives–their backgrounds, personal histories, strengths, and current situations. In many adult ESL programs, students are interviewed during in-take and composite profiles of the student populations are constructed for assessment and placement purposes. However, once students enter the classroom, these profiles, which include general information about years of schooling, occupational status, reasons for immigration, and so on, may be ignored in the push to work on competencies or survival skills for the new life in the U.S. Our experience is that each of these aspects of students' lives has real consequences for what happens in the classroom, and, further, that these general profiles only tell the beginning of the story. Behind every student profile there are powerful stories that affect learning and participation, stories which can only be uncovered through classroom interaction. Thus, the starting point for participatory curriculum development must be learning about the students, and understanding the contextual factors that shape their literacy acquisition.

job situations

In terms of the general profiles of the students in our project, as we said in Chapter 2, there was a great deal of variation both within and among sites. The differences in students' situations at different sites had direct implications for the development of the curriculum: for example, while at the HMSC some classes focused on strategies for looking for work (because unemployment was so high), classes at the JMCS and Harborside, where more students were working (but in marginalized jobs), focused on workplace rights and discrimination on the job.

The fact that so many of the literacy students at the HMSC were unemployed had very real consequences for both the atmosphere and the content of classes. On a very practical level, it meant that students sometimes had to miss classes because they didn't have the bus fare. At one point in the spring, enrollment fell drastically because many of the students had to leave to work in the fields. This disrupted the continuity of classes and was sad for the students (because they wanted to continue studying, but these were the only jobs they could get).

In addition, unemployment meant that students were often preoccupied with worries about how they would be able to survive, which, in turn, affected their ability to concentrate. As one student said, *"I could learn more, but because I have a lot of problems, my mind is not here."* This presented a dilemma and a challenge for teachers: although they wanted to help students address this problem, the reality is that, during a time of recession, prospects for Haitians with few English or literacy skills are bleak. Julio responded to this situation in one of his classes by inviting a job counselor to talk about the process of finding a job in the U.S., as well as by discussing the whole economic situation in the U.S. Teachers gave students space to talk about their concerns and linked them to literacy teaching. Students talked about coming to class so they wouldn't have to stay home and think about their problems by themselves: they have nothing at home, no TV, no music; as one of them said, "My house is like a jail." In one class, they wrote about these concerns in their dialogue journals. Many said that the class was the only place they could really talk about their problems.

immigration status

Issues relating to immigration status and regulations also affected teaching. At Harborside, many of the students had been granted temporary residence under special INS provisions for Salvadoran refugees. There, too, enrollment dropped suddenly at one point when students heard that the INS had changed the date that their temporary residence permits would expire; many left classes because they decided to get as much work as they could (part-time jobs in addition to their regular jobs) before they had to leave the country. Recruitment was also affected, because potential students chose to try to find work rather than go to school. In addition, some students had to leave the country for extended periods in order to comply with INS regulations or to tend to family business. Because students were often separated from their families for either economic or bureaucratic reasons, learning to write letters to family members became an important focus of classwork.

political situation in home country

Another factor that shaped student participation in classes was the political situation in their home countries. Thus, for example, because students from Central America had often been directly affected by war or other aspects of political repression, discussion of their past lives had to be handled with great sensitivity. Some of the participants in the first group of students at Harborside had previously enrolled in another literacy program but left it because the methodology focused heavily on direct discussion of the political situations in their countries; they were upset when the teacher introduced these topics as the primary vehicle for literacy development. Yet, in the Harborside classes, when students had more control over selection of the curriculum content, they sometimes introduced these issues themselves. Understanding the complexity of students' responses to their backgrounds was key in knowing when and how to talk about issues of immigration.

Likewise, the changing political situation in Haiti had an enormous and pervasive influence on both the content and atmosphere of classes at the HMSC. For example, at the time of Aristide's campaign and election, there was a great deal of energetic class discussion about various political perspectives, the history of Haiti, the processes of political change (and especially the role of literacy in this process) in many of the classes. Even day-to-day events in Haiti became the focus of classwork: once, when a political meeting about preventing violence was interrupted by gunfire and assassinations in Port-au-Prince, the students generated a language experience story about this event which became the focus of a week-long unit.

Of course, the coup against Aristide affected both the mood and the content of classes. The first step for teachers was to figure out how to go on despite the overwhelming desolation and anger that they and their students felt. As teachers said in a teacher-sharing meeting, there was no way to proceed without dealing with students' feelings about what had happened. Teachers responded in a variety of different ways. One teacher linked the coup to a discussion about the importance of education (the role of education in building a new Haiti) and this became a way to get students motivated to get back to literacy work. In another class, the teacher linked the current situation to the history of Haiti, the assassination of Dessalines, and then brought in proverbs that represented the situation in Haiti; these proverbs became the basis for some literacy work which, as the teacher said, began to "renormalize" the class. A third teacher invited students to express their feelings about the coup in English; they started by writing an English account of the story and then generated their own *wh-* questions (e.g., What happened? How did it happen? Who is responsible? When did it happen? Where is Aristide now? Why did it happen?) The teacher then brought in an English newspaper article which the class read and answered *wh-* questions about. He went on to relate the current situation to Haitian history, including important dates and events relating to Haitian independence. By the time of the CTAFL project, students were so demoralized by the repression and seeming hopelessness of the situation that they did not want to discuss it in class.

violence

The issues of violence and neighborhood safety also shaped teaching. Students often talked about being afraid to come to class at night; evening classes got smaller as it got dark earlier. They told about having their purses snatched or their apartments broken into, and there were periodic fluctuations in attendance corresponding to particular incidents of crime in the neighborhood. In many cases, this issue was incorporated into lesson content: students talked or wrote about their experiences and fears as well as generating strategies for addressing them (carpooling, walking in groups, etc.). One of the classes, for example, wrote a language experience story about a student who was robbed; they then wrote about an attack that had taken place in Haiti; finally, they analyzed the differences between violence in Boston and that in Haiti, concluding that the former was economic while the latter was political.

men's and women's roles

At one site, an entire class was composed of men (except for one woman). In the community of that class, it was common for men to go out to work, socialize, or attend school while the women stayed home with the children. At times, men specifically forbade their wives to come to school. This dynamic had an effect on the issues that arose in class and on the nature of discussions. It came up as an issue for dialogue as the class talked about how to recruit more students. As students discussed what keeps people from enrolling, the question of why women stay home but men don't was explored.

funding

The unstable nature of funding for adult education in general and native language literacy in particular influenced teaching both affectively and substantively. Students, Interns, and Mentors were demoralized by the fact that there was so much uncertainty about whether classes would be able to continue. At the HCC, this contextual factor was integrated into the curriculum as students decided to form a committee to raise money once the end of the National Institute for Literacy funding was in sight. They instituted weekly meetings, elected officers, and developed a range of strategies for addressing the problem.

What tools did Interns and Mentors use in teaching?

The very power of these contextual factors in students' lives means that they have to be taken into account in teaching. Traditionally problems caused by unemployment, immigration, or family concerns might be dealt with primarily through structures external to the instructional process (by counseling, attendance regulations, legal assistance, etc.); in a participatory approach, issues that preoccupy students are central to the content of instruction itself (although, of course, support services are also important). Because students' real issues and concerns vary from group to group, teachers cannot rely on traditional textbooks, with a pre-determined, form-focused sequence of lessons, as the mainstay of the curriculum (although certainly there is a place for using published materials). This section shows how teachers in a participatory approach move from the context of students' lives to curriculum content. It presents tools and activities teachers in our project used in place of a set curriculum or textbook.

uncovering themes

The first step towards developing a participatory classroom is learning about students. Often, however, students only share their concerns, needs, and preoccupations once a basis of trust has been built. As such, part of the art of teaching is creating an atmosphere where students feel comfortable about sharing their stories. Paradoxically, many students feel most comfortable at first in a traditional classroom where teaching is rote and decontextualized (focusing on vocabulary lists, grammar, textbook exercises, etc.). Although some of the Interns initially thought that the way to find students' needs was just to ask them what they wanted to do, whenever they asked this question, the response was, "You're the teacher, you're supposed to tell us what to do." They quickly discovered that finding compelling issues in students' lives entails more than just asking students for their input: it entails moving gradually from the traditional model that learners may expect to a more participatory one, consciously listening for opportunities to build on issues of importance to students, as well as creating a structured framework for eliciting these issues. The following excerpt from the minutes of a staff meeting describes how Felipe addressed this dilemma with a beginning Spanish literacy class:

The transition to a participatory approach has not been easy because the students are used to a "ma-me-mi-mo-mu" approach and don't feel that they can learn unless they are using a book. This week, Felipe brought a paper with drawings of family members for the beginning class. At first they didn't want to work on it, saying, "What are we going to do with these pictures?" Felipe said, "Let's try it and then we'll see if you learned from it." They first read the words under the pictures and then Felipe used them to introduce new letters and showed them how to make words. Next, he then gave them some pictures with blanks under them and asked them to write the words for family members. They then wrote the names of their own brothers and sisters, etc. They were excited when they saw their family members' names in writing. Next, they plan to write stories about their families.

conscious listening

One way that teachers and Interns were able to find students' issues was through **conscious listening.** This process entails being tuned in to classroom dynamics and off-the-record spontaneous conversations that occur before, during, or after class. Teachers would often walk in on heated discussions of events in the news, in students' personal lives, or in the community as class was starting; alternatively, a debate might erupt unexpectedly during the course of a lesson. In some cases, teachers would follow up on these issues immediately (by incorporating the discussion into the lesson, pulling out key words, or developing a language experience story); in other cases, the teacher would think about the issue, discuss how to handle it, and develop a lesson related to it for a subsequent class.

In one class, a student who had been absent came in talking excitedly because he had seen his ex-wife with another man; he had hit the man's car; they had argued and fought. This prompted a class discussion in which others talked about quarrels they had had and their experiences with the court system. They discussed ways of resolving conflicts that didn't involve violence and would not end up in court.

However, it is not enough to rely on conscious listening as the main way to find student issues. First, it is hard to predict when issues will arise spontaneously; especially at the beginning of a cycle, before students are comfortable bringing their experiences and concerns into class, the times that issues emerge in this way may be few and far between. Further, learning how to "hear" these issues and then utilize them is a skill which develops over time. Even when students' concerns have surfaced, students may not feel that discussing them is "real" school work: no matter how compelling a discussion may be, students may see it as a diversion from what they are "supposed" to be doing (worksheets, dictations, etc.).

tools

Thus, a central way to legitimate an issue-centered approach involves introducing structured activities (or **tools**) that draw out dialogue while at the same time developing literacy and language. Deborah Barndt (1986), a Canadian popular educator, has suggested the notion of a **tool kit** of resources that teachers can draw from to elicit or develop themes. For her, tools are concrete ways of representing an issue (photos, drawings, socio-drama, etc.), designed to generate active responses, dialogue, and language or literacy work. We extended the term to refer to any artifact or activity that triggers student participation through a structured process with an open format. These structured activities serve two important functions: they provide a format for uncovering issues, and they serve to legitimize discussions that might otherwise seem to be diversions. By linking loaded thematically based content with structured literacy work, they provide a concrete format to focus dialogue so that it counts as "real work" in students' eyes. The following list includes tools that were utilized in both the BCLTP and the CTAFL at various points:

- *Charts*
- *Pictures and photos*
- *Key words*
- *Language experience stories (LEA)*
- *Published materials*
- *Codes*
- *Role plays*
- *Student-generated writing*
- *Photostories*

In practice, a combination of different tools was usually used to explore any given theme. Thus, for example, a class may have started with a discussion prompted by conscious listening on the teacher's part; they may have then pulled out key words, developed a language experience story, read a related published text, and written about the topic in journals. In addition, participatory tools were often integrated with traditional activities like grammar exercises in the ESL classes, handwriting or spelling work in the literacy classes. Further, many of the students requested math work and this was incorporated on a regular weekly basis in many of the classes. Finally, in the L1 literacy classes, as students became more confident with their first-language reading and writing, they also requested some ESL instruction.

Charts

Charts are useful because they provide a structure into which students can insert content from their own lives and experiences. They were used in a variety of ways in our project: to gather information about students' life histories, to compare cultural practices among different groups, to identify places where students used English or L1 literacy, and to elicit students' goals. The basic process in using charts is this:

- chose categories or questions as the focus (students can participate in this)
- elicit information from each other regarding the questions (through peer or teacher questioning in pairs, small groups, or whole group work)
- write the information for each individual on the chart
- follow up with both form- and content-focused work

Follow-up work focusing on form might utilize the information in the chart to develop sentences, practice grammar, or do reading/writing exercises. Content work might compare students' information, look for patterns, discuss their causes, and plan future work based on the information. The following excerpts from workshop minutes describe how several Interns used charts with their classes:

- In one of the ESL classes, an Intern divided the class into three groups (each of which had one fluent English writer in the group) and gave them a set of questions about their life histories. The groups discussed the questions and then interviewed each other in pairs within the groups. They then shared the information they had discussed and the fluent English writer wrote it on a chart. For follow up, the class worked on the past tense (used to forms). They discussed similarities and differences between their jobs in the U.S. and at home. The Intern then wrote a story using information from the chart and gave students copies of the stories with follow-up exercises.

- In one of the Spanish literacy classes, the Intern made a chart asking students their name, country, arrival date, important family members, persons affected by students' learning, and what you miss most from your country, jobs, and home. He had students write their answers on small pieces of paper; then students stuck their pieces of paper onto a large piece of cardboard with the blank chart on it. They then took turns reading each others' answers off the chart. For follow-up, they made games from the charts, and discussed jobs in each country.

- One Intern developed a chart about Valentine's Day with questions like: Do you have a holiday like Valentine's Day in your country? How do you celebrate it? Who is your valentine?

Pictures and photos

Unlike traditional visual aids, the function of pictures or photos in a participatory classroom is to uncover themes or to evoke powerful responses. As such, the pictures themselves should represent a loaded, easily recognizable issue or dilemma from students' lives. Use of the picture should start with very concrete questions about what students see in the picture and move on to experiences and issues evoked by the picture. Once again, this tool can trigger dialogue which, in turn, may lead to a range of literacy activities: language experience stories, student writing and reading, as well as vocabulary and conversation development in ESL classes. The following excerpts from workshop minutes describe several variations on the use of pictures in our project:

•*Teacher-drawn pictures:* Felipe drew a picture of a farm/country scene because most of the students in his beginning class are from the countryside and he wanted to get ideas about their pasts and interests. He gave the picture to students face down and then asked them to talk about what they first noticed when they turned the page over. They liked the picture; some said it reminded them of their homes. After they discussed the picture, they wrote about it. They wrote their stories on the board, made some revisions, and did some corrections. They asked Felipe to type their stories. These students often say that they can't write, but they wrote a lot in this activity. The most beginning student wrote the most.

•*Student-drawn pictures:* Ana gave students newsprint and asked them to sit in pairs and draw a picture together without talking. Afterwards, they sat in small groups and discussed questions: How did you feel while doing this? How did you come up with the picture and how did you agree on what to draw without using words? Everyone was involved and talked about how it felt to have to communicate without words, mentioning issues like the confusion that you feel when you're on a train and have to ask directions. This activity led to the identification of places where students need English.

•*Photos:* The BCLTP Mentor at Harborside brought in a picture of a shovel (representing the key word *pala* in Spanish). Though he thought he might get a response, he didn't imagine it would be so strong: students talked for at least 45 minutes about the uses of shovels in their lives, telling stories about being forced by the police to bury people in their villages in El Salvador. They went on to discuss using shovels in the fields, crops, the various agricultural methods they used in their countries, and so on. As they spoke, he wrote down what they were saying, including other key words which became the focus of subsequent lessons. See Appendix A for a full account of how pictures and key words were used in this class.

Key words

Key words provide a bridge between dialogue and decoding activities for literacy and ESL classes. They are chosen for their powerful meaning in students' lives (representing some important concept or issue for them) as well as for their structural features. Once the significance of the words and issues they represent has been explored, the words themselves become a way to link the discussion to further literacy activities. They can be broken into syllables, used to generate new words, or used as vocabulary for follow-up language experience stories, dialogue journal writing, and so on. Teachers can elicit key words in the students' first language as a bridge to English. The following excerpts from workshop minutes describe some of the ways key words were used in our project:

•*teacher-selected key words:* In this case the teacher introduces a key word based on his or her own knowledge of what may be important to students. A concept which has been introduced by a key word can be elaborated by a clustering exercise in which students free-associate the word with other words/ideas it brings to mind (the teacher may ask "What does this word make you think of? How have you experienced this?"); they may go on to explore the commonalities among people's experiences, their social causes, etc. Interns at the JMCS introduced the word *food* in a beginning ESL class, discussing food in different countries, cheap and expensive food, and why there is so much food in the U.S. but so little in other countries.

•*key words emerging from student dialogue:* In this case, the teacher pulls key words out of a discussion that has been triggered through some other means (a picture, a news story, etc.) or asks students to select them. For example, after viewing a video about the inauguration of Aristide in Haiti, a beginning ESL class discussed the video, first in terms of what they had seen and then in terms of how it related to their lives. The teacher wrote what the students were saying as they spoke. The teacher then asked them to find five words that they "liked best" in the story. They chose: *president, money, freedom, Tonton Macoute,* and *peace.* They proceeded to write stories based on the words.

•*as follow-up on a reading:* Key words can be selected from a reading to generate further dialogue and writing. After identifying problems with employers as an issue at Harborside, the Mentor introduced a reading about workplace rights. Once the group had read the text together, he put the key word *discriminación* on the board as a way to facilitate discussion of the text and elicit students' own experiences. The group then did a clustering exercise to elaborate the concept and went on to write about particular problems at work and strategies for addressing them.

Language experience stories (LEA)

One of the most effective tools for connecting dialogue and literacy work is the Language Experience Approach (LEA), in which the teacher acts as a scribe while students dictate whatever they want to have written. When Interns were first introduced to the participatory approach, they often were quite successful in engaging the class in dialogue of current events or critical issues in their lives. However, there was sometimes a gap between discussions and literacy activities (which focused on decoding and mechanical skills work). The LEA provided a concrete bridge from discussions to reading and writing activities. The following are some of the ways LEA was used in our project:

•*to follow-up a class discussion of a heated topic:* Thus, for example, if students were talking about the Gulf War, the teacher might ask, "What would you like to write about the war?" The students would then dictate a story which the teacher wrote on the board. This, in turn, might be followed by a range of literacy activities (selecting key words, working on corrections or a particular grammar point, generating student writing about the topic, etc.). Alternatively, the teacher might take notes while discussion was in progress and type the story for further work and reflection in later classes.

•*to tell the story of a picture:* Teachers often started by introducing a picture and asking some concrete questions about it. They then facilitated dialogue about issues that were implicit in students' responses. The challenge at this point is to get beyond a physical description of the picture. At the HMSC, one class used a Polaroid camera to take their own pictures. The task was to take a picture of "something important in the lives of Haitians in Boston." Thus, their photos became a way of both identifying important themes for the students and generating LEA stories. Questions used to start the process included: *What does this picture make you think of? What does it mean to you? Why is it important for Haitians in Boston?* As students talked, the teacher wrote key words on the board. Then students responded to the question, *What do you want to write about this picture?* Each student contributed one sentence to the story. The teacher read the story to the group; the group read it together; individuals read sentences with others' support. The story was typed with follow-up questions and key word exercises (grouping key words into patterns, etc.) and followed by more group and individual reading.

An important debate in the LEA process centers around the issue of corrections: should teachers write exactly what students say (even if it is not grammatical) or correct it? Many Interns felt uncomfortable writing anything that was not correct. This question (and the way we handled it) is discussed later in the section on Teaching Issues.

Published materials

Students want books; books make them feel that their learning is real. They provide a sense of security and continuity. In addition, teachers often don't have the time or the experience to continuously generate their own materials; they want the structure that a textbook provides (even if they don't rely on it exclusively).

However, there are a number of problems relating to materials. The first, of course, for native language literacy classes, is that few textbooks are available, and those that do exist are often not suitable for literacy acquisition in the U.S., for adults, and/or for a participatory approach to literacy instruction. Most adult literacy texts for Haitian Creole or Spanish were developed for literacy campaigns in Haiti or Mexico, and, as such, use key words and concepts that relate to realities that are not always relevant for immigrants or refugees in the U.S. Other L1 literacy books may be written for children and have content or pictures that are patronizing and irrelevant for adult learners. Many of those written in North America are based on Puerto Rican or Mexican culture and on vocabulary which is unfamiliar to Central American students. Many focus on mechanical approaches to literacy. Even texts that aim to promote a participatory approach may have such an explicitly political agenda that students are put off by them.

For beginning ESL, where there is an abundance of commercial texts, finding a single, appropriate text was also problematic, again because the texts may be patronizing, mechanical, and not geared toward a participatory, learner-centered approach. Of course, many experienced teachers reject the notion of relying on a single text anyway: they say that, by definition, no text can meet the evolving needs of students and texts should be seen as resources rather than backbones of the curriculum. In our project, published materials were generally used to support the development of a theme (rather than as lessons in themselves). Issues relating to materials were addressed in several ways:

• *using published literacy texts:* Texts that had been developed for other contexts were used with adaptations for the U.S.; dialogue was framed in terms of how an issue related to students' lives here (with questions like, "How do you experience this problem in Boston?"). Interns and Mentors frequently asked family members in their home countries to bring back materials which could be used in L1 literacy classes.

• *using authentic materials:* Newspaper articles, cartoons, and leaflets were used as texts. Ana regularly asked students to bring in news articles that they wanted to read and discuss.

•using published student writing: Among the most powerful published materials that interns used were texts written by literacy and ESL students. Some of these had been published elsewhere (e.g., Voices, a magazine of student writings from Invergarry, British Columbia, and I Told Myself I am Going to Learn, by Elizabeth Ndaba, a photostory about a South African woman's struggles with her husband as she decides to go back to school). These materials are glossy and beautiful (satisfying students' desire for "real" texts) as well as powerful and relevant in terms of content. In addition, classes used locally published magazines, such as Need I Say More, a journal of Boston-area literacy students' writings, and magazines published at their own sites.

•adapting ESL materials for L1 use: Native language literacy teachers often used ESL texts to get graphics and ideas for exercises. For example, ESL materials on body parts were used in the Spanish literacy units on health.

•generating L1 materials for the U.S. context: The Mentor and Interns at the HMSC used some of their teacher-sharing time to develop Creole literacy materials for the U.S. context. Most of these were readings with thematic content, followed by questions about the text as well as opinion questions.

•using children's literature: Unlike literacy texts (basals) written for children, real literature often has beautiful illustrations and compelling stories which may have relevance for adults. Participants used some of these books with the Spanish literacy classes.

•using culturally familiar genres (proverbs, riddles, songs): Because of their own familiarity with the cultures of the learners, teachers and interns were able to integrate into instruction both forms and processes that were culturally congruent for learners. For example, during the BCLTP, the Mentor and Interns at the HMSC developed a Creole proverb book based on one that had been started by a group of teachers at another Creole literacy program several years earlier. At the JMCS, Ana often used slogans to elicit discussion. For example, she introduced the Spanish slogan, "*El pueblo unido jamas sera vencido*" and invited the Spanish-speaking students to explain its significance to the others; then she asked people from other language groups if they had slogans in their countries and, if so, to share them with the class.

Codes

Another tool used to explore themes from students' social reality is a *code*; this term comes from Freire's concept of codification by Nina Wallerstein (1983). In this case, the teacher selects or creates materials that represent a problem or dilemma facing students. Rather than suggesting solutions to the problem for students or referring them to an outside support service/expert, the teacher poses the problem back to the group in the form of a picture or a short dialogue. This re-presentation of the problem depersonalizes it (framing it in a somewhat abstract way so that it doesn't refer to the specific dilemma, but captures its various aspects); in this way, learners can get some distance on the issue and generalize about a specific problem.

Once reactions have been triggered by the code, the teacher guides students through a structured five-step dialogue process in which they

- **describe what they see in the code:** Who is talking? What is happening?
- **identify the problem represented by the code:** What is the problem here?
- **relate the problem to their own experience:** Do you know anyone who has been in a similar situation? How have you experienced this problem?
- **discuss the root causes of the problem:** How has this problem come to be? What is happening in the broader society that causes this problem?
- **share strategies for addressing the problem:** What have you done in a similar situation? What can we do about this problem? In this final stage, collective action is stressed over individual action because this is often more effective and reinforces collaboration.

Teachers in our project used problem-posing codes to address a wide range of themes they had identified as significant for students, including the following:

- **issues of classroom dynamics:** how to deal with a student who talked too much; how much ESL the literacy classes should do each week; whether students should use their first language in ESL classes; what to do with hot topics like religion or politics when they come up in class

- **family issues:** men expecting women to stay home and watch the children while they go to school or socialize; kids acting as interpreters for parents; health issues like cancer, birth control, and AIDS

- **workplace issues:** discrimination at work, finding work

- **community issues:** dealing with the legal system, immigration, day care

94

Role plays and theater techniques

Some Interns used role play and theater techniques to explore themes while at the same time providing contexts for language development. The description of the workshop on sociodrama in the Appendices includes the rationale for this tool as well as other ideas for how to use theater techniques in ESL and literacy classes.

• An Intern at the JMCS planned a week of classes around the theme of work; however, after the first class, the lesson for the rest of the week developed from what had happened on Monday. The Intern started by bringing in a reading about a case involving discrimination in the workplace. The class worked on vocabulary from the case *(prejudice, benefits,* etc.). The Intern used a picture of a store with a "Help Wanted" sign where a woman was telling someone, "No jobs." The class divided into three groups, discussed the picture, and then developed role plays about similar situations that they had been in. The Intern had been worried that the lesson would be too difficult for beginning students, but they had all experienced similar situations and were eager to talk about them. She said, *"I gave them the vocabulary and they went from that."*

• After a theater workshop in the BCLTP, one Intern used theater techniques to motivate her students. She came to class one night and noticed that students seemed to be tired and without energy. She decided to do a warm-up activity to get them motivated. She started by explaining that the first activity would get them energized for work and asked them to stand in a circle and clap their hands with each other. After they had done this, she explained the purpose of the next activity, saying it is easier to have a dialogue by acting out the idea first. She then asked them to form two groups and choose a word which was meaningful to them. Each group acted out the word; the other group described each act afterwards and then guessed what the word was. One group chose the word *malad* (sick) and the other group chose the word *pov* (poor). After the acting, the students dictated a story about each word. She then typed up the stories and formulated some questions as a follow-up activity.

Student-generated writing

Despite the fact that many of the students in the literacy classes knew only a few letters and were not comfortable with the physical aspects of writing (holding a pencil, letter formation) when they began classes, most were able to do some independent, meaningful writing after about 6 months. Several factors seemed to support the development of their writing. The first was the **modeling** that took place in class through the group LEA process: students collectively went through a composing process, linking their ideas to written form with the support of the teacher and peers; they moved through various stages from this supported group writing to individual writing which, in turn, progressed from words to sentences to longer pieces. Second was the stress on **meaning over form**: students were encouraged to take risks, and teachers responded to their writing in terms of its content more than its surface features. Third, students were encouraged to write for real **communicative purposes**, for real audiences and about topics that were important to them. Fourth, they were immersed in contexts where **student writing was valued**: they read published pieces by other students, and saw peers working on writing and having it published in site magazines; they were included in this community of writers as their own writing sometimes was published. Several formats or genres were utilized by different classes in the project to promote the development of writing:

•**dialogue journals:** Dialogue journals are a place where teachers and students can have a written conversation on a private, one-to-one basis. In theory, students write about whatever they want to (although, in our experience, they may need to go through some guided steps before they are comfortable initiating topics of their own); teachers write back to students just as they would to a peer, responding communicatively in terms of the meaning or content, rather than attending to form. Their responses model correct usage, but don't explicitly correct students' mistakes.

•**letters:** One of the main goals expressed by many students when they started classes was to be able to write letters to family and friends by themselves, without having to depend on others. At the HCC, this process started with students writing letters to another Spanish literacy class in NYC. Although the exchange itself was sustained only for a few months, it gave students the confidence to begin writing letters to their families and friends.

•**articles for publication in site magazines:** All three sites in the project published their own magazines of student writings. Being invited to write for the magazine turned out to be a strong motivation for literacy students. As they became more proficient, they moved from submitting LEA stories written by the whole class to individual pieces of increasingly greater length.

Photostories

A photostory is a story which is about a key issue or set of issues identified by learners, accompanied by photographs. Interns in the BCLTP were introduced to the idea of photostories through a workshop by an outside presenter. One Intern at the HMSC decided to follow up on the idea with her own class. They made a photostory about the life of a Haitian family in Boston using the following process:

1. **Picture plus analysis:** The Intern started by showing students a picture of a Haitian man looking pensive. She asked students to give their reactions to the picture: what did they see? They responded by saying they saw a man who is thinking and looking sad. Using a clustering format, she then asked why he might be sad and what he might be thinking. One student said he doesn't like the country where he lives. Others said he may have social problems: problems with the educational system or prejudice, no money, no food, no family; he may have sentimental problems like a wife who cheats or whom he doesn't trust. They then discussed the results of these problems, mentioning things like frustration, loss of confidence, humiliation, alcoholism, and drug problems. They went on to discuss possible solutions: go to school, be open about his problems, seek advice, and so on.

2. **Key words:** The Intern then pulled out some key words for syllable work and told the students that they would continue to discuss and write about the problems students had identified.

3. **Further exploration and writing about themes generated:** In subsequent classes (for about an hour each day), students discussed and wrote about various themes that had been identified in response to the picture: problems with their children's education, lack of respect and confidence, family problems, work, and so on.

4. **Writing their own photostory:** Students then gave the man a name and connected his various problems into a story. As the Intern said, "The sad man came alive."

5. **Looking at a model of a photostory:** The Intern brought in a South African photostory (I Told Myself I am Going to Learn by Elizabeth Ndaba) as an example of something that they could do with the story they had written.

6. **Taking pictures:** The students then assigned roles for the various characters and took pictures to go with each part of the story.

7. **Lay-out and copying:** The pictures were laid out with the story and copied.

8. **Revision:** There was some debate about the ending of the story; the students discussed the ending and revised it somewhat.

What themes did classes explore?

As Interns became more skilled in conscious listening and drawing out student themes, and students became more comfortable with the notion of centering learning around their concerns, a rich tapestry of themes and topics emerged. The following list gives a sense of the kinds of issues from the context of students' lives around which curriculum was developed in the BCLTP and the CTAFL.

educa-tional issues	• why L1 literacy is important • students' prior educational experiences • issues of classroom dynamics: use of the L1 in ESL classes, students who talk too much, child care (for learners' children) • funding for classes
personal histories	• reasons for immigrating • family situations • jobs in the home country vs. jobs in the U.S.
culture	• cultural phenomena (e.g. mythical animals from Central American folklore) • cultural comparisons (food in various countries, medicines) • men's roles, women's roles • the significance of holidays in learners' lives/cultures (Mother's Day, Valentine's Day, Martin Luther King Day)
history and politics	• important events in Haitian, Salvadoran history • current events: the Gulf War, Aristide's election, the coup against him, children from Haiti being forced to work in the Dominican Republic, the political situation in Central America • English Only laws
community issues	• violence and safety: a Haitian cab driver being shot, a mugging • the court system; handling disputes without involving the legal system
housing	• homelessness; finding housing
employ-ment	• workplace discrimination and other workplace problems • reasons for unemployment • strategies for finding jobs
health	• AIDS, nutrition, cancer, the reproductive system
family issues	• men's and women's roles; participation in schooling • domestic violence • family literacy: children as interpreters for parents

Teaching issues...

Many of the issues that Mentors and Interns encountered in working with students in the classroom were strikingly similar to the issues that arose in the training workshops: just as Interns had started by expecting a methods-oriented training, students started by expecting a mechanical approach to literacy and a grammar-based approach to ESL. Just as we had to work with different needs and starting points among Interns, they had to work with a range of levels and needs among students. Just as we had to balance planning with responsiveness, Interns had to find a similar balance in the classroom, and so on. This section summarizes the teaching issues touched on above and examines how they were addressed in our project.

"What are we going to do with these pictures?" Many of the initial issues centered around students' expectations of schooling and the transition to a participatory approach. Even if they hadn't been to school before, students often had an internalized notion of education that was quite traditional: school means sitting in rows, having a text book, doing exercises from worksheets, speaking only when called on, listening and copying, taking tests, and so on. Some Interns, as well, felt that until beginning literacy students had "mastered" the basics of decoding (through a rote learning approach), they could not do meaningful work. Mentors addressed this by slowly demonstrating what could be learned by integrating mechanical and participatory approaches. For example, Felipe brought drawings of family members to class; students who were used to the "ma-me-mi-mo-mu" approach questioned what they could learn by using pictures, but as he showed them how to generate and write their own words, they became excited.

"Why don't I have an American teacher?" Some students (especially ESL students) are disconcerted at first when they find that their teacher isn't a White North American native speaker of English. They may feel that they can learn better from someone whose grammar and pronunciation are "perfect"; or, as Julio said, they may have internalized the view that a Black person's English isn't good enough. Interns and Mentors responded to this in a variety of ways: by inviting students to try the class with the option of changing if they didn't think they were learning, by inviting native speakers to class on a regular basis, by explicitly discussing variations in dialect and pronunciation, and by discussing when "correct" pronunciation is and isn't important. When one student complained about not having an American teacher, his Intern sent him to the class of an American teacher (who was a volunteer). He came back the next day, saying "All that teacher knows is how to speak English." In another case, a Guatemalan Spanish literacy student didn't want Felipe as a teacher because he is Salvadoran. Felipe responded by saying, "Well, let's see if I can teach you"; they ended up being good friends. In virtually every case, students were comfortable with non-native speakers as teachers after only a short time.

99

"Where's the book?" As mentioned earlier, a key issue was the desire of both Interns and students for textbooks. However, most of those available, especially for L1 literacy, were not appropriate in terms of content or level: they were often geared toward a non-U.S. context, were too overtly political or too mechanical, too elementary or too advanced. Some L1 Interns tried to address this by using basals for children. Mentors and Interns developed a variety of other strategies to address the need for materials: at the HMSC, they met together to develop their own materials. As a whole group, we had two workshops focused on appropriate materials for adults; as they became more comfortable with the participatory approach and methods like LEA and dialogue journals, increasingly, Interns used learner-generated materials. Even so, both the Spanish and Creole literacy teachers continued to feel the need for good L1 texts.

"You're the teacher....You're supposed to tell us what to do." Students often initially viewed the teacher as the authority who is supposed to transmit information, ask questions, correct students' errors, enforce discipline and have the answer to any question. This posed a challenge in terms of developing a student-centered curriculum. For example, students were initially uncomfortable with the idea of helping to select topics. They felt that a good teacher should know what to do without having to ask. As Interns developed more structured ways of eliciting themes and issues, students became more comfortable about contributing their ideas and experiences.

"What's the right answer?" A related issue concerns students' notions of what counts as "real" knowledge. Often students didn't see their own knowledge or opinions as valid; they thought the teacher was the only one with the "right" answers. This meant that initially many were uncomfortable with dialogue or helping each other. At times, tensions arose when students answered each other's questions or corrected one another: some felt that others were trying to show their superiority. In one class, when asked their views in a discussion, students went through a period when each one would repeat exactly what the first one had said. Some students were uncomfortable with the idea of disagreeing, or debating ideas; many had come from cultures and/or political contexts where they hadn't had experience with dialogue or where it may even be dangerous to disagree with an authority figure, to state one's true beliefs. One way that teachers addressed this was by stating explicitly that they didn't know all the answers and by talking about the participatory approach to teaching. Another way was to try to turn students' questions back to them or to the group as a whole, eliciting their own answers to each other's questions.

"Homeless people are lazy." Once Interns felt comfortable facilitating dialogues, they began to wonder whether they should give their own opinions or keep silent. For example, if students made statements that they strongly disagreed with (e.g., that homeless people are lazy or that women who are abused deserve it), should they

intervene? Some Mentors felt that our responsibility as teachers is NOT to express our views because it will silence students. Others said that sometimes you have to participate as a person, not a teacher, and this means saying what you think. Ana said that the trick is to express your views without imposing them: you can be a facilitator and a person at the same time. One way of doing this is by asking questions that prompt people to think about their own statements or views.

"Let's stop talking and do our work." Another issue that arose once Interns became more comfortable eliciting discussion and integrating it into class time was that students didn't always see this as legitimate learning. In ESL classes, dialogue was seen as conversation practice, but in L1 literacy classes students sometimes felt that open-ended discussion was not "real work." It was seen as a diversion from the lesson, rather than part of the lesson. Interns, too, sometimes saw it as outside the curriculum and didn't always know how to link it to literacy acquisition (as was the case with the Intern who elicited a heated discussion by introducing a picture of a jail, but then abruptly stopped the discussion, saying it was time to get back to work). As Interns learned to connect discussion with more structured learning activities, students began to see it as legitimate.

"Let's get back to the lesson plan." A related dilemma was whether to stick to lesson plans or go with the flow when something interesting came up. The two extremes of this tension were having no plan (waiting for a lesson to emerge spontaneously) and sticking to a plan rigidly without allowing for the lesson to take its own direction. In order to insure coherence, some Interns decided to set a schedule for a whole week in advance; however, often whatever happened the first day caused them to revise the plan for subsequent days. Once Interns were familiar with a set of tools that could be drawn on in response to spontaneous dialogue, they were able to modify plans as needed.

"This class is too easy." The differences in levels, needs, and wants within a given class may create tensions between students. In one of Ana's classes, the more advanced students wanted her to give a test to screen out lower level students; in Julio's advanced Creole literacy class, some students wanted transitional ESL every day while others wanted it once a week. Sometimes, the more advanced students did all the talking, leaving the others silenced. Strategies for addressing differing needs included preparing separate activities for different groups, developing peer teaching activities, getting tutors, and doing whole group activities which incorporated a range of student strengths (some students speaking, others writing, etc.).

"I can't concentrate. I'm too distracted." Often students come to class preoccupied with worries that blocked their participation. Some Interns initially tried to get students to leave their problems outside the classroom door (telling them to stop talking about things unrelated to the lesson). Later, they became increasingly skilled

at integrating these concerns into the lessons, asking questions like: *What makes it hard for you to come to class? What makes it hard for you to concentrate?* From these questions, they developed LEA stories, journals, and so on. At times, the students' problems seemed so great that the Interns felt overwhelmed by them.

"We don't have Indians." When learning is centered on participants' experiences and social issues, tensions taking a variety of forms inevitably arise: there may be tensions based on historic differences between ethnic or nationality groups, differences in belief systems or even religious differences. This kind of tension arose in one of the Spanish literacy classes: in Guatemala, there is a great deal of pride in Indian culture (with traditions and customs having been preserved); this is not the case in El Salvador where Indians have been more assimilated. So when the teacher began to talk about Indian word origins, some of these students were offended and tried to dissociate themselves, saying, "We don't have Indians in El Salvador." At the HMSC, there were sometimes tensions between students from different religious groups. These tensions were addressed in various ways: sometimes teachers tried to avoid them in class; sometimes, the class explored them from a historical perspective; sometimes, they were addressed through cultural sharing. Other tensions relate to classroom dynamics (e.g., students bringing their children to class or students who talk too much). Students initially expected the teachers to intervene to fix these problems, but teachers moved toward a problem-posing stance, presenting the issues back to the class so they could collectively generate solutions.

"It's embarrassing to talk about breasts." In some cases, the issues themselves were difficult to talk about because of cultural taboos. For example, as students began to talk about health care, the reproductive system, and breast cancer, the Interns found themselves having to explain vocabulary and concepts that were embarrassing in mixed gender classes. In many cases, they dealt with this by laughing and using humor to dispel tensions.

"If we wanted to learn about war, we would have stayed in El Salvador." An additional dilemma concerned how to connect literacy work with the social or political context of students' lives. Students often explicitly resisted political discussions when they were initiated by teachers; however, over and over, our experience was that they became very engaged when discussion of the same issues emerged spontaneously or in the context of language work. As Julio said, *"It's important not to impose your views because students think they have to agree with you because you're the teacher."* Further, once Interns came to understand how politics manifests itself in everyday life (rather than just through wars, elections, etc.), it was easier to integrate analysis into teaching.

How did we address teaching issues?

Just as the teaching issues themselves mirrored training issues, ways of addressing them paralleled ways of addressing training issues. Interns used many of the same processes with each other and with students to address teaching issues that we had used to resolve training issues. Through the following processes, Interns generally came to rely on their collective resources (rather than "university experts") to address classroom issues, adopting a stance of inquiry, posing problems back to students, and negotiating solutions with them.

• ***Combining traditional and innovative approaches:*** The primary strategy for dealing with students' expectations for traditional activities, materials, and student-teacher roles, was to integrate the more traditional and mechanical format (grammar, workbook, dictation) with more participatory activities. Likewise, a key way of legitimating dialogue, learners' knowledge, and critical thinking was to link discussion with structured literacy/ESL activities.

• ***Teacher-sharing and problem-posing with each other:*** The primary strategy Interns used when dealing with issues of classroom dynamics was to bring the issue back to their site-based group or to the workshop, drawing on each other's ideas and expertise to address problems. For example, when some Interns were having trouble figuring out how to follow up on a student's heated account of a personal problem, the group generated the following suggestions:

-Listen a while and then ask if other students can relate similar experiences.
-Write the story, or key words from it, on the board.
-Ask for support/ideas from others about the problem.
-Change the lesson and come back to it the next day.
-Make a list of vocabulary from the discussion and use it the next day.
-Ask students to speak slowly and watch to see who is participating; shift the focus to the dynamics of the discussion.
-Change the subject but make sentences related to the topic the next day.
-Avoid giving your own opinion as a teacher; set rules for dialogue so students learn to respect others.
-Use the Language Experience Approach to record the discussion.

103

When the issue of whether or not to correct students in writing Language Experience stories arose, the group generated the following possible strategies:

-Write exactly what they say first and correct it at a later stage.
-Compliment students' language and then say, "In English (or in Boston), they say it this way...," or "That's good but it's better to say...."
-Repeat their exact words and then say, "Is that what you want to say?"
-Note errors silently, but don't correct them; then use that point in the next day's lesson.
-Invite students to help each other, come to the board together to make changes.

•*Reflecting on ways of learning (metacognition):* Often when teachers tried a new activity, they would integrate discussion about why they were doing it and invite students to compare their own responses to more traditional versus innovative activities. For example, when students asked to have their dialogue journals corrected, one Intern explained why she would not focus on errors and then told them she would note language areas that needed work for future lessons. This kind of ongoing evaluation and meta-talk about learning strategies helped to legitimate the new approaches.

•*Problem-posing with learners:* Interns often chose to address problems of classroom dynamics by creating a problem-posing code about the issue as a framework for language/literacy work and as a way of involving learners in the resolution of the problem. For example, Interns at the JMCS developed a code about use of the native language in the ESL classroom. This approach of involving students in addressing classroom problems moved classes toward sharing responsibility for learning. Further, it reinforced the underlying principle of the project, drawing on the resources of the community to address community needs.

Chapter Five: Evaluation

Because the focus of this project was on training (rather than on instruction), the evaluation mainly examines its impact on Interns and Mentors. Of course, assessing their effectiveness as teachers entails to some extent looking at how much their students learned. However, because the project was not long enough to yield or document significant changes in the literacy/ESL acquisition of beginning literacy/ESL students, we did not assess the progress of each individual learner involved in project classes; we did, however, gather some data on general changes among groups of learners. Thus, this chapter looks at the impact of the project on Interns, Mentors, groups of learners, and participating sites.

What was our approach to evaluation?

the guiding principles

Although more has been written about the evaluation of adult literacy *instruction* than about the evaluation of adult literacy *teacher training*, we felt that many of the same principles apply. One of the guiding principles in literacy evaluation theory is that *evaluation processes and tools should be congruent with the instructional approach* (Lytle, 1988). Because our approach to both instruction and training was a participatory one, emphasizing participant involvement, meaning-centered learning, and the relationships between learning and the social context, an evaluation model focusing only on the acquisition of discrete, decontextualized skills (measured through tests or formal assessments) would be inappropriate.

When instruction itself is responsive to participants' needs, evaluation must look at how they use what they've learned in their everyday lives. Likewise, the evaluation of Interns and Mentors must look at how they use what they've learned in their practice. We wanted the participants themselves to be involved in assessing their own learning; in addition, we wanted to see how they developed over time and integrated what they learned in their daily interactions. We felt that measuring outcomes of the project only in quantitative terms would be misleading and intimidating for participants. For these reasons, this report stresses qualitative evaluation in order to capture the varied ways that the impact of the project manifested itself. It was guided by the following principles that were originally formulated for assessing learner progress, but that apply equally to assessing teachers-in-training.

Participatory evaluation is*...

•*contextualized,variable*...It doesn't try to measure isolated decontextualized skills, but rather examines actual usages and practices. Assessment tasks have a purpose. The particular forms that assessment takes can vary accordingly.

•*qualitative*...It involves reflective description, attempting to capture the richness of learning, rather than reducing it to numbers. It looks at metacognitive and affective factors.

•*process oriented*...It is concerned with how and why participants develop.

•*ongoing, formative*...It aims to inform curriculum development and training, or to explore a particular problem.

•*supportive*...It focuses on participants' strengths, what they *can* do rather than what they *can't* do. It starts with what they know and reflects their successes.

•*collaborative*...It is done *with* participants, not *to* them. Self-evaluation is an important part of developing metacognitive awareness and involvement in learning. Participants are subjects, not objects, of the evaluation process.

•*multi-faceted*...It invites various participants to evaluate each other. Not only do teachers evaluate students, but students evaluate teachers and program dynamics. Interns evaluate training as well as their development being evaluated.

•*open-ended*...It leaves room for and values the unexpected; non-predictable and one-time manifestations of change count.

In accordance with these principles, project evaluation emphasized self-evaluation, group dialogue, peer observation, interviews, and ongoing documentation of project work (through minutes of meetings and workshops, anecdotes, and samples of participants' work). In addition, evaluation was integrated as much as possible with training and instructional activities so that it did not impose additional time demands on participants.

---

*adapted from Auerbach (1992, p. 114)

What tools were used in project evaluation?

The following section presents a brief description of tools used to evaluate the workshops themselves, as well as the impact of the project on Mentors, Interns, and the sites. As you will see, in many cases, the same tool was used to gather data about Interns, Mentors, and training processes. Specific tools used to assess the impact of the project on learners are included in the following section on changes among learners.

interviews

Mentors and Interns interviewed each other early in the project about reasons for participating in the project, educational and work histories, goals, fears, concerns, needs, and future plans. They were interviewed again at the end of the project about their views of the training (to what extent it met their needs, its strengths and weaknesses), their views on teaching, their views of their own growth (self-evaluation), their views of the project as a whole, the impact of the project on their lives, and their career or educational goals. These interviews were audio-taped and transcribed. Quotes from these interviews are included in the following sections. In addition, each Mentor interviewed one learner about the impact of the classes on his or her life.

minutes of meetings and workshops

Teacher-sharing meetings and workshops were documented through minutes. Minutes of **meetings** recorded feedback from site-based evaluations of training workshops, Mentor observations of Interns' applications of training content, and issues arising from practice at the sites in order to inform future workshops. **Workshop** minutes included accounts of what happened, participants' responses, discussion, questions, and reactions.

samples of participant work

Mentors and Interns often brought in samples of exercises that they had developed, lesson plans, examples of their students' work, and accounts of activities from their classes. Mentors brought in site-based evaluation forms that they had developed and/or documentation of training activities that they had facilitated.

evaluation discus- sions

At the mid-point and the end of the workshop sequence, we included group exercises in which participants identified issues they were struggling with in their practice, goals for future training sessions, and priorities for the workshops. Site-based teacher-sharing meetings included evaluations of workshops as well as evaluation of practice (assessing how classes were going and the transition from training to practice). Mentors sometimes structured evaluation sessions to trigger self-reflection by Interns.

peer observation

One of the early trainings focused on peer observation. Participants then observed each other and reported back to the whole group at a subsequent workshop. In addition, Mentors did ongoing informal observation of Interns and reported observations at staff meetings.

Each site filled out a questionnaire to gather data about the impact of the project on the site. It included questions about the number of students served, types of student (literacy levels, nationality, language background), neighborhoods served, number and type of students on the waiting list, changes in the waiting list, family data, number of family members impacted by the project, and so on. In addition, each site provided a statement about their needs and goals for the project. The sites responded to the questionnaire to the extent that they had data available; in some cases, they were unable to provide data that we sought for project purposes. For example, we had hoped to gather information about the family situations of learners in order to assess our family literacy objectives, but this information was not always part of site record-keeping.

Samples of student writing posted on a bulletin board at Harborside

What was the impact of the project on Interns?

One of the most important lessons we learned in our training process is that changes don't occur linearly or evenly: individual Interns reacted differently to the same training experiences (as indicated in Chapter Four). A number of factors–their prior educational experiences, their current life situations, their reasons for participating in the project, the context of their sites (including the influence of other teachers and activities at the sites)–all shaped the ways that their ideas and practice developed. Thus, how they changed cannot simply be attributed to the training itself.

In addition, the impact of the project was not always visible during the life of the project; many of its positive effects only surfaced after it was over. For example, one of the BCLTP Interns said that she only realized the value of the training when she was hired as a teacher months after the project ended: it was then that she appreciated having been given a *framework* for curriculum development, rather than a specific *methodology*, so that she could adapt her practice in accordance with students' needs.

By the same token, successes cannot be counted by looking at outcomes at only one point in time. In one case, for example, a BCLTP Intern started with quite a traditional, mechanical approach to literacy instruction; through the course of the project, she moved toward a more learner-centered style of teaching; however, when she continued as a volunteer after the BCLTP funding (and the support of a Mentor) ended, she reverted to a mechanical approach.

All of this is to say that to reduce Intern changes simplistically to a *before* and *after* analysis (framed strictly in terms of 'outcomes of training') would be misleading: it would miss the uneven development of the process and fail to capture the cumulative, cyclical nature of growth. Thus, the following analysis of the impact of the project on Interns will look at various stages of their thinking and practice, rather than just at results.

The next section examines several broad categories of change among Interns: changes in their ways of thinking about and participating in **training**; changes in their **conceptions of literacy and literacy pedagogy**; changes in their actual **classroom practice**; changes in their **self-concepts**; views of themselves and their goals; and changes in their **roles outside the classroom**.

TRAINING

changes in
expectations

Many of the Interns came into the project expecting and wanting a transmission model of training. Perhaps because of their own prior educational experiences and their lack of confidence about teaching, they wanted to be told what to do and given a "method" to apply in the classroom. As one Intern stated in the interview at the beginning of the CTAFL, *"I want to get techniques."* This expectation may have been reinforced by the fact that this was called a *training* project: the word *training* itself implies that a skill will be transmitted. After the BCLTP, we recognized this danger and specifically addressed it in the letter welcoming Interns to the CTAFL project, stating that we would be exploring an approach, not focusing on methods.

Interns embraced the participatory model of training at various rates; quite early in the project, some not only accepted it, but actively took on responsibility for explaining it to others. For example, at a site evaluation of one of first workshops, when one Intern said that she had expected a more formal presentation of methods, another responded that the purpose of the workshops wasn't to present only one way to do things, but to provide a place to share ideas and debate with each other.

changes in
notions of
expertise

As the workshops created a context for Interns to reflect on their own experiences and generate the collective knowledge of the group, their notions of what counts as expertise began to change. Gradually they began to value their own knowledge and gain a sense of themselves as experts. In place of asking us to tell them what to do, many began to see each other as resources and appreciate opportunities to hear from each other. As one Intern said, *"Sharing with others makes me understand how to work with my own little group."* Toward the end of the BCLTP, Interns had enough trust in their own knowledge and practice to directly challenge the expertise of an outside presenter; they did this through a series of questions designed to highlight the relationship between theory and practice, indicating that even though the presenter knew a lot about theory, they had a stronger base of practice and, in fact, could teach her a lot. The following excerpt from an interview sums up the process that many of the Interns went through:

> *To tell you the truth, in the beginning, when I started to go to the training, I was expecting that you would give us the materials and show us the way to teach. That was my idea. When I started going, I thought, gee, this was different. Why*

110

did they come with these different ideas, why didn't they tell us "you have to do this and that"?

...to tell you the truth, the more I went to the trainings, I really enjoyed it. I saw the different ways you were introducing and I think that was the best idea–not the way we are used to doing it: you do this and you follow. You gave us the opportunity to grow–not to depend on somebody else. The workshops gave us the ideas and we wanted to apply them. At least they give you the ideas, and it's up to you...So, I think it works better that way. In my opinion, it's been wonderful. I look through the notes and when I read them, I know I can apply them. If I think it would be too difficult, I try to do it another way where it would be more simple and they [the students] would understand. But the ideas are great... I didn't expect that in the beginning.

Another Intern described the change as follows:

That's what I was expecting when I first started–I said, you know, "well they don't tell me what I'm going to do so how can we implement it?" Maybe because we were new; but now that I know how you work, it was easier to understand what you were doing. Now you are more able to use the tools and you can bring your own ideas and then you can do different things. I can abstract them and not use them exactly the way you tell us; you do a little change, but it works the same way. This comes easy when you know how the project works.

changes in
participation
in training

By the end of the CTAFL, conceptions of training had changed to such an extent that one of the Interns' criticisms of the workshops was that too much time was spent on presentations, and not enough allotted for Interns to share their practice with each other.

Interns' ways of participating in the training also changed: where at first they saw themselves as passively absorbing "received knowledge," they increasingly took on responsibility for bringing their own knowledge and experience into the trainings as content for discussion and dialogue. They brought in samples of their work, actively participated in exercises, and, in some cases, led workshops (in the BCLTP, one Intern designed a session on using games and, in the CTAFL, an Intern co-facilitated a session on a breast cancer curriculum). Perhaps the strongest indication of their sense of participation and "ownership" of the training was their increasing ease in critically evaluating workshops.

LITERACY AND LITERACY PEDAGOGY

changes in conceptions

Changes in Interns' conceptions about training were mirrored by changes in their conceptions about what literacy is and how it should be taught: just as they had started by expecting a somewhat traditional model of training, many were preoccupied with mechanical aspects of literacy instruction at first. Many viewed literacy acquisition as a linear process starting with the smallest units (letters and sounds), moving through decontextualized subskills and achieving mastery at each level before moving on to the next. For them, acquiring these skills preceded reading or writing whole meaningful texts, thinking, or connecting literacy to life experiences. Some saw their own role as transmitting skills to students.

from decoding to meaning-centered teaching

Again, however, there was unevenness among Interns; those who grasped a participatory approach to literacy pedagogy first actively took responsibility for challenging the others' ideas. For example, when one Intern said that she thought that the approach to education was too informal (*"I don't think we can solve the problems of the world. Why do we talk about unemployment–this is not a jobs agency"*), another Intern responded,*"So where is thinking left if you present worksheets and follow formal methods?"* When one Intern argued that talking about social issues is okay for teaching literacy in "third world" countries but not in the U.S., another countered, *"But isn't that part of life? And life is what we use to teach them!"*

from problem-solving to problem-posing

Once Interns began to see the value of connecting "the word" (the written text) and "the world" (students' life experiences and concerns), many of them felt overwhelmed and inadequate. They wondered how they could address students' enormous problems in class and, at the same time, felt the need or desire to solve the problems *for* students. Gradually, however, as they gained more experience in developing codes and using participatory tools, and heard about others' successes in the workshops, many of them began to try new things in their teaching. This, in turn, pushed them to change their ideas. Thus, changes in their thinking triggered changes in their practice, and vice versa (changes in their practice are described in the next section). Through this process, they began to see their role as one of posing rather than solving problems.

Evidence of changes in Interns' conceptions about literacy comes from the ways in which they talked about literacy pedagogy at various points. For example, the same Intern that expressed the desire for techniques in the beginning of the CTAFL, said, at the end of the project, *"Teaching is an art. When you become a teacher, you become an artist."* He went on to say that he liked reading Freire's writing because, *"I see so many thing I could learn from those books... You don't learn procedures, steps that you could follow for teaching adults. I see the books in terms of general philosophy, not specifics."* Early in the first cycle of training, for example, after an entire workshop on drawing out student issues and using them to develop LEA stories, when Interns were asked if there was anything else they wanted to talk about, they focused on a spelling problem in Spanish; just a few months later, however, when the group did a brainstorming activity about literacy pedagogy, the key concepts that they mentioned included *learners' contexts, critical thinking, content, respect, discover, explore, problem posing, codes, issues.*

changes in conceptions of teacher-student roles

Interns' ways of talking about learner and teacher roles also changed; increasingly they began to talk about learners as central to the educational process. Whereas, at the beginning of the project, some Interns said that being a "good" teacher entails having a lot of knowledge, at the end, they said that a good teacher is someone who listens to students. At the end of the project, one Intern talked about the roles of the teacher as a facilitator and guide, *"someone who unveils or awakens the soul"* and the student as *"someone who guides the teacher."* Another, in describing how he teaches initial literacy in Creole, said, *"I don't say anything. I find all that I want in students' mouths. I write sentences on the board after they give them to me."* A third one said about students,

> *Their judgment is good; they might not be able to read and write, but when they talk, their logic is good. When you first start teaching, you see a lot of people older than you, and if you have something to tell them, you don't know how to tell them. You learn that you can't impose on adults, you have to exchange with them.*

One Intern said that rather than deciding students MUST learn a certain way, he tries to find out what they need and want. *"My job is not to give them knowledge; they're not empty–here is some knowledge in them which is not conventional knowledge that we need to develop."*

The following excerpt is a particularly telling example of how Interns changed their views of teacher–learner roles. It comes from an end-of-project interview with an Intern who had started with a traditional and somewhat top-down style of teaching:

At the beginning I didn't know what to expect from teaching even though at home [in Guatemala] I did it before. But down there we used a different way to do it. This way, over here, instead of being structured, it's like you are part of the classroom too, like the students. You belong to them...You do what they feel comfortable with and if you see that something is not working you try to change it to work.

I feel like family with them. It's like I belong to them. It's not like, "I'm here to teach you and you have to learn." I think they feel comfortable with us too. You can tell the way they express themselves. It's the way you teach them. You don't go over there and say, "Well I'm here just to teach." No, you tell them, "If you think that we're not teaching right let us know; that's what we're here for because YOU people are the teachers," I tell them. "I'm the student, I'm learning from you guys." And it is true, you learn from them. They learn from you, but you learn from them too because their ideas sometimes work more than your ideas.

At the beginning, it was very difficult for me to change the way I was teaching because I was afraid to implement it. I was like, "Will that work or no? Let me try." Maybe because the way I was brought up and the way I went to school, the way they teach. But to be honest with you, I think the best way to teach is the way you people taught us to do it. You can see that the students learn.

You get them to know their ideas too, to see what their ideas are. You work with their ideas. That's what I do most of the time, I get their ideas, "What do you think we have to do now? What would you like to do?" I say, "I'm not here just to teach; I'm here to find out what is happening." Like if somebody has a headache, what to do when you go to the doctor. That's the way you start communicating with them. And it has been easy that way. You get their ideas and that's the way you start teaching.

A related change concerned Interns' conceptions about a pre-packaged vs. a context-specific curriculum. In place of wanting a particular method to apply across the board, Interns came to realize that each context is different and that the curriculum must emerge from work with a particular group of students. They began to resist simplistic prescriptions, as the following comments illustrate:

The techniques in the video might not work for everybody. It is up to each teacher to try out what will work with your group. Any time someone presents a technique like in this video, it's always very limited. Whether it will work depends on the context of your class.

This shift from a transmission model of literacy pedagogy to a learner-centered, context-specific one is captured by the following quote from an interview with an Intern:

You cannot transplant, you cannot think, "Hey, E. tried this, and I am gonna try it in my class because it worked for her." No, it doesn't work like this. You have to know your own students in such a way to really get something good out of them. There aren't any specific tools that will always work because each learner has his own problem and I am supposed to find it. What I learned from all those workshops–here is a problem and you as a teacher are like an investigator–you have to find it and once you get it, then you say, "This is how I'm going to work." The context of the students is very important.

CHANGES IN CLASSROOM PRACTICE

from
following to
taking
initiative

What the Interns actually did in the classroom also mirrored their changing reactions to training. At the beginning, some relied heavily on the Mentor, passively observing, waiting to be told what to do, or following the teacher's lead. Gradually, however, they began to take on more responsibility (first working with individual students, then with small groups, then with the whole class under the Mentor's supervision, and finally with their own classes). They began to adapt training activities to their own contexts (e.g., developing a chart activity around Valentine's Day, developing games to introduce the reproductive system). One Intern invited a friend who had been involved in Haiti's literacy campaign to come to the HMSC to meet with students and Interns. Others took the initiative in developing lessons and introducing new activities. The following excerpt from workshop minutes shows how one Intern developed her own tools for learner assessment:

E. said that periodically she gives students 20 minutes of free conversation time in order to evaluate themselves; she says, *"Today, I want a soup."* This means they have to sit in mixed language groups and talk while she leaves the room. When she comes back, they have to report on what they discussed.

integrating planning and responsiveness

Interns' practice also changed in regard to curriculum and lesson planning. At first, many didn't feel confident about teaching without a predetermined curriculum. Yet often, when they had a plan, it didn't work out in reality. For example, one Intern started by trying to implement a weekly sequence (teaching writing on Mondays, vocabulary on Tuesdays, reading on Wednesdays, etc.); when this didn't work, he began each day by asking students what they wanted to do. He evolved toward drawing themes from their lives and developing them through the routine use of certain tools (LEA, codes, etc.). Another Intern describes how she addressed this tension between planning and responsiveness with the support of a Mentor:

I would go to class with the idea, "O.K., this is my plan" but I would just cover one thing. I would feel bad because I had this plan and I wanted them to learn more. At the beginning, I felt sort of tense because I felt, "Now what should I do? Should I go with the flow or should I cut them." But I realized that, in many cases, you learn more when you are actually thinking. For example, if I saw that most of the students were on that one topic, I would just let them stay on it because they were interested in that, whereas, if I cut them, they would probably get bored....

I also could see Ana: sometimes she would come in and say, "This is what we are more or less going to do in class today." Once we were in the class, the same thing happened. She would be O.K. If I were in her shoes, I wouldn't know what to do or how to do it. Sometimes I felt pressured. But once I was actually there, I had to have all my five senses awake and see if I could actually do something. I pretty much went with the flow. I would come to class and have this in my mind and I would work from that. I could see reactions in the students. Sometimes they were bored; they didn't want to talk, so I had to change it. What I always tried to do was

116

see how students reacted. Before I would just freeze. I wouldn't know what to do. I would just follow the textbook: "O.K. Keep reading," but it helped a lot to see how Ana dealt with the classes, because in so many cases, she'd have things prepared and then completely change because someone just came in and asked for something and they would concentrate on that.

One group of Interns got to the point where they consciously chose not to develop an a priori curriculum until they had met their students because they couldn't know what to prepare until they knew more about their students. Later, when one of them was hired as a teacher, she asked if she could throw out the site's general curriculum guidelines for her class and create a new one appropriate for her students. In general, by the end of the project, Interns became more comfortable both with developing their own plans and with going with the flow. Julio captured the essence of this approach when he said, *"It's important to plan and let the improvisation come from the class reaction to the plan."*

from form to meaning

Many Interns tended to focus mainly on decontextualized skills in their work with students when they started; they were preoccupied with form and accuracy (correct grammar, spelling, punctuation, etc.). In one case, an Intern even went so far as to correct students' papers for them, erasing incorrect forms and replacing them with the correct ones. Gradually, however, the question of correct form stopped being a central preoccupation. Interns began to see that students wrote more and developed more quickly if meaning was the focus. They began to experiment with other activities, introducing pictures, eliciting stories, and so on. As they saw the effectiveness of these activities, they became more confident in using them. One Intern, in talking about changes in her practice in an end-of-project interview, said:

We use pictures now for them to write about; it was kind of difficult for them at the beginning, but the more you introduce the pictures, the more ideas they have and they start writing. That was a big advance for us. Before, they used to write just a word or small sentence. Now what they write makes sense. So the pictures help a lot.

A particularly telling example of the shift from preoccupation with form to focus on meaning comes from the beginning and final interviews of an HMSC Intern: where at the beginning of the project he said, *"When you teach writing it's important to focus on spelling the words clearly, without mistakes,"* at the end, he said:

117

The dialogue journal is a good process of teaching because you get in communication with the students. You develop ideas from them. You are on the same level with them, and when you are on the same level with the students, they feel comfortable to express their ideas or their thinking. If they write and you only correct, without giving them any response, it will be like STOP–no more ideas. When you respond and tell your students to respond, then you keep on going, getting ideas from it.

ability to use a range of tools

Even when Interns began to see the importance of drawing out learners' ideas, they were often at a loss about how to connect discussion to literacy learning. Some classes would have heated debates about world events and then go back to rote work on sound-symbol correspondences (like the Intern who elicited an animated discussion about a picture of a jail, but cut it off to "get back to work"). As Interns gained skill and confidence in using the tools, their ability to integrate the mechanical and meaningful aspects of teaching increased. In terms of finding topics or themes, where many had started either by just asking students what they wanted to do, or by imposing topics, they learned how to elicit issues from students through structured activities. Interns learned to make mechanical exercises interesting by connecting them to learners' lives (e.g., an ESL Intern taught *wh-* questions by eliciting what students knew about a Haitian singer performing in Boston). One Intern summed up this change in ability to use tools as follows:

Now I have more tools. I can have a topic and I can take it in any direction I want. At the beginning, no, I just got the book and did it the way it was. Now I have this new skill because of the experiences that we have shared. I don't even have to look at readings or books. I just get the topic and I can change it the way I want.

from teacher- to learner- centered roles

Interns' practice also changed with regard to teacher-student roles and classroom dynamics. In some cases, Interns began by seeing themselves as the center of all interactions. Side conversations between students were considered discipline problems. One Intern, for example, initially had students work quietly at their seats while she went over each one's homework individually with them. If there were problems with particular students or tensions between students, Interns felt that they had to intervene as the authority to handle the problem. Differences in levels between students were seen as problematic; groups were separated by level.

118

As time went on, however, Interns began to reconceptualize issues of classroom dynamics and experiment with different participant structures. Side conversations sometimes came to be seen as opportunities instead of diversions. In one case, an Intern noticed that one group was having an excited discussion while she was working with another group and asked them to write about whatever they were talking about; this became the basis for a group story. Some Interns began to see differences in level as a resource rather than a problem. The Intern who had required students to work quietly at their seats invited advanced students to work with beginners. Several Interns moved toward building peer learning and mixed-level groups into their classrooms.

Interns also began to involve students in addressing teaching problems. In several cases, Interns brought issues of dynamics back to the group (e.g., use of the L1 in ESL class, uneven participation, children in class, etc.), and students developed guidelines for handling them. Interns' new way of seeing their relationship to learners is captured by the following words:

> *In my teaching, I try to really do the things we learned or heard in our training. I tried to do them because they were new to me. And in those things, I see that the students are the bosses. They have to participate in giving us the materials for teaching...It's like we listen to them. That's what I do in my teaching.*

ability to find and create materials

Another area in which Interns' practice changed concerned finding and creating materials. Although at first, Interns hoped to be given the perfect text to guide their teaching, they gradually began to take greater initiative in finding and developing their own materials. Native language literacy Interns often asked for friends or family to send materials from their home countries. One Intern developed her own method for incorporating pictograms into sentence exercises. Others invented games. One developed an entire math curriculum for his literacy class. The HMSC Mentor and Interns decided to form a materials development group because they felt they were just as capable of creating materials as their counterparts in Haiti, and probably in a better position to do so.

a stance of inquiry toward practice

Many Interns began to address questions and push forward their practice by experimenting with various activities or tools. For example, one Intern tried two ways of presenting pictures as a catalyst to writing, once with structured questions and once without; afterwards she concluded (contrary to her expectations)

119

that the open-ended way worked better because it allowed space for students to write about their own experiences. One ESL Intern summed up this newfound stance of inquiry as follows:

> *Before, I would present pictures but wouldn't feel that that's O.K. to do. In this project, I realized that it's O.K. to try even if it doesn't work because that's the way you find things out, you find either people learn or they don't learn.*

Interns not only engaged in this type of exploration but recognized its value and came to see it as one of the strengths of the project. At a conference presentation, when someone in the audience noted the great range of methods presented, Interns responded by saying that one of the great things about the project was that it gave them the freedom to explore and investigate their own ways of doing things–that they could try whatever made sense for their own groups and evaluate how it worked. One Intern said that she felt the best way to learn to teach was by observing students.

As Interns became more reflective about their work, they also became more self-critical about their own practice. They began to acknowledge when classes didn't go well and analyze the reasons. In one case, an Intern hypothesized that students had had difficulty with a particular reading because he hadn't done enough preparation linking it to students' experience; in his words, *"Each story has to be in the students' context."* Interns began to look to their peers for insights; for example, an Intern reported that his students had resisted writing an LEA story, and asked others for insights about why; they wondered if the story might have been too personal and suggested doing it in the third person. Another Intern criticized her own way of giving feedback to a peer after observing his class (telling him what she thought before asking for his insights). As one Intern said,

> *Sometimes you don't recognize your mistakes until you have them in front of you or maybe in the end. We have stereotypes and then, by the conversation, you start to realize what you were doing wrong and wonder, why did I do that?*

SELF-CONCEPT

confidence

Many Interns entered the project with some hesitation or fear about their own ability to teach. As one said, *"In the beginning, it was kind of hard, not only for me but for the students because they do not feel very confident in you, and I felt not that confident too because I didn't have experience working with them."*

120

Interns were nervous about standing in front of a group, and about teaching people who, in many cases, were older than they were. They were worried that the students wouldn't listen to them, that they wouldn't know what to do or be able to answer questions. In addition, the ESL Interns were concerned about whether their English was good enough and whether their students would respect them because they weren't native English speakers.

Once Interns started teaching, many were pleasantly surprised by how quickly they felt comfortable and how readily students accepted them. One Intern expressed it this way, *"I couldn't see myself as a teacher, but I discovered that students were my allies."* Virtually all of the Interns said that gaining confidence in their ability to teach was one of the most important outcomes of the project for them:

> *This was a very exciting experience. I learned more than I thought because when I started, I didn't feel confident with myself and, you know, I thought I couldn't do it. And now I know that I can...I have more experience. It doesn't take m e as much time to prepare classes. I have a lot of ideas now. Of course, I think about what I am going to do, but it is easier, not like before. I didn't know what to do, what would be fine for this day. Should I do this, should I do that? Is this going to be right? I don't feel that insecurity that I had.*

autonomy and expertise

A further indication of Interns' self-confidence was their growing sense of ownership and autonomy over their own work. Interns came to see themselves as peers with the Mentors; in one case, for example, an Intern told the Mentor to be careful about the words he used with students because they might not be familiar with them. In another case, Interns questioned whether they should accept the critique of a university professor (concerning the proverb book) just because he was an expert. Changes in responses to outside researchers also indicated an increasing sense of control and empowerment. For example, when one of the Interns went to a conference in Washington with biliteracy experts from around the country, he felt quite comfortable in criticizing the way the conference was organized.

sense of identity

Increasingly, Interns gained a sense of their own expertise, talking about their identity as professionals:

> *Now I know what to ask and what I need to be able to teach. At the beginning, I was teaching empirically–like a non-professional teacher; I feel now like a professional teacher. As a nonprofessional, you use what you have; you use your*

121

personal way. Now I follow things that other have done before and I adapt them to my way. Now I'm able to shape them to my own way of teaching. I feel that's a new skill that I have gotten from these workshops.

Many Interns began to reconceptualize their own histories and take a new pride in who they were. Early in the project, some didn't want it mentioned that they were housekeepers, factory workers, and so on, because they saw these low-status jobs as a stigma; through the project, they came to realize that this stigma was socially constructed and that their movement from these positions to teaching showed their strength. They realized that their situations in the U.S. were not something to be embarrassed about. One Intern said that since she had been in the U.S. she had tried to avoid her identity: *"I didn't know who I was."* As a Brazilian, she had tried to separate herself from Hispanics and, as she said, "deny who I am so I wouldn't be discriminated against." Through the project, she came to see her unity with other Latinos and to claim it. Another Intern said that the project allowed her to assert her identity as a Central American; she began to see herself as a model for her peers. As she said, *"It gave me the opportunity to show other people from Central America that they can do more than just earn money here."*

changing
feelings
about work

This sense of helping one's community, in turn, helped to transform the meaning of work for some, giving them a new sense of purpose and joy, as this quote from an Intern who worked in a hotel during the day indicates:

My life has changed a lot. Now I feel better because I helped them [the students]. I feel nice. When I come to work, I don't say, "Oh, it's time to work," I say, "Oh! It's time to go to class. I like it!" I come happy.

In addition, several Interns mentioned learning how to work with others as one of the most important ways they changed during the project. One Intern, for example, said that midway through the training she had almost quit because it was so hard to come to agreement with the other people in her group who had strong ideas about what to do; but she realized that no matter what job she has in her life, she would have to work with other people and get along with them, so she should try to learn how to do this. She told her partner in the interview that for her, one of the most important parts of the project was learning how to listen and figuring out a way of working together.

122

BEYOND THE PROJECT

changes in
career and
personal
goals

Many Interns changed their plans for the future as a result of the project. As Ana said, *"The project helped Interns clarify their goals. It gave them the opportunity to look at their skills and what they are capable of doing."* Some undergraduate Interns who came into the project undecided about their majors decided to major in education. One who had been interested in electronics decided to become a math teacher as a result of teaching math in a Creole literacy class. Several who had been working in factories or as housekeepers decided to continue their education and enrolled as undergraduates at UMass. Some who had started this project as a "sideline" were surprised at its impact. As one said,

> *I didn't think I would be so involved. Just to think about further education or to change my field–I didn't expect that. I thought that it would be something on the side. I thought I might pursue another field, but not education....But I'm really pleased that I participated in this project because it helped me in myself to find a career. I was kind of undecided what I was going to do. But I feel that I have become more stable now, because I tried what I learned in the project and it really worked. And that left me with the feeling "All right, I'm going to try other things..." That brought me confidence.*

Another said:

> *I think my plans have changed because I feel like I want to learn more things. I want to go back to school. I have to see other alternatives because this whole project made me realize that I need to know a lot of things that I don't know, explore things that I haven't explored. I think it's a very serious thing to teach. I used to think, "I know Spanish, therefore I can just go teach." But it isn't just teaching the language. It implies a lot of things besides that. Personally I wouldn't like to stop developing that.*

In addition to concrete changes in career or educational plans, Interns spoke about new ways of thinking about their long-term goals. One Intern, for example, talked about wanting to work with other Latinas because of having overcome obstacles herself:

> *Now I would like to do more things–I feel more motivated to do things for women, for Latina women, because now I see that there are not barriers if you want to do something*

123

with all your heart. I think our women need hope, they need to set up goals. I feel like a kind of role model. I feel so angry that young women could do so many things, but they don't have this hope, they don't have this motivation. Especially when we are in a strange country that's very hard, new for us, we have to try to shine in a new world. Maybe someday we can change the world—we won't have machismo anymore in our countries, in our culture. I just hate looking at young women here doing nothing—just waiting for somebody to marry them or have children.

Another Intern spoke about gaining new insights about her own life and new personal goals:

Going through this project made me realize that I have lot of other things that I need to work on personally, like being flexible. I felt I was learning so many things, but at the same time, how to put that all together.... I felt frustrated in many cases because I realized that I didn't know how to deal with time, pressure. I realized I was trying to be too rigid: I thought I had to go from 1 to 10. I guess that's the way I always tried to do things. But in many cases it didn't work out that way because of time. It made me think.... With this whole project, I didn't have the chance to be systematic, to do things the way I was doing it before. I would come to class and have the idea in my mind and work 5 minutes, and it would be different. That was really interesting because I realized that there are so many ways to get to your goal.

For many Interns, the project offered concrete experiences that directly helped them acquire other jobs. As one Intern said, *"The project gives you a ladder; it opens doors."* Participants could put their work with the project on their resumes. One, who was hired as a community liaison for a health education project, said:

When we had the first interview 6 months ago, I wasn't sure what my goals were; since that day my life has changed a lot. I have a new job that I never expected to have. I never thought I would get this kind of job. One of the things I'm grateful for is that being in the project helped me to get it. Just to be able to tell them in the interview that I was doing this kind of workshop—that showed them that I was working with the community and that I could develop sensitive curriculum and multicultural curriculum. And now, in my new job, I have to develop curriculum, educational material oriented to a multicultural population.

NEW ROLES AND RESPONSIBILITIES

at the sites

Interns not only grew in personal and professional ways, but they also contributed to the development of their own communities and the field of adult literacy as a whole. As they became more self-confident about their practice, they took on new roles both at their sites and in the broader literacy community. At the sites, Interns began to help with recruitment, in-take, assessment, and site publications: Harborside Interns conducted an open house for potential students; Interns at the JMCS were largely responsible for the publication of the Center magazine; HMSC Interns helped to organize center-wide discussions of Creole literacy. Many Interns showed incredible commitment to their students by taking on additional responsibilities without pay: they stayed late to tutor them after class, took them to the hospital or lawyers, and helped them with personal problems. As one Intern said:

I feel like the center is my other home. It's so comfortable with the students. You get used to them and you see the need. They bring their letters in English and you can translate it for them, the bills, the phone calls; so it's not only teaching them, it's the other extra help that we can give them. I know about taxes so they come to me. If they need a letter to send out, I do it for them.

Another talked about the project changing her perspective on her relationship to the community. In the process of learning how to listen as a teacher, she became more involved in the lives of the learners and her commitment to the community grew:

[The teaching] makes me change in my relationship with other people. By listening you think more, you think more of other people, you become more a listener, you listen more to people. And I also think that being involved in the project, I am always talking about it and I think that that does change me in a sense that I'm always encouraging other people to be more involved in the Haitian community. At first I didn't care, but now I take time just to get people to volunteer and to speak with them about the project. In the beginning I wasn't really interested in that. And it not only changed me but other people told me, "I can see that you are doing something useful or something wonderful" and that is really encouraging.

125

in the community

Several Interns took the initiative to extend what they had learned in other community contexts. Interns applied what they learned in ESL to L1 teaching and vice versa. A Spanish literacy Intern started an ESL class in his church, saying, *"I use ideas from the workshops in that."* Likewise, an ESL Intern began teaching Spanish literacy when she noticed that some of her ESL students couldn't read and write. She spoke about this experience:

> *This man went to first grade in his country. His wife, his sister, his children tried to encourage him to go to school.... When I was teaching him, I noticed that he didn't know how to write and read and he wanted to do it in English, but I said you have to do it first in Spanish. And then I started developing a very basic curriculum in Spanish and he liked it. Every time he liked it more. Then I noticed I had another one–he was acting "lazy"–he didn't want to read and write. But that was the problem: he didn't know how to read and write in Spanish. So I had two students. That's how it started. One day I talked to the wife of the first one and she said, "Thank you very much. I think you must be very nice because now Pedro is very motivated to read and write and we feel so good about it because now he's asking us to help him." That's the thing that makes me want to keep going.*

in the broader literacy community

Interns participated in various projects and activities that contributed to the development of the field of adult literacy (particularly during the BCLTP). Some became involved in a State Department of Education assessment project; others shared their work at state-sponsored workshops. One was a member of a Breast Cancer curriculum team. During the BCLTP, Interns participated in an international conference in New York to celebrate Paulo Freire's 70th birthday, made conference presentations, and attended a Native Language Literacy working group meeting in Washington.

Interns changed from being part of the audience at conferences to becoming presenters. At first they were quite nervous about presenting, spending long hours rehearsing what they would say. By the end of the project, they had gotten to the point that they could speak spontaneously with ease and field questions. They developed their own handouts, flip charts, and role-plays as well as being to discuss conference presentations critically and to redesign presentations for changing contexts. In many conferences, people from our project were the only language or racial minority representation. As such, the Interns' voices served an important function in raising the issue of diversification of the field.

TABLE 4: Categories of Change Among Interns

Table 4 summarizes the ways in which Interns changed during the course of the project. Even though every Intern did not demonstrate change in each of these categories, they represent the overall growth of the group.

Conceptions of training	
	Expectations of workshop content and process Notions of expertise
Participation in training	
	Ability to share and debate ideas Responsibility for workshop activities Preparation and planning of workshops Ability to evaluate training critically Ability to challenge experts Ability to explain workshop content to peers
Conceptions about literacy and literacy pedagogy	
	Mechanical vs. meaningful aspects of literacy Problem-solving vs. problem-posing Teacher/student roles View of the role of methods Uniform vs. context-specific curriculum
Classroom practice	
	Taking the initiative Approaches to and skill in lesson planning Emphasis on meaning vs. form Ability to use a range of tools Skill in facilitating discussion Skill in connecting dialogue to literacy work Teacher- vs. learner-centered roles Ability to vary participant structures Ability to facilitate peer learning Problem-posing ability Ability to find and create materials Stance of inquiry toward practice Ability to reflect on and criticize own practice Ability to address problems of classroom dynamics
Self-concept	
	Self-confidence Autonomy and expertise Sense of identity Conceptions of and feelings about work Ability to work with others
Roles outside the project	
	Changes in career and personal goals Responsibilities at site (recruitment, in-take, etc.) Community participation Participation in local/state literacy projects and conferences

What was the impact of the project on Mentors?

a
cautionary
note

Although the CTAFL objectives included Mentor training, we conducted no formal training sessions specifically geared toward this objective. Rather, we focused on issues of mentoring through informal interactions in staff meetings, on-site experiences, and workshops. In fact, at one point Felipe criticized the fact that we had not done enough specific training for the Mentors. As Coordinator, I was somewhat surprised by this comment, because my perception was that we had integrated Mentor training all along the way through our discussions of supervision and teaching issues in staff meetings. An additional factor was time: because funding arrived late and Interns were not on board until January, we focused most of our energy on preparing for workshops.

Thus, it would be misleading to claim that the changes that Mentors' underwent were a direct result of any specific Mentor training. Rather, a number of factors shaped their growth, not the least of which was their own initiative and creativity in addressing challenges presented by their jobs. In many ways, what the project did was give them a chance to develop skills that they already had, but which had not been recognized or nurtured in prior jobs. In a sense, it could be said that they trained themselves and were trained by the demands of their positions.

Another important point to note about the Mentors' roles is that they were shaped by contextual factors. For example, time constraints affected Mentors' roles in training workshops. During the BCLTP, because workshops were held on a monthly basis and we had staff meetings bi-weekly, there was much more time for Mentors to participate in planning the workshops and actually facilitating different segments of them. In the CTAFL, we barely had time to evaluate each session and plan an overall framework for the subsequent one at staff meetings because they were at 2-week intervals. Thus, Mentors took a less active role in conducting the workshops. An additional factor that shaped Mentors' participation was the context at their sites. The amount of initiative that individual Mentors took depended to some extent on their sense of control at the sites. The more responsibility they felt was vested in them, the more they invested in developing the work at the sites and the project.

The following analysis of the impact of the project on Mentors is based primarily on what they said during interviews and on examples of actions they took at the sites or in workshops.

CHANGES IN TEACHING

creativity

During the course of the project, Mentors changed their teaching in many of the same ways that Interns did. They experimented with new approaches in class and tried out activities that they encountered in workshops, as Julio explains here:

I can say that I learned a lot from the workshops....There are a lot of things that I would never never think of doing by myself. I can give an example...the free writing, it's something that works very well. I tried what we did in the last workshop–the dialogue journals–in my class yesterday. Without attending those seminars, I would never be able to think about those things. And I love to create things, like the bingo things in my class. That was something I created by myself. I don't mean that I was the first teacher who tried bingo, but at the Center, I was the first one maybe who did it. And I've been thinking about what's new to do. By attending those workshops, I always have something new that I learned. Eh–that doesn't mean all of them work; some don't work, but most of them work.... What's important about it is–from one thing you learn, you can create another thing.

In addition, Mentors stressed that because they were modeling for others, being a Mentor shaped their practice as teachers. Ana, for example, said that this modeling caused her to become more reflective and more consistent in her teaching:

reflective-
ness

Before I was a Mentor, I wasn't as conscious or rational in what I was doing as a teacher. In a way, I think the best way to learn about something is by trying to teach it. When you try to teach somebody else, you have to be clear in what you are doing and you have to have a way of explaining it. I've gotten more reflective about what I do. When you reflect on just about anything, there is a change, a change in attitude, a change in style.

consistency

And, I think, to some extent, that has happened with me. When I am sitting with the students, trying to overhear what is happening at the next table where the Interns are working, I am letting myself be loud so that the Interns can hear what I'm doing and can somehow follow the path. I think it reflects also a certain new consistency in what I do. I used to try a lot of new things just about every night. Now I try to follow certain paths over and over.

curriculum
and
materials
development

Mentors also took on curriculum development responsibilities, creating and adapting activities and materials to fit their own contexts. Felipe, for example, adapted what he had learned about the participatory approach as an ESL Intern in the BCLTP to his work as a Spanish literacy Mentor in the CTAFL:

The only difference teaching ESL and Spanish literacy is that the material for the Spanish literacy class has been a little bit complicated to put together. The teaching part is the same. You use the same methods and you deal with students' issues. Using the participatory approach in Spanish literacy has been complicated because you have to be creating the material or trying to use students' issues all the time and there is not much [supporting material] in Spanish. You have to create a lot. We have to keep our ears open.

Felipe took the initiative in adapting this approach for his component in several ways: for example, he developed a survey form to elicit topics from the advanced class; he brought in picture activities to facilitate the transition from a mechanical to a meaningful approach in the beginning class. He was also particularly creative in integrating programmatic, contextual issues into the teaching itself: for instance, when enrollment was down, he worked with Interns and students to develop a video to be used for recruitment purposes; when funding was threatened, students worked on fund-raising strategies for one class period each week. In each case, these activities were linked to literacy acquisition. Likewise, Julio took on responsibility for developing appropriate materials with Interns. As he said, *"We used to have the tendency to think that when we need to get materials, we need to go to Haiti."* He and the other Creole literacy teachers began to write their own materials to respond to the needs of Haitians in the U.S.

ADMINISTRATIVE RESPONSIBILITIES

Mentors talked about several ways in which their position differed from their prior jobs as teachers. Felipe felt that one of the challenges of a Mentor was taking on new responsibilities for program administration and project documentation:

Being a teacher meant less responsibilities; being a Mentor, there is a lot more to do. A lot more to learn.... The difference will be paperwork and making sure that you're collecting what you will need for the final report and that kind of thing.

130

In fact, Felipe took the initiative in terms of these paperwork and documentation responsibilities to the extent of creating his own Spanish literacy in-take assessment form; he was particularly creative in taking on recruitment and fundraising responsibilities. Julio, too, spoke about the project as increasing his sense of responsibility:

In a sense, my participation in this project is a continuity with my life, but at the other side, it's also a change because it gives me what we call the sense of responsibility because I am the person in charge. I have to think about the project, I have to think about what the Interns are doing. I don't want to sound bossy, but what's important, I have to keep contact with them, to know if they have any problem, if there's anything that they need. This gives me an opportunity to evaluate myself as a responsible person, to evaluate myself if I can deal with people without letting them feel that I am their boss, which I don't want. I don't want to be their gendarme.... I got this from this project because when I was working before, I was not in charge. All I had to do was do my job. So now I have to–I don't want to say supervise–but at least to show my presence as a responsible person. I have to know if everything is all right, if they are not confronting any kind of problem.

For him, the most challenging part of this responsibility for program administration was balancing conflicting needs:

I think the most difficult part of it is that I was not and am still not able to satisfy everybody's demands. Some of the Interns would like to have tutors in their classes; some of them are working with 20 students in the classroom. This is not recommended; this is impossible to work with 20 students doing native language literacy. When they talk to me about it, sometimes I feel guilty, but what helps me a lot is that they trust me. I say, "I do understand that, but we cannot afford to pay anyone else. You have a choice: if you want, you can reduce your class from 20 to 12 students." To be honest with you, I take advantage of them, because I know they will never do that. They will say, "I would never do that–what about those 8 people–you don't want me to ask them to stay home? This is not possible. I would not feel O.K. to do something like that." This is the most difficult part of the program.

TRAINING AND SUPERVISORY ROLES

Julio's comment about not wanting to sound bossy reflected a general concern that Mentors had in taking on responsibilities for training and supervising Interns. Each of them talked about learning to supervise or train in a participatory, nonhierarchical way–learning to be a guide without being a boss. Ana, for example, said that one of the ways she did this was by trying to be a role model, by *showing* rather than *telling* Interns her way of teaching:

> *As a model and as a facilitator, when I work with people who are like me, I think I have the opportunity to show them that we're in the same place, and I have this skill–I am working in this field in spite of whatever has been against us both. This reassures the person who is working with me. I work more as a guide. When they are in my classes, they see what I'm doing and the way I do it. When we sit down to talk, we rationalize what we have done in the class and when there are confusions, we try to clarify them.*

Because Ana was a Mentor in both the BCLTP and the CTAFL, she had several years experience in refining her role. In the following lengthy interview excerpt, she talks about changes she underwent during this time:

providing
more
guidance

> *When we started this project, I think my attitude was more like, "Well, here they are, five more people. Let's work together." In the beginning, I assumed that they had a mentality that was more attuned to mine. As time went by, I realized that people had great skills (some of them that I don't have) and I also realized that they needed more guidance than I was giving.*

gaining
confidence
in own
knowledge

> *I have gotten much more at ease with what I am doing. I feel much more confident. In the beginning, I felt, "I'm going to work as a team with this group of people and they know as many things as I do so let's put them together and make a team." As time went by, I realized that I knew much more, and that everything has to go through a process and they were as confused as I was when I started. In the past I would ask, "What do you think we should do?" Now I say, "This is what makes sense to me. Based on this, what do you think?"*

132

demystifying training	*The workshops gave me the framework for solving the problems and also for guiding Interns. To some extent, I think before you enter this kind of project, there are certain mystiques, a certain mysticism, and as you get into it, as you participate, you understand and get at peace with it, less afraid. For me, the project demystified the training part. I have learned to be a supervisor without being a boss. I come forward more with ideas. I think that the way I demystified the training was that I understood that there were things that I knew that had some value.*
change in understand-ing of participatory training	*As time went by, I started relating to the participation part of the participatory stuff, and coming forward with what I think. Now when people ask me what I think, I <u>say</u> what I think. And then they can take it or leave it. I suggest stuff to do.... I don't want to tell them what to do, but I suggest things that can be done. I think I participate more, given that I articulate my ideas much more confidently.*

Julio defined his training role in terms of sharing what he knew with Interns and encouraging them to learn:

I don't have the pretension to say that I am teaching other people to become a teacher, because being a teacher is something natural. It's like being a priest. But what I can do, or what I think I'm doing, I can lead them a little bit; I can share my knowledge with them, I can share my experience with them, and I can refer them to some books; I can refer them to some people that I know, people I learn from; I can encourage them to participate in some seminars. Even when they are boring, it is very important to attend them because I never participated in any seminar where I can say "I regret my participation." No way. Even though what the guest speakers were talking about was not that helpful, I met people that I can exchange knowledge with. So, therefore, I also encourage them to attend all those seminars.

For Felipe, being in a supervisory or training position was especially challenging because he had been a peer of the Interns at one point. He dealt with this in creative ways, for example, by having Interns do self-evaluations, so they came to their own conclusions about issues they needed to address in their practice.

BEYOND THE PROJECT

changes in
career and
personal
goals

Like the Interns, Mentors talked about the project as giving them new ways of seeing themselves and recognizing their own capabilities. Felipe, for example, said:

> *For me, being a factory worker when I began, I thought that was the job that I would do for the rest of my life. I didn't know anyone to help me. Since then, my life has changed. The project gave me the opportunity to use my skills, not just my hands. This is the other me. I can be a role model for people who want to do something. People look at me and say, "Well, if he did it, why can't I do it?" They see role models and they want to improve, to get better in their lives.*

The project helped Ana to gain a new sense her own capabilities:

> *I have learned and see much better what I know... Before I didn't think that I knew that much. I know now that I really know a lot about this stuff.... When I see the interns teaching, I'm observing myself. The new teachers have made me reflect a lot on what I do and how I do it. Who did she or he learn this from? Where did he or she learn this? There are times you feel so proud! Other times you see your own mistakes so clearly you want to hide! ... So I know I can be a good trainer. But it is a continuous reflecting exercise.*

As Felipe says, the project also gave Mentors skills and work experience that they could use in future jobs:

> *In my life in this country, the project has meant a lot. Being an Intern was the first opportunity I had to express or to let people know the skills that I had. Now that I'm a Mentor, I consider it like an open door for me to get a good job in this country. In the factory, I used my hands to work. That was basically it.... Now I have changed to a new [day-time] job with special education. I didn't have experience from my factory job that would help me in special education, but through this teaching experience, they looked at my resume and said, "Wow, this is something that he might do." I had shown that I had skills.*

the
downside:
uncertain
futures

The Mentors also said, however, that even though they would like to work in adult education as a career goal, they were not optimistic about a future in this field. As Felipe said:

I am interested in becoming a teacher in adult education, but unfortunately, in this country right now, funding is a problem. I don't see that as becoming a full-time job. For the time that I've been working here, the most frustrating part is waiting for more funding at the end of the project. There is a pressure. Am I going to have a job or am I not going to have a job? Should I wait? Shouldn't I wait? That's the part I don't like.

Ana, too, felt that despite all she had learned in the project, these skills would not be valued in the broader society:

Now I find myself with more skills and, given the economy, not much future in this particular field. I feel much more strongly than I felt before about having people from the communities themselves be part of the staff–and not on a volunteer basis! For myself, the project has opened up a whole new panorama, but it has also made me realize how little we are really appreciated.

contributions to the field of adult literacy | As with the Interns, the Mentors participated in various other projects, conferences, and organizations. Ana was part of a Breast Cancer curriculum project; Felipe was part of a Smoking Cessation literacy project. They participated in the same conferences that Interns did during the BCLTP, as well as a giving a presentation at the international TESOL Convention after the end of the CTAFL.

TABLE 5: Categories of Change Among Mentors

Teaching	
	creativity reflectiveness consistency curriculum and materials development
Administrative responsibilities	
	recruitment assessment and documentation coordination liaison with other site staff fund-raising
Training/supervisory roles	
	guidance confidence in own knowledge demystification of training
Self-concept and goals	
	self-confidence sense of self as role model changes in career and personal goals new job opportunities participation in local/state literacy projects and conferences

135

What was the impact of the project on learners?

As we said earlier, the time frame for the CTAFL was too short to fully assess learner progress: particularly with beginning literacy students, significant progress takes time. Children acquire literacy over a period of years; there is no reason to assume that adults will make dramatic changes in less than a year. However, by looking at the work of both the BCLTP and the CTAFL, as well as approaching learner assessment in a qualitative way, we were able to make some generalizations about the impact of the model on learners. Our approach to assessing learners focused on evaluating classes and groups rather than on assessing individual students. We asked, "How are learners' literacy practices and uses changing?" rather than "How much are they changing?" We were concerned about what learners said or showed about literacy and English in their lives rather than with test scores.

**context
shapes
outcomes**

Before analyzing specific changes in learners' proficiency and uses of ESL/literacy, it is important to note one general finding that emerged as we analyzed student progress. Over and over, we found that *the context for assessment shaped its outcomes:* what students could demonstrate about their knowledge or abilities depended on how they were evaluated. For example, beginning literacy students could readily respond to, "How much will it cost to buy 7 pounds of potatoes if each pound is 30 cents?" but might not be able to do the same operations on decontextualized paper and pencil tests or if asked to multiply 7 x 30.

Likewise, if writing tasks had a purpose, focusing on meaning and issues of substance, even the most beginning students could produce rich, substantive pieces; in addition, formal aspects of their writing (spelling, grammar, etc.) became increasingly accurate. For example, very beginning Spanish literacy students could write several sentences about a compelling picture even though they didn't know the whole alphabet yet. ESL students who struggled with textbook exercises about reporting emergencies spoke with ease and eloquence when asked to discuss real emergencies that they experienced in their own lives (utilizing more complex grammar and vocabulary). Similarly, students' ability to read a passage depended on the content of the text rather than on any "inherent" skill level. What they could read depended on the relationship between the text and their own lives. For example, beginning students at the HMSC eagerly read passages from texts with compelling content (e.g., <u>Voices</u> and <u>I Told Myself I'm Going to Learn</u>, Ndaba, 1990) even though they were syntactically more complex than other texts that the same students found difficult. These findings reinforce the notion that *students' competence depends on the context in which they are asked to demonstrate it.*

What tools were used to assess student progress?

charts lifelines	Information about learners' educational, employment, and family histories was elicited through classroom activities like the profile charts that Interns did in the training. This information became the basis for subsequent lessons as well as for composite class profiles.
samples of student work	Although portfolios never fully took hold as a system for collecting and analyzing student writing, teachers kept track of changes in student writing by collecting samples of student work. For example, one Intern photocopied sequences of entries in her students' dialogue journals and analyzed changes in accuracy and quantity of writing. An ESL Intern traced the changes in the use of verb tenses in his students' journals. Another Intern gave each student a notebook to write his or her own words or sentences and collected them from time to time to see how they were progressing. Comparison of submissions to site publications at the end of each cycle also provided evidence of changes in writing proficiency.
informal observa-tion	Teachers did ongoing assessment by looking at students' homework and by noting their oral participation in class and responses to in-class activities. They noted at regular intervals what learners were able to read (from words to sentences to texts; the kind of text, and the length of text). The development of both affective factors (self-confidence) and skills were noted in this way.
formal assess-ment	Some teachers routinely integrated dictations, spelling tests, or worksheet pages from a text as quizzes to see whether students were ready to go on to something new.
contex-tualized tasks	Sometimes students were asked to do specific tasks that would demonstrate their knowledge; for example, at the HMSC, one Intern asked students to help make the attendance list (by writing their names, addresses, and phone numbers). At HCC, students made a video for recruitment purposes. Each of these tasks had a purpose other than assessment, but yielded assessment data.
critical incidents	Spontaneous, unexpected incidents may occur in class, indicating changes in learners' literacy/ESL proficiency or use. For example, when a new student joined the class, old ones realized how much they had learned; when an Intern returned after observing another class for a month he saw great changes; when the site coordinator dropped into class and spontaneously asked students to read

something on the spot, he was impressed with how well they could read. In one case, students identified spelling errors in a U.S.-published Creole text, indicating the extent to which they had mastered the orthographic system.

anecdotes Students often reported incidents reflecting new uses of literacy or ESL in their lives outside of class. They told stories about what had happened at home, at work, in their communities, or with their children's schooling.

posted journals Posted journals are large pieces of newsprint on which participants can write accomplishments at regular intervals. Interns introduced posted journals in several classes as a way for learners to reflect on their own progress and document it for project evaluation.

student self-evaluation Student self-evaluation took a variety of forms.

•*Class evaluations:* Class evaluation exercises were conducted during and at the end of cycles at each site. In some cases, they were written (e.g., for ESL classes). In others, they were group discussions that became language experience stories.

•*Individual interviews:* In several cases, individual students were interviewed at the sites.

•*Testimony:* In public meetings, students sometimes stood up and gave testimony about their progress; for example, in a site meeting about why Creole was being taught at the HMSC, one student spoke at length about how literacy had changed her life.

checklists During a CTAFL training evaluation exercise, Interns identified the question,*"How do we know our students are learning?"* as a training issue. In response to this issue, we developed checklists to systematize their assessments of student progress. The process for developing these checklists unfolded as follows:

•Interns and Mentors brainstorming two lists:*What students could do when they first started classes*, and *What they can do now.*

•We then categorized these lists into types of changes: *In-Class Changes* and *Out-of-Class Changes*. Some of the In-Class Changes included:

changes in writing (length, ease, genre/type of writing, ability to copy, knowledge of letters, what students can write, thinking while writing)

changes in reading (length, ease, genre, ability to decode, understanding, ability to explain text, ability to use punctuation in reading, ability to read own stories)

changes in how students act (participation, comfort, helping peers)

changes in learning strategies (understanding role of L1 reading, guessing, taking risks)

Some of the *Out-of-Class Changes* included:

changes in what participants can do with literacy/ESL (reading bills, making budgets, writing money orders, communicating with family, sorting mail, etc.)

changes in how they feel about themselves (self-confidence, etc.)

changes in responsibility for the program (participation in recruitment, fund-raising)

•Seeing the changes categorized in this way triggered the realization that there were probably many more kinds of change within each category that could be added to the list.

•Before the next workshop, the Coordinator typed two versions of the category lists, one that included each of the items specified under the broad categories (as well as some blanks under each category) and one that only listed broad categories and had blanks for Interns to add their own itemization of changes under each.

•Interns then chose the format they preferred and summarized learners' changes during subsequent weeks, adding subcategories and keeping the checklists as a tool for ongoing assessment. Many Interns said that they preferred the more open-ended format because it allowed them to represent the richness, complexity, and variation of student changes more fully. The checklist with pre-specified categories of change seemed very limiting and reductionist once it had been generated.

IN-CLASS CHANGES

changes in
reading
proficiency

Students demonstrated a variety of changes in both the quantity and quality of what they could read. The general pattern of progression was from reading key words, to self-generated sentences, to sentences in a textbook, to longer passages in a textbook and teacher-generated passages, to authentic materials. They progressed from mechanical decoding to reading for meaning. As one Spanish literacy Intern said, *"Now they can think while they're reading. They didn't use to pay attention to what they were reading, but now they are paying attention and they can explain."*

In both the Creole and Spanish literacy classes, students who knew only a few of the letters of the alphabet when they started classes were able to read authentic material (e.g., an AIDS flyer, a healthy baby brochure, and a newspaper in Creole; a workplace rights flyer, and newspaper articles in Spanish) within about 8 months. Creole students with minimal exposure to English eagerly read a book (in English) by a South African literacy student, because, as one student said, *"All the book is my life."* In addition, students who at first did not want to read anything outside of a literacy book, gained confidence in reading other kinds of materials.

In ESL classes, Interns reported that their students could understand increasingly complex readings; they brought in newspaper articles that they found interesting as texts for the whole class. One beginning ESL teacher said, *"Now when I read the class a story, I don't need to repeat it; they understand it the first time."*

changes in
writing
proficiency

Students' writing changed both in terms of what they wrote about (the content) and in terms of its accuracy (form). Often, students' first tendency was to see writing primarily as copying. The extent and rate at which this view changed depended a great deal on how writing was taught: students in classes where accuracy and spelling was stressed progressed more slowly; when teaching stressed writing as making meaning, students wrote longer and more substantive pieces. For example, Interns at Harborside had initially tended to focus on learning the alphabet before doing more substantive writing; however, when the second group of beginners at Harborside started classes, the Interns invited them to write about pictures, even though they didn't know all the letters of the alphabet, and responded to the content of what students had written. The result was that each student was able to write several meaningful sentences about each picture. As one Intern said, *"Now you can understand what they're writing... and now, when I ask them what they wrote, they can explain it. That means that at the same time that they're writing, they're thinking, and this is a step that's very difficult to get to. So I can tell that they've improved."*

There was a diversification of genres of student writing through the course of the projects. By the end of the project, students had written journal entries, LEA stories, magazine articles, letters, and photo-stories. In some cases, students began to do personal expressive writing, bringing in pieces that they had done for their own purposes outside of class. In letter-writing and writing for site magazines, students started by generating ideas and went through various phases of revision, thus moving toward a process approach to their writing.

One clear indication of changes in Creole literacy students' writing proficiency can be seen in the kind of submissions to the site magazine. In the first issue after the project started, the teacher wrote a description of the Creole component; the next issue included several language experience stories written by groups of students; the subsequent issue included a few short sentences by individual students; more recently, issues have included a range of entries from Creole students ranging from sentences to paragraphs and page-long pieces.

changes in English proficiency

ESL students progressed in terms of the traditional kinds of change in grammatical proficiency (e.g., acquisition of verb tenses, vocabulary, etc.). But they also progressed in their communicative ability–their ease and fluency in conversing about meaningful topics. In describing these changes, beginning students said things like, *"Now I can talk about Russian history with my classmates"* and *"I understand the teacher in class now."* When themes were compelling, their ESL proficiency seemed to increase (as in the case of the students who had difficulty doing workbook exercises about emergencies, but no difficulty talking about real emergencies in their lives). They were able to explore sensitive topics like breast cancer and workplace discrimination. As one Intern said, *"I gave them the vocabulary and they went from that."*

meta-cognitive changes

In addition to changes in proficiency, students also underwent changes in metacognitive aspects of their learning: they became less preoccupied with form, corrections, mechanics and accuracy, and more concerned with expressing meaning as time went on. They began to value their own knowledge, experience, and dialogue as integral aspects of learning. One reflection of this is the following excerpt in which students describe their process of writing stories based on photos:

We got together in the class and studied everything that was in the picture. We chose what was important in the picture so that we could make a lesson because what comes from within us is better than anything else. We discussed the picture and the teacher wrote our words on the blackboard. What is important in that method is that it allows us all to participate in the work of the class.

The following is a Mentor's account of what one student said during an end-of-cycle interview when asked to describe the most important thing he had learned:

He responded that when he had started class, he didn't think he would learn anything because of the nonformal approach (having discussions in class); however, he realized that he had thought this because he was used to a traditional approach. Now, he feels that it is good that he has learned to analyze things and be more critical of what's going on around him. He said that this is the most important thing he learned because this is something that will stay with him.

AFFECTIVE CHANGES

self-confidence

One of the main ways in which students changed related to their self-confidence and ability to contribute their ideas to class discussions. Looking back, they said things like, *"I was shy in class. I didn't feel happy in school."* But gradually, as one Intern said,

They open up and tell you their needs....They feel like family. The class is a lot of support for them. A lot of them say that as soon as they come to school, they see the difference. Their life changes. You can see that they're losing their fear and getting more into reality. It's like the light comes to them.

changes in classroom roles and participation

When they started classes, many students refused to write on the board or to draw because they thought it would reveal how elementary their skills were. If they were asked an opinion, they would often repeat whatever the person before them had said; it was difficult to draw out their ideas. Gradually, they became less afraid to make mistakes and take risks. They began to express their own opinions, disagree with each other, and respect each others' opinions. The beginning classes began to bring in their own topics (e.g., the causes of the Gulf War). At times they actively critiqued the Intern or materials, for example, telling an Intern to be on time for class, pointing out errors in textbooks, and making suggestions about lessons.

Students took on increasing responsibility for the class as a whole, developing it as a community and helping each other. When a new student came in and didn't have a job, the others collected money and bought him some groceries. One ESL student who was ready to go on to a higher level asked to stay in her class because, as she told the Intern, *"You need me."* One of the advanced Spanish literacy students began tutoring beginners 1 day a week. The Intern who worked with him said:

> *Now he can understand more, write more, and he wants to be like a teacher, helping other people. He knows their problems, because they've happened to him. He's concerned about his life; he wants to change.*

use of L1 literacy as a learning tool

Literacy students increasingly began to use their knowledge of L1 literacy to support their English acquisition. For example, Spanish literacy students insisted that the teacher write all new English words on the board at the end of each ESL conversation class. Students also used the metalinguistic knowledge that they had gained in L1 literacy classes (their ability to talk about language and its functions) in supporting their acquisition of English. For instance, because they had discussed pronoun use in Creole, one of Julio's students was able to explain the use of pronouns in English as follows, *"You use 'she' if you want to talk about a woman but you don't want to repeat her name."*

OUT OF CLASS CHANGES

functional uses of ESL and literacy

Students reported many ways that they could independently accomplish various functional tasks as a result of class participation. ESL students said things like, *"In January, I couldn't understand TV or the radio; now I <u>like</u> to watch TV and listen to the radio! I can go to the store and ask prices now."* They mentioned being able to call long-distance, call 911, ask an American neighbor for help when locked out, understand the weather forecast on TV, and go to the bank or grocery store independently. L1 literacy students mentioned being able to sort and distribute mail to other household

143

members, write letters home, and use public transportation more easily. Several Creole literacy students got their driver's licenses after organizing a special Creole Driver's Education class. One Spanish literacy student said,

Before, I needed to find somebody to write a letter for me and now I can try to write it. I can go to the bank and try to fill out papers; I can try to find out where I am by reading. I can communicate more with my family.

self-
sufficiency

Again, being able to accomplish these tasks was important to students not just for their functional value, but because of the new sense of self-sufficiency they gained. Many students reported that one of the biggest changes in their lives was they no longer felt that they could be exploited as easily: for example, they could read documents like tax forms, day care agreements, and inheritance papers before signing them. They no longer had to depend on someone else to tell them what they were signing. As one student said, *"Now, if someone says $50 and you see $100, you can say 'No, that is not correct!'"*

changes in family relationships

They also said that their new proficiency and independence shaped their family relationships and interactions. One student said, *"I used to go shopping with my husband; now I go alone."* Being able to write letters signified powerful changes in family relationships. Writing the first letter to a family member was an emotional experience, serving almost as an announcement of a new self. In one case, a student wrote her first letter to her husband and then put it on his pillow; he cried when he read it. Another woman wrote to her son, who is an engineer, for the first time. Many students said that one of the most important changes in their lives was that they were no longer dependent on family members (or others) to read mail and official papers for them. As one student said, *"You're not able to write your real feelings when somebody else is writing for you."* Many felt that their children respected them more because they could read and write.

changes in the workplace

Another domain where students applied what they learned to make changes in their lives was in the workplace. Many students reported having problems at work that resulted from their limited English. In some cases, they had to rely on others because they couldn't understand the boss: for example, one student said that when her boss had said, "You don't have to work tomorrow," someone had translated, "You have to work tomorrow." In other cases, students couldn't make themselves understood. One student,

144

for example, had been working on Sundays even though it was against his religion because he didn't know how to refuse overtime. As a result of classes, he reported later that he had been able to tell his boss successfully, *"I go to church Sunday. No overtime."*

site roles and responsibilities

Students also took on increasing responsibility at their sites. In addition to tutoring other students, they became involved in recruitment. At Harborside, they conducted an open house for prospective students; in addition, they made a video for public television to publicize the program and organized a fund-raising committee so that classes would be able to continue after CTAFL funding ran out.

community roles and responsibilities

In addition, many students took on new roles in their own communities. For example, one student, who could write only a few words when he started in the program at Harborside, began taking minutes at his AA meeting after about 6 months of classes. He went to a state-wide convention and took notes so he could report back to his group. Many of the refugees in Creole classes participated actively in community events as a way to integrate themselves into Boston's Haitian community and express support for democracy in Haiti. JMCS students took part in community hearings about the closing of a bilingual program at a local school.

The following excerpt from an Intern interview sums up many of the changes that students experienced, pointing to perhaps the most important change of all–the desire to continue learning:

learning goals

I can see the improvements with the students that we have. When they start learning, they are very afraid of communicating, they're very afraid of everything, but as soon as they start learning, you can see how they open themselves, how they can really face life with less pain. They can see things more clearly. When they learn to write and read, it gives them strength to continue and they get a little ambitious. They want to keep learning. I can see the changes in their lives. They know how to communicate with their family–that's very important, especially because most of the people, they leave their families in their countries. They feel proud with their children because they feel "Well at least my kids they know I know how to read." They're proud of themselves too because they went a step ahead. A lot of the students are already in an ESL class–students that started with us when they didn't know nothing at all. So they learned Spanish and now they're learning English. They're really improving themselves.

TABLE 6: Categories of Change Among Learners

In-Class Changes	Examples
Reading proficiency	
	quantity/length of text (letter identification, key words, sentences, paragraphs, stories, articles, books) diversification of genres (proverbs, LEA stories, news articles, brochures, student-written texts, etc.) conception of reading (focus on meaning rather decoding) ability to link texts to lives ability to respond to text
Writing proficiency	
	quantity of writing conception of writing (focus on meaning rather than form/accuracy) self-selection of topics process development (prewriting, drafting, revision) diversification of genres and purposes (journals, letters, proverbs, writing for publication)
ESL proficiency	
	grammatical development communicative fluency ability to discuss sensitive, loaded issues
Affective changes	
	self-confidence willingness to take risks and make mistakes classroom roles (contributions to class discussion, selection of topics, peer teaching, critique of lessons)
Metacognition	
	conceptions of literacy acquisition conceptions of teaching approach attitude toward dialogue/discussion
Use of L1 literacy as a learning tool	
	use of literacy as a memory aid use of L1 literacy for L2 acquisition use of grammatical/metalinguistic knowledge for L2 acquisition
Out-of-Class Changes	**Examples**
Functional uses of ESL or literacy	
	sorting mail, shopping, banking, telephone use, TV and radio, communication with neighbors, driver's tests, documents
Family relationships	
	independence self-respect and respect of children
Responsibilities at site	
	recruitment, peer tutoring, work on site publications fund-raising
Roles in community	
	responsibilities in community organizations participation in community events
Workplace uses of ESL	
	understanding directions communicating needs

What was the impact of the project on the sites?

Any evaluation of the effectiveness of this model must also consider its impact on the participating sites. The following section presents some of the ways that the sites were affected by the project.

number of classes and students served	The BCLTP and the CTAFL increased the number of classes provided and students served at each site in accordance with the number of Interns whose training was funded at the time. Because the BCLTP paid stipends to four Interns per site, its impact was significantly greater in this regard: during BCLTP, several new classes were added as well as weekly math literacy sessions, and, for a time, Drivers' Education classes at the HMSC. The JMCS had three new classes (taught by Interns) and the Harborside had two new classes; both of the native language literacy sites were able to offer two levels of literacy classes by the end of the project. A total of 200 students per year were enrolled in project classes during the BCLTP. As one of the Mentors said, *"The sites got a lot of mileage out of the project."* Of course, the increase in course offerings created a dilemma for the sites once BCLTP and CTAFL funding ran out, because they had no ongoing source of support for these classes.
formerly unserved students served	Second, the project enabled the sites to serve new populations of students. In the case of the JMCS, the BCLTP allowed the site to reconnect with the Brazilian community in the Allston-Brighton area during a time when two of the Interns were Brazilian. At the HMSC, students from the waiting list were able to enroll. In East Boston, a population of students who had never come to the Center because they felt unprepared for ESL now became part of the learner population.
L1 literacy components institutional-ized	Third, in the case of the HMSC and Harborside, the project was instrumental in achieving the sites' goals of institutionalizing native language literacy instruction. The Creole component at the HMSC, which had existed for several years, was expanded. At Harborside, the Spanish literacy component, although still small, became a site priority in subsequent funding requests.
community needs served	The project also enabled the sites to respond to community needs. For example, when a local hospital wanted to start a new ESL program for its staff, it hired Interns from the JMCS to staff this new program. An Intern was hired as community outreach worker and health educator by a local health center.

147

staff diversification

Further, the project supported the sites' goals of diversifying their staffs and developing community leadership. In a context where there was considerable local and state attention to multiculturalism and diversity, the project was one of the few concrete initiatives to make these goals a reality. At the HMSC, where several of the Interns had already been working, the project provided supplemental training; it allowed for continuation of training initiatives begun prior to the onset of the project. At the JMCS, several of the Interns who were former site students were subsequently hired by the site. Felipe, who was an Intern at the JMCS during the BCLTP, was hired as a Mentor at Harborside for the CTAFL project.

enhanced quality of instruction

The sites also identified the enhancement of the quality of instruction as a benefit of the project. According to Jean-Marc Jean-Baptiste, the Director of the HMSC, the emphasis on connecting students' reality to reading and writing meant that students became more involved in classes and made teaching more comfortable for both students and teachers. One indication of the impact of the quality of instruction was the fact that student retention was very high in many of the Interns' and Mentors' classes; at the JMCS, for example, Ana reported that retention in her class was 100% during the CTAFL; the HMSC reported a retention rate of 95%.

opportunities for collaboration

Another benefit for the sites was the opportunity it gave for collaboration and networking between agencies. This collaborative work took place on the instructional level, in terms of cross-fertilization between classes and teachers. Spanish-speaking ESL teachers depended on Haitian teachers for insights about their Haitian students. Teachers from one site adapted materials and activities from another for their students. Teachers referred students from one site to another at times. Collaboration also took place on an administrative level: the project provided an informal context for site coordinators to meet on a regular basis to share concerns and address program-based issues. The sites worked together to develop funding proposals and to develop strategies for promoting native language literacy instruction. Although the dynamics of collaboration were not always smooth, the Mentors mentioned the participatory way that the project itself was conducted as a factor in its impact. Ana, for example, said:

> *I also think that the way we did it, the participatory approach, I think it was good to go through that, having so many parties involved, really trying to be as participatory as you can be with so many people from so many different places and still coming out alive.*

I also think that the University played a very vital role... I think the trust the University gave the Centers was vital to the success of the project. I think by the Centers being able to have their own curriculum, to do the trainings the way they are used to doing it, by giving that kind of trust to the real people, the real work–I think [the University staff] showed that they believe in participation. At least for me that is one of the best things that can happen.

national attention for sites

Further, the project contributed to bringing national attention to the sites, which, in turn, was beneficial to them in seeking further funding to build capacity and expand services. Partly because of its work to develop Creole literacy instruction (which the BCLTP and the CTAFL helped to develop), the HMSC was featured in three federally funded studies. The BCLTP Spanish literacy Mentor at the Harborside was invited to participate in a national biliteracy roundtable forum in Washington, DC, and in a Spanish literacy working group in New York City.

the downside

Perhaps inevitably, the collaboration was not all smooth sailing. Because of the recurring issues of time and funding limitations, there was ongoing pressure about how to continue the positive initiatives that had been nurtured by the project. The fact that Interns were not included in the CTAFL budget meant that each site had to develop its own proposals and strategies to fund them. Both project staff and site Education Coordinators spent enormous amounts of time trying to figure out strategies for the continuation of funding. Although there was generally a positive sense about the collaboration among participants, some site personnel had differences of opinion regarding the process of documentation and the history of the project. At times, the prospect of termination of funding led to tensions between the sites, between Mentors and Interns, or between staff and students. At one point, several students dropped out of the Spanish literacy classes because of uncertainty about whether Intern funding would continue (however, others then organized their own fund-raising committee to address the problem). As Ana said, *"In spite of how helpful the project could have been, the shortness of the CTAFL and the lack of secure funding worked against it."*

Chapter Six: So What?

The work reported on in this Guidebook confirms and extends the findings of other practitioners and researchers indicating that a "from the community to the community" model is a powerful and promising approach to adult literacy education for immigrants and refugees in the United States. This chapter summarizes what we learned in implementing the model as well as the issues we struggled with in the process. For each key aspect of the model, we will discuss our findings, related dilemmas and challenges, and recommendations.

Regarding community literacy instructors...

One of the most promising findings in our project was the effectiveness of community-based literacy teachers, both for L1 and for ESL instruction. They represent a powerful untapped resource for serving the large numbers of immigrants and refugees in need of adult literacy and ESL services. Our project suggests that opening the professional ranks to include community instructors may significantly increase both the quantity and quality of available services. In addition, such a model has enormous benefits both for those being trained as instructors and for the field of adult literacy as a whole.

findings

> *It is very important that we speak the learners' language and we have suffered all the problems they have, because in a way, they can come to us and tell us their problems and we will understand because we have passed by them. We have suffered them.*
>
> Felipe Vaquerano, Intern (HMSC), Mentor (HCC)

•*Community teachers are particularly effective because of their life experiences and cultural resources:* We found that community-based instructors (both Mentors and Interns) were particularly suited to identifying issues, building trust, and linking literacy with community issues. In addition, they were role models for learners. As one Mentor said, *"People look at me and say, 'Well if he did this, why can't I do it?'"* Our project confirmed research findings indicating that shared background knowledge with learners, as well as the ability to create an atmosphere of trust, are key qualifications of adult educators.

•*Training community-based Interns is a cost-effective way to address increasing demands on the adult education system:* The apprenticeship model in which a Mentor trains several Interns can greatly increase the number of students receiving services without a proportionate increase in cost. As one of the Mentors said, her impact is multiplied by five during the term of the project. In the last year of the BCLTP, 200 students were served who would not otherwise have received services; 100 students who would not have received services participated in CTAFL classes.

> *Students have a fear right now. They keep asking, "Are we going to another class? I don't want to go to another class. I want to be with you next cycle." I tell them they have to experience another teacher and learn how someone else speaks English.... Everyone is recommending to their friends that I am a good teacher. I feel good about it.*
>
> Estela Matute, Intern (JMCS)

• *Teachers from the communities of the learners are effective not only for L1 literacy instruction, but for ESL instruction as well:* Over and over, ESL students commented on how much they learned in the classes of Interns. Although it is often assumed that ESL teachers should be native speakers of English, our experience indicates that the non-native teachers can be effective teachers in both transitional ESL classes (where they share the learners' L1) and in mixed ESL classes (where participants come from a variety of language backgrounds). Limitations related to the instructors' non-native English were more than compensated for by strengths: their commonalities of experience with learners promoted empathy and trust, as well as enhancing the relevance of curriculum content.

> *I see this project as a way of opening doors. I wanted to go to college but I couldn't [for financial reasons]. I didn't want to work in a factory forever. Without the project, I would still be working in a factory. The project got me where I am now.*
>
> Felipe Vaquerano, Intern (JMCS), Mentor (HCC)

• *The project provided access to professional and educational development for people from immigrant and refugee communities:* By recruiting adult education students, community activists, and undergraduates as literacy Interns, the project enabled participants to embark on a professional path that would not otherwise have been open to them. It was the first opportunity for many to move out of unskilled manual jobs into teaching or community service: an ESL student who was working in a plastics factory became an Intern and went on to become a Mentor and a Special Education teaching assistant; another former ESL student who worked as a housecleaner when she started as an Intern went on to become a community health educator; other Interns were hired as social service workers, day care workers, and, in several cases, ESL or native language literacy teachers; one Intern set up an ESL program at his church. In addition, the project prompted many to further their own education: an Intern who was getting his GED when he started the project went on to enroll in the University; two Mentors reentered the University to complete their undergraduate educations. Several Interns decided to major in education and/or changed career goals toward teaching. Thus, this model offers the opportunity for people with otherwise underutilized skills to become resources for community development, as well as giving them a way out of the unskilled jobs to which immigrants and refugees are often relegated.

• *Community teachers contribute to the development of the field of adult literacy:* Because of the background and experiences they share with adult learners, community teachers can provide insights into the concerns, needs, and learning processes of learners, adding to the knowledge base of the field. Not only can the field learn from their perspective, but they can contribute to the much needed cultural diversification of the field. Interns and Mentors made numerous conference presentations about their work; frequently, they were the only language minority representatives at conferences they attended. This model provides a clear structure for the development of people with the potential to enrich and diversify the field of adult literacy.

dilemmas and challenges

• *Increasing responsibilities without increasing stipends:* As Interns progressed, their skills and responsibilities increased up to the point when they began to teach independently. They then had all the responsibilities of regular teachers (planning, materials development, teaching) in addition to training meetings, workshops, conference presentations, and, in some cases, additional site tasks (assisting with recruitment, work on the site magazine, etc.). Yet, they continued to receive stipends for a fixed number of hours per week at a rate of pay lower than that of teachers. Thus, the fact that the model is cost-effective (because it extends the number of students served through the use of Interns) has the potential to result in an exploitative situation for Interns.

• *Shortage of jobs and funding for trained teachers:* Interns sometimes had difficulty finding jobs for which they had been trained. The insecurity of funding for project classes after the end of the grant period meant that Interns who were eager to teach sometimes left for other jobs. Both Interns and Mentors felt conflicted: on the one hand, they loved their work; on the other, they were discouraged about future possibilities in adult education. There was no system to place them once they had been trained or to follow up on them beyond the end of the project.

recommen-
dations

• *Training opportunities for people from the communities of adult learners should be expanded:* Community teachers are an untapped resource with significant potential to address the growing need for ESL/literacy services. Resources should be made available to replicate the model so that communities and Interns can benefit.

• *The ranks of the ESL profession should be opened to include more people from the communities of the learners:* Whether or not community teachers share the first language of learners, their common experiences are a significant resource which can more than compensate for non-native speaker status (given a certain threshold of ESL competence). The myth that native-speakers of English are the best ESL teachers must be reexamined.

• *Teacher-learners should receive adequate compensation for the services they render:* The pay structure for Interns should reflect actual responsibilities and take into account variability as Interns increase their workload. As Interns become more experienced, their pay should be on a par with teachers who do similar work.

• *New job categories should be created and job qualifications revised to ensure that the resources of community people can be utilized in adult education:* The traditional notion of hiring only teachers with college degrees and/or certification must be reexamined because it excludes people who have much to contribute to the field. Qualifications such as familiarity with learners' cultural and linguistic backgrounds, life experiences, and community issues should be given consideration in hiring adult ESL/literacy teachers.

• *Resources should be earmarked for the hiring of trained community instructors:* Job categories for community instructors should be created so that people who have received literacy training like that provided in the project will have a career path open to them upon completion of training. Adequate funding should be allocated so that Interns will have job opportunities once they have received training.

153

Regarding training...

Our project indicated that, given adequate training time, a participatory, inquiry-based model for training literacy instructors can be highly effective and empowering for participants. Combining observation, mentoring, workshops, and teacher-sharing meetings allows a range of contexts for developing teaching proficiency and for addressing teaching issues.

findings

• *Observation, mentoring, training workshops, and teacher-sharing meetings complement each other in supporting the development of teacher-learners:* The effectiveness of the training derived in large part from the combination of site-based training guided by Mentors and university-based workshops in which participants from various sites shared experiences. Providing a range of training contexts allowed Interns to see, participate in, and discuss teaching. They could move back and forth between theory and practice, participation, and reflection. Mentors can both serve as models and offer feedback to Interns about their own teaching; workshops can present and model approaches, as well as providing a context for exchanging ideas; teacher-sharing can promote a problem-posing stance toward practice and allow for peer exchanges. None of these in themselves would have been as effective as the combination proved to be.

I realize now the best thing in the teaching process is to observe the students, to find the thing you need to know to help them.

Ernst Germain, Intern (HMSC)

• *The participatory training model encouraged teacher-learners to become problem posers and researchers of their own classrooms:* Because the workshops modeled a participatory process, rather than transmitting skills or techniques, Interns learned to investigate the issues and dynamics of their own teaching contexts and develop context-specific instructional strategies. They moved toward valuing active learning for themselves as well as their students. Interns learned to be creative in responding to student needs and generating lessons/materials; they developed a stance of critical inquiry in addressing classroom problems.

> *We learned more useful things, things that are really going to help us teach [in the later workshops]. I don't know if the same things were in the others [earlier ones] and I just wasn't aware of them. I really wasn't ready or I didn't recognize those things because of my lack of confidence. Now I am more open to everything in the workshops because I have more experience. Now I know what to ask.*
>
> Estela Matute, Intern (JMCS)

• *Learning to become a teacher takes time:* One of the most significant differences between the BCLTP and CTAFL concerned training time. The length of the training cycle (number of months of training) is critical in determining the extent to which Interns become independent, reflective, and responsive teachers. Because it takes time to unlearn much of what they have internalized through their own education, and become socialized into a new way of thinking about teaching, we found that at least a year is necessary for this process. Not until Interns have participated for several months are they really open to the approach of the workshops.

• *Logistical factors relating to workshop timing are critical to their effectiveness:* Again, based on our experience with the two projects, we found the energy level, sense of community, and participation in workshops varied according to factors such as time of day, day of the week, and number of workshops per month. During the BCLTP, workshops were held once a month on Saturday mornings for 3 hours, whereas, during the CTAFL, they were held twice a month on Friday afternoons at 3:00 for 2 hours. The fact that they were late in the day on Fridays meant that people were rushing from other jobs, often tired and preoccupied about getting home to family responsibilities. The fact that workshops were only 2 hours long meant that there was less time to get into topics in depth, and often the sharing between participants was curtailed so the sessions seemed less participatory. The fact that the workshops were held twice a month meant that there was less planning time for project staff between sessions (resulting in less participatory planning), and that participants had less time between workshops to try out and gain experience with ideas or activities presented in the sessions.

dilemmas and challenges

There were both substantive and logistical challenges in implementing the training model. The former stemmed from Interns' expectations and internalized notions of education. The latter revolved around variability in individual and site-based backgrounds and needs, as well as factors relating to timing.

•*Uneven responses to a participatory, learner-centered approach:* In some cases, Interns' prior educational experiences caused them to be uncomfortable with a participatory approach—they expected to teach and be taught in the ways they themselves had learned, which may have been quite traditional. Thus, some wanted the training to provide them with techniques and tended to rely on mechanical approaches in their own teaching. The rate and extent of change from a teacher- to a learner-centered approach was uneven. In addition, even when participants seemed very engaged in workshop activities, the extent to which they transferred workshop ideas to their own teaching contexts was variable.

•*Impracticality of fixed observation, co-teaching and independent teaching cycles:* Although the original proposal stipulated 3 month segments of observing, co-teaching, and teaching independently, this sequence did not correspond to the realities of participants' needs and backgrounds. They started with various degrees and kinds of experiences (some having already taught for many years or volunteered in Mentors' classes) and were ready to teach at different points (some needing minimal observation time and others being reluctant to teach independently even after 6 months in a Mentor's class).

•*The multifaceted demands of becoming a teacher:* The transition to teaching involves changes on many fronts for Interns: becoming comfortable with the role of teacher, revising their own notions of education, learning to implement teaching processes, becoming familiar with resources, generating materials and lesson-plans, and so on. The rate at which Interns are ready to take on new responsibilities is variable and uneven, which may cause logistical problems or tensions between Interns.

•*Coordinating conflicting scheduling demands of participants and addressing training needs:* It was difficult to balance participants' needs with training needs (scheduling adequate time for workshops and coordinating their various schedules in terms of day of the week and time of workshops). Likewise, scheduling was a recurring problem for site meetings because of Interns' limited hours and full time jobs.

> *Sometimes I felt like people... didn't have a chance to explain their opinion, to talk about what they would like to discuss. Sometimes we spent too much time on the agenda. Yes, we always tried our best to fit their demands into the agenda..but we didn't solve this problem. If the workshop is 2 hours, we should give 1 hour for them to talk....I think, if we had a chance to do it again, we should allocate more time to the Interns than to the agenda.*
>
> Julio Midy, Mentor (HMSC)

**recommen-
dations**

•*Balancing covering the training agenda with allowing for spontaneous sharing:* At times, due to time pressure, we tried to pack too much into workshops, resulting in inadequate time for unanticipated dialogue and sharing among Interns.

•*Training and practice should include specific exploration of mechanical approaches to literacy as a basis for comparison with participatory approaches:* One way to address discomfort with participatory models is to invite Interns to try teaching both ways and to compare results. Promoting only one approach without evaluating the other may not demonstrate their differences.

•*Training should include explicit strategies to support the transition from workshops to classroom practice:* Workshops themselves should incorporate planning time so that participants can explore how they may want to apply what they have learned. Site-based follow-up should include structured discussions of workshops at site meetings, site-based sessions dealing with site-specific issues, and multiple opportunities for peer observation.

•*The transition from training to teaching should to be flexible and context specific:* Because Interns come with different backgrounds and develop at various rates, their responsibilities should be increased as each is ready for them, rather than according to a pre-determined timeline. In place of a uniform 10-month cycle divided into three segments of observation, supervised co-teaching, and independent teaching, Interns should assume greater responsibilities as they are ready and comfortable with them (and in accordance with site needs).

• *Adequate time should be allowed for training:* At least a year (and preferably more) should be allowed for training; each session should be long enough to allow for dialogue and sharing.

Regarding participatory literacy instruction...

Participatory literacy instruction and curriculum development is a particularly powerful model for newly literate adults because it connects their life concerns with literacy acquisition. It allows learners to move relatively quickly toward using and producing texts for their own purposes; as they use literacy to address their concerns, literacy becomes socially significant in family and community life.

findings

•*Participatory curriculum development is a powerful model for adult learners:* Work in our project suggests that a participatory approach is appropriate for adult literacy and ESL students: very often, they are immersed in the struggles of adjusting to a new culture, separation from families, preoccupation with the political situation in the home countries, trying to find work, and so on. Rather than seeing these preoccupations as obstacles to learning, the participatory approach allows learners to focus on them as part of learning. Because the acquisition of skills is contextualized, they may be less frustrated with limitations of memory, and more engaged with content. The participatory approach allows them to draw on their own experiences, contribute to their own learning, use literacy to accomplish their own purposes, and explore issues of importance to them.

> *The students were evaluating the class last night and comparing places they had studied in the past. They were talking about particular textbooks that they had used; at one point, they said, "The nice thing about this program is that people are more important than books are." The curriculum has taken that power of making the person really important, as opposed to just the written word.*
>
> Ana Zambrano, Mentor (JMCS)

•*Meaning-based instruction facilitates literacy acquisition:* Work with our classes confirms studies which find that when the emphasis on learning focuses on meaning rather than form, learning is facilitated. Most beginning students in our classes who knew only a few letters of the alphabet when they enrolled were able to read authentic texts and to write sentences about pictures, journal entries, language experience stories, and letters to relatives after relatively short periods of time.

dilemmas and challenges	*A participatory approach is time-consuming and requires skill to implement. In addition, the lack of readily available materials to use as resources intensifies the challenge. These challenges demand substantial preparation time and support.*

•*The time-consuming nature of participatory curriculum development:* The strengths of a participatory approach are also what make it particularly challenging; precisely because the curriculum is tailored to each group, and emerges from a particular context, its implementation demands a great deal of time and skill. For people who are just learning to teach, this can be especially challenging.

•*The lack of resources and materials:* Because participatory curriculum development and a socially oriented approach to adult literacy instruction is relatively new, there are few available support materials, particularly for native language literacy instruction. In addition to not being text-driven, this approach is labor-intensive in terms of finding or creating materials. Materials that are appropriate in terms of both linguistic accessibility and engaging content are few and far between.

•*The inadequacy of preparation time and support:* As Interns took on increasingly greater teaching responsibilities, they had less meeting time (because their paid time was fixed). They needed additional time, not only to prepare classes, but to discuss how to implement a participatory approach and to develop materials.

recommendations

•*Training opportunities for participatory curriculum development need to be expanded to become more widely implemented in adult education programs.* While participatory curriculum development is a powerful approach to teaching adult literacy, there is relatively little ongoing teacher preparation available for it. TESOL programs should institutionalize course offerings for prospective teachers to prepare them for the influx of adult learners with little prior educational background.

•*Teachers should be provided support and paid time for participatory curriculum development.* Teacher-sharing meetings should become institutionalized as a regular part of job descriptions. In addition, teachers should be adequately paid for planning and materials preparation time. Further recommendations regarding materials development and curriculum support are elaborated in the following section on L1 literacy.

Regarding first language literacy...

Our project indicated that provision of L1 literacy services addresses the needs of previously unserved populations, is effective in developing the basis for ESL acquisition for adults who are minimally literate in their L1, and contributes to community development.

findings

•*L1 literacy provision addresses the needs of previously underserved or unserved learners:* Sites in our project found that offering native language literacy instruction allowed the sites to serve students that they had not been able to serve before. Learners had often quit other programs because their needs were not met or had never attended adult education classes before because they were intimidated by their own lack of prior schooling/literacy.

•*L1 instruction is critical for the transition to ESL:* The project demonstrated that students with minimal L1 literacy can, after 6 months to a year of L1 literacy instruction, successfully make the transition to beginning ESL. We found that a bilingual ESL class can be a significant support for this transition. It is critical to stress, however, that there may be a great deal of individual variation in the actual amount of time needed in L1 literacy classes; the rate of literacy acquisition and readiness for ESL depends on a range of background factors including the learner's prior educational experience, age, exposure to non-L1 communities, and so on.

•*L1 literacy can contribute to individual and community development:* L1 literacy acquisition allowed learners to meet many personal goals (ability to write letters to family members, use literacy at work, participate in community organizations, etc.), as well as gain an increased sense of self-confidence and independence. At the same time, it enhanced the sense of community cultural pride and enabled learners to become more active in addressing community issues. Through the context of L1 literacy classes, participants were able to engage in dialogue about socially significant issues in their own lives (e.g., political developments in Haiti, workplace rights, AIDS), which they would not have been able to address in ESL classes (due to language limitations). Through this meaningful contextualization of literacy acquisition, they were able to become active participants in dialogue, develop critical thinking skills, and link their classwork to issues outside the classroom.

dilemmas and challenges

Precisely because the L1 literacy classes were so successful, new challenges emerged: As beginning students progressed, there were demands for additional courses and spaces in existing courses; in addition, expanded resources to support the proliferation of courses and increased numbers of students were required; further the project entailed additional administrative responsibilities for the sites, which were not adequately supported by the project itself.

•*The need for additional course offerings:* As students came closer to being ready for ESL, transitional bilingual ESL classes became necessary to bridge their L1 and L2 learning experiences. Thus, the project engendered the proliferation of classes (beginning and advanced L1 literacy, transitional bilingual ESL). Once L1 literacy students were ready for beginning ESL classes, existing classes had to accommodate them in addition to the students already on waiting lists. The result, in many cases, was a logjam or bottleneck. In addition, rather than reducing the waiting lists, the program was so successful that the waiting list actually increased as more and more students realized that their educational needs could now be met.

•*The lack of ongoing support for L1 literacy and its spin-offs:* Although the sites were able to initiate a number of new classes during the project, finding support for this proliferation of classes once it ended was a challenge. In addition, there were not enough spaces for literacy students once they became ready for beginning ESL classes. Thus a whole new set of demands for the site was triggered by the project which the project itself did not address. The political climate is such that funding for L1 literacy classes is an uphill battle: the priority placed on quick job placements means that it can be difficult to find support for the lowest level students (who take longest to be employable).

•*The increased administrative burden for the sites:* Institutionalizing the L1 literacy components at the sites entailed additional administrative responsibilities; however, because the project was primarily a training project (rather than a service delivery project), it was not always clear into whose domain these responsibilities fell. Although there were substantial administrative tasks accompanying the additional services, there was no provision for funding this administration of services in the grant.

•*Lack of materials and support for L1 literacy curriculum development:* Where ESL teachers may be able to draw on existing materials, integrating them into a participatory process, L1 teachers often have few resources to guide them. Existing materials are few and far between, and are often not geared to a U.S. context.

•*L1 literacy instruction should become a regular, institutionalized option in adult education settings:* The work of our project suggests that it is critical to ensure the provision of L1 literacy services for adult immigrants and refugees with limited prior educational experience. Without it, these adults will have little chance of accessing ESL services and the accompanying benefits in terms of employment, community, and family participation. At the same time, however, service delivery models need to be flexible and tailored to the changing needs of sites: this means that there may be different course offerings and schedules at each site, depending on circumstances, and that the offerings may change over time within a site as student and community needs change, the number of students ready for ESL increases, and so on.

•*Funding for L1 literacy should be increased and institutionalized:* Pilot or demonstration programs can only be as successful as their follow-up. Policymakers must be committed not only to supporting innovative pilot projects, but to supporting their continuation. The stability of programming is necessary not only from an institutional perspective, but also for the sake of students: unless there is continuity of service provision, the gains that they make in literacy classes will be lost. In addition, stability and continuity of programming is necessary for research purposes: without long-term services, it will be impossible to seriously evaluate the impact of various instructional options.

•*Site-based curriculum specialists should be hired for L1 literacy programs:* Whereas all sites would benefit greatly from having site-based curriculum specialists who could assist in materials collection and development, they are particularly important in L1 literacy programs where few existing materials and resources are available. One of the responsibilities of curriculum specialists should be to develop curriculum tool kits that include teacher- and learner-generated materials as well as authentic materials on a variety of topics; these tool kits can then become resources from which new (and experienced) teachers can draw. Once a greater body of knowledge/materials is available, the role of curriculum specialist may become less necessary.

•*Funding should be allocated for native language curriculum development:* Projects to develop curricula and materials for key languages with large nonliterate adult populations in the U.S. (e.g., Haitian Creole, Spanish, Vietnamese, Hmong, etc.) are necessary to provide teachers with resources. Each teacher cannot be expected to generate his or her materials from scratch for L1 literacy programs.

Regarding family literacy...

Our project indicated that an approach to adult literacy instruction in which learners' needs and concerns guide curriculum development can result in an enhanced role for literacy in family life. A broad approach that defines family literacy as using literacy to address family concerns and strengthen adults' ability to care for their families is more effective than a narrow, prescriptive approach that focuses on parent–child interactions around literacy.

findings

> *Family literacy is teaching parents to fill out money orders, not just read to their kids.*
>
> Felipe Vaquerano, Intern (HMSC), Mentor (HCC)

•*By focusing on their own literacy and ESL acquisition, adults are enhancing the role of literacy in family life:* As adults develop their own capacity to use literacy and English, they are increasingly able to address family needs and strengthen family ties. Frequently, their goal was to become increasingly independent of their children and able to manage without them (rather than to read to children or help them with homework). In our project, participants used literacy and English to communicate with family members outside the U.S., to find jobs, to secure services for their children, to become more active in their communities, and to discuss difficult topics with their children (e.g., sexuality). Thus, literacy became socially significant in family and community life, embodying the concept of family literacy in its truest sense.

> *At least my kids know that I know how to read now.*
>
> adult learner, HCC Spanish literacy class

•*The development of parents' literacy and ESL has important consequences for family dynamics and parental confidence:* As participants in our project became increasingly proficient in ESL or literacy, they relied less on their children, freeing the children to pursue their own development, as well as enhancing the parents' role within the family. By becoming less dependent on children, parents strengthened family ties and gained self respect.

163

•*Exploring family literacy issues as curriculum content is more effective if it comes from the participants rather than being imposed by teachers/trainers:* Students may resist teacher-initiated lessons focusing on family literacy practices, while they respond positively if similar topics emerge through dialogue. Likewise, if trainers impose family literacy as their own agenda, they may be met with resistance or disinterest, whereas the topic may be compelling for Interns if it they bring it up themselves.

> **Family literacy is not a week, a label, a lesson; it's a concept that's part of everything we do.**
>
> Ana Zambrano, Mentor (JMCS)

dilemmas and challenges

•*Tensions between grant and participant priorities:* Because the grant included family literacy training as one of its goals, staff felt at times that we were not focused enough on family literacy content. At the same time, our adherence to participatory principles meant that we did not want to impose the topic if it was not a priority for Interns. Through discussion of the real meaning of family literacy we came to see that this was a false contradiction: in fact, as Interns were promoting learners' ability to use literacy to address their own and their families' needs, they were promoting family literacy. W e didn't have to have a session labeled "family literacy" to be doing family literacy training. We were doing it on an ongoing basis.

recommen- dations

•*Family literacy must be defined broadly to include all the ways that literacy is used to address family concerns and strengthen family life:* Programs that focus narrowly on parents reading to children or helping them with homework miss the essence of family literacy –the ability to use literacy to take care of one's family. Rather than defining it as a particular set of behaviors, activities, or family interactions, family literacy should encompass any literacy practices that enable adults to take on the struggles of everyday living.

•*Training in family literacy must include a focus on participatory curriculum development so that adults' own concerns can drive instruction.* Basing training on the above definition of family literacy entails focusing on eliciting participants' concerns and finding out what they need literacy for in their own lives. Thus, family literacy training should be integrated rather than limited only to particular sessions.

164

Regarding collaboration and dissemination...

One of the positive and unexpected outcomes of the project was the cross-fertilization that occurred as a result of collaboration between sites. This was a benefit for participating teachers, administrators, and for the sites themselves. Further, dissemination tasks enhanced participants' skills and confidence, as they documented and presented their findings to colleagues.

findings

•*Collaboration gave participants the chance to work with colleagues from other programs on substantive (not just bureaucratic) issues:* Whereas site representatives usually only have the chance to meet with each other to discuss administrative issues (e.g., to hear about guidelines for proposals), this collaboration provided an ongoing context for dialogue about programming, curriculum development, long-term planning, and policy priorities. Mentors and Interns particularly benefitted from hearing about issues that other sites were addressing, learning about other cultures, and utilizing each other as resources for their own teaching. ESL teachers from Latin America, for example, drew on their Haitian colleagues' knowledge to better understand their Haitian students.

•*The participatory nature of project administration enhanced the collaboration:* Internally, in terms of staff decision making and project administration, the fact that university and site personnel worked together in a participatory way supported the development of project staff. The guiding principle for project functioning, collaboration without control, promoted the sites' sense of ownership and control in most cases.

•*Mentor and Intern participation in dissemination of information about the project enhanced their skills and contributed to the diversification of the field:* Our goal in dissemination was that the process itself would contribute to participants' sense of ownership of the their own work, as well as their increasing skills and confidence. Thus, most dissemination was participatory, with Intern and Mentor involvement in documenting and presenting our work. Further, their participation at professional conferences promoted diversity within the profession; their insights and perspectives made important contributions to the knowledge base of the field.

165

dilemmas and challenges	*The dual administrative structure of the project yielded tensions at certain times. In some cases, the needs of the sites came into conflict with the aims of the project, and the Mentors were caught between these conflicting demands. In addition, service needs and dissemination sometimes conflicted with each other because of limited time and resources.*

•*Lack of clarity regarding responsibility for added administrative requirements of new components:*   In sites where the project funded a new component, there was some uncertainty over who was responsible for administrative tasks associated with it. Mentors faced various challenges because of the duality of their roles as both project and site staff.

•*Conflict between service and documentation/dissemination demands:*   Although, on the one hand, we wanted everyone to participate in dissemination (especially in writing about their own work for this report), the reality was that Mentors' time was limited; they felt that limited resources should be directed toward providing services for students.

recommen- dations

•*Opportunities for networking between sites should be enhanced:* Collaboration and networking are powerful ways to address shared concerns and push forward the knowledge base of the field. They can help to overcome the "reinventing the wheel" syndrome and allow for the pooling of resources and experiences. In the case of pioneering work (such as native language literacy), the need for a forum for dialogue is all the greater; funding must be allocated not only to support local collaborations, but to support national conferences where native language adult literacy practitioners can meet to discuss their work. This sharing of ideas can go a long way toward building the knowledge base in adult ESL and L1 literacy.

•*Administration of site-based project responsibilities should be clearly delineated:* Job descriptions of site-based Mentors should include participation in site meetings to ensure adequate communication between the project and the site. Paid time to administer services funded by the project should be included in the job description of a site staff member.

What's next?

> *This project is like a flower.*
> *We have planted the seed,*
> *the flower is starting to grow,*
> *and now we are cutting it.*
>
> Roberto Flores, Intern (HCC)

As we confront dramatic changes in the demographics for the 21st century, we need to find equally dramatic new ways to address the increased demands for adult literacy and ESL provision. Hopefully, this report has shown that the "from the community to the community" model has the potential to be one such approach. It is a model that promotes leadership from within language minority communities, provides effective services for underserved populations, and opens   career opportunities for immigrants and refugees.

Yet, as Ana said, *"This model has the potential to be a powerful model, but it can only work if it is adequately supported."* Unfortunately, our experience has not been entirely positive as we have attempted to continue the work of the project beyond the grant period. The good news is that many of those who were trained by the project are now teaching ESL or literacy, or have other community service jobs. Both of the L1 literacy components are continuing (although at reduced levels). The bad news is that finding funding for this work is an ongoing struggle demanding enormous expenditures of time and energy on the part of the CBO's, and the returns are decreasing. The training and collaboration aspects of our project are also no longer in place. Although there are other local and state training opportunities, none focus on training community people to teach in their own communities.

The single biggest obstacle, not only to our efforts but in literacy provision for adult immigrants and refugees across the country, is inadequate and unstable funding. Although federal agencies encourage providers to seek state funding, the states are limited by budget cutbacks. At the same time that national support for an English Only political agenda seems to be increasing , there is decreasing support for services which would enable people to learn English. Competition for scarce resources pits agencies against each other, undermining collaboration between organizations that should be working toward similar goals.

In a political climate where a great deal of lip service is paid to cultural diversity and to "breaking the cycle of illiteracy," obstacles to institutionalizing services for immigrants and refugees continue to be enormous; efforts to secure funding are so demanding that they take away from the actual delivery of services. There is constant pressure to develop innovative projects but these projects last for a few years, only to be replaced by new ones that suffer the same fate. It is clearly important to promote innovation, but it is equally important to support its institutionalization. We hope that this book will contribute to securing stable, ongoing support for training and hiring community literacy teachers, as well as for native language literacy and participatory curriculum development projects.

It seems appropriate that the last words of this Guidebook should come from the Interns. This poem, written by several Interns from the JMCS is a reminder of the power of a learning that comes from the community and goes back to the community.

```
               "THANK YOU"

   As time passes by and life goes on,
   As long as we are alive,
   As long as our goals seem to be hidden,
   As long as our hopes are not finished,
   We can struggle to survive.

   As long as we stay awake
   To see Today's sunset and Tomorrow's
                          sunrise,
   As long as we remember what we've done
   And what we want to do,
   We can struggle to survive.

   As long as there is someone to hold on,
   As long as we can get up from a failure,
   As long as somebody believes in us,
   As long as we can show who we are,
   We can struggle to survive.

   As long as people like you exist
   It is going to be difficult to fall;
   Because you're the person we can count on
   To encourage us to struggle to survive.

   Thank you for supporting us,
   In our long-long walk,
   For sharing your knowledge with us
   For being who you are.

   Thank you again and good luck!

        Ediane,Estela,(Felipe),Laudize
```

Poem written by Interns at the Jackson-Mann Community School

Appendices

Julio and Marilyn St. Hilaire (Intern from the HMSC) with Paulo Freire in New York

Appendix A: The Spanish Literacy Component

by Byron Barahona, Master Teacher
Harborside Community Center

The need

The Spanish Literacy project at Harborside Community Center knew its early development in the fall of 1990 as a result of being part of a Title VII-funded collaboration with UMass and two other adult education agencies. Prior to this funding there had been some native language instruction. However, it was extremely limited because students who needed this type of instruction were part of the amnesty program whose main purpose was to teach ESL/civics. Students came in order to fulfill a requirement to become permanent residents of the U.S. Classes were functioning to their fullest capacity, 25 to 30 students per class. In the beginning, students came to this program for only 3 months and then later for only 7 weeks. Thus, in addition to not being adequately served, students who had limited literacy skills could only stay for a short period of time in that program.

Moreover, classes were multilevel and multilingual, though the majority of students were Spanish and Portuguese speaking. It was difficult to give proper instruction to those students (mostly Spanish speaking) who had limited literacy skills in their native language. The situation was remedied by giving them some Spanish literacy tutoring before or during class time.

The necessity for native language literacy instruction resulted from the fact that the ESL/civics students were not the only ones who could benefit from more native language literacy instruction. Regular ESL classes also experienced retention problems due to students having low or limited literacy skills in their mother tongue. All this is to say that Harborside had many reasons for seeking funding to establish native language literacy instruction for underserved Spanish speaking students.

Justification of the praxis

The goal of this project was to provide appropriate instruction to those who had been, in one form or another, denied access to what many consider an entitlement: education. It must also be noted that the instructional approach for reaching this goal had already been determined by the time Harborside decided to participate in the project. The approach would be a Freirean or a participatory approach. Even though this instructional approach was already articulated by the project, it coincided with the Center's and my own pedagogical orientation to teaching and learning. The following are some of the ideas that I found informative and illuminating in order to implement the Freirean approach.

First, Paulo Freire articulates an educational theory which is concerned with liberating individuals from forces that deny their humanity. However, in this particular process, what I found innovative is the fact that it is not about some individuals liberating others. For Freire, the crucial step is for the oppressed to become aware of his or her dehumanized state of being. For, in order to change an oppressive reality, one must be aware of it to later attempt to transform it. Further, another influential idea is Freire's view of dialogue in education. For Freire, dialogue is at the core of any real and true transformation of any educational program that attempts to "educate" the oppressed. It is through dialogue, as described later, that teachers discover students' concerns and issues.

Moreover, in *Pedagogy of the Oppressed* (1970), Freire proposes a model of education called problem posing. This model aims at guiding individuals toward thinking critically about their own reality and reflecting upon it. Therefore, he proposes a total questioning of the existing educational structure. In his view, current educational systems usually manifest only the views and prejudices of the oppressors, whose purpose is to domesticate individuals by training them to perform and perpetuate an oppressive system. In problem posing education, social and educational change are essential for any type of transformation. The latter was particularly influential, for it could be applied to the reality of marginalized immigrants in this country. The way these ideas were applied to our particular context will be explained in more detail in the following sections.

The project: Implementation of Freirean approach

One of the ideas that Freire strongly articulates in *Pedagogy of the Oppressed* is the necessity of investigating the area where teachers or coordinators are going to work. However, this notion mainly addresses massive literacy campaigns as they take place in Latin America or in other parts of the world. In our particular context, because classes met at a school located in the area where the students or learners live, teachers did not have to come to investigate the area. It was assumed that we were already familiar with the issues relevant to the people that we would teach and learn from.

This assumption was based on key information about the students, teachers, and interns who participated in this project (namely, the fact that teachers, interns and students come from similar cultural backgrounds). Moreover, the situation in which I and other teachers have been immersed is very different from the one Freire describes. While in Brazil, the dominant social group and the marginalized literacy learners come mainly from a homogeneous linguistic and cultural background, the community of people we worked with is located within a linguistically and culturally diverse society. This fact raises new difficulties. Because the students in this project are not literate in their native language, linguistic barriers limit the possibilities for teachers speaking only English to be directly involved in the teaching-learning process. Hence, it was essential to find teachers or interns who had cultural and linguistic bonds with the students to be involved in the process. This matter reinforces the importance of including teachers from the community of the learners, for they may be in a better position to understand the learners' reality.

Indeed, given this cultural and linguistic commonality, one might infer that teachers understand the reality of the students. However, the danger with this assumption is that it may not always be true. Because most of the literacy students at Harborside come from rural areas in their countries, social class distinctions and rural or urban backgrounds play an important role. As a result, the process of selecting teachers becomes more complex, for there is a dual reality at work: the reality where the students come from and the reality in which they might be immersed in actuality.

In conclusion, teacher or interns cannot be assumed to understand the totality of the participants' reality, both in this country and their own. It is not sufficient to have teachers or interns involved in the process based solely on cultural and linguistic bonds; they must also be individuals who are willing to struggle with the learners along the process of learning, as well as to engage in co-investigation as part of the instructional process. For the danger, as Freire points out, is that coordinators may adopt a paternalistic attitude.

Once this problem has been tentatively addressed, and assuming that teachers or interns are conscious of the area in which the students live, then the process can get started. Freire proposes guidelines that could be utilized to investigate the conditions of the area where one is to work. For example: a) investigators should meet and discuss with the participants their objectives in the area; b) investigators should make clear that mutual understanding and trust is necessary; c) investigators should call for volunteers or assistants to gather a series of necessary data about the life of the area; d) investigators may not impose their own perceptions on the reality they are facing, much less to transform it; e) investigators should consider the area of study as a totality and then proceed to decode it in order to understand every component through observation and informal conversation with the inhabitants.

It is clear that our realities are very different, so the classroom has been the medium for investigating the issues listed above, for instance, the way people talk, lifestyle, their idiom (*expressions, vocabulary, syntax, the way they construct their thoughts*). Accordingly, the classroom becomes both the place for dialogue and the research area of all those aspects.

Teacher-student encounter

The first day of class, interns and I started with a small group of seven adult participants from El Salvador. We tried to get to know the participants by discussing the purpose of the project and making clear that *mutual understanding and trust was necessary*. Then, we asked them about their previous experience at school - if they had one - and only if they felt comfortable talking about it. At first, they seemed hesitant about saying anything, but once the first participant started, the rest followed. Through this conversation, we found out that some of them had not gone to school at all, others went to school 1 year when they were children, and others had had a recent experience which did not last very long.

Students talked about different reasons for not going to school, such as: "We were so poor that our parents needed us to work in the fields since we were children, so there was no time to go to school. When we could go to school we had to walk kilometers to get there and that made our going to school more difficult." The reasons they gave us were known to us in one way or another, so we were particularly intrigued about their most recent experience here in the Boston area and asked why it had ended so soon. This was their response: "We did not feel like we were learning anything. The instructor would show us pictures about the war in El Salvador for the most part. We left El Salvador because of the horrors of the war or because of economic hardship." One student said, "If I wanted to know more about the guerilla, I would have stayed in El Salvador and become one, it was so easy to do it." They proceeded, "We are here and don't want to know much about it. We went to that school because we wanted to learn to read and write in Spanish, but instead of doing that we felt that the teacher only wanted to discuss the war between the government and the guerilla and the reasons the guerilla had to fight the military forces. We thought we were wasting our time." This was an indication that something was wrong, so we tried to establish as much dialogical interaction as possible in order not to disappoint them while we proceeded to implement our ideas.

In relation to the experience they described, my immediate impression was that perhaps the former instructor had tried to use some of Freire's ideas but was not taking students' input into account while using them. It is true that Freire suggests using codifications in the classroom, but when they are not connected to the students' life and what they wanted

172

to learn, they become what Freire calls "*brain-washing propaganda*" regardless of whatever good intentions the teacher may have. The pictures the former instructor used might have been overly explicit or might not have offered possibilities for interpretation. Furthermore, they might have not been connected to learning how to read and write. However, because I did not witness the classroom situation the students were describing, I can only infer what might have happened, with the danger of not doing justice to the former instructor.

Initial generative words

After this discussion, we also talked about the types of work students do now and what they used to do in their country. A lot of data was collected from these conversations. The men had been, for the most part, fishermen and others, including women, had worked in the fields growing different vegetables. The language or "idiom" they used to describe their fishing activities was unique. There were words that we had never heard. Many of those words referred to the same objects they used to use for fishing. Their explanations were carefully registered so we could use the information later.

From the very first day, the classroom became both the center for learning and the site to gather or investigate available data about the students' lives. There we found that one of the main reasons for learning how to write and read was to be able to write letters to their families, relatives, and friends. So far they had been recording cassettes to communicate with their families in El Salvador. We also discovered that this is a common practice among illiterate individuals; otherwise they have to ask someone to either read or write a letter for them. They did not seem very happy about having to depend on someone else. In one of the students' own words, "*Having to ask someone to read or write a letter for us means having to disclose our private life to others; sometimes this is very frustrating. There are things others do not need to know.*"

In the beginning we also wanted to have an idea of how much they knew. In order to find out, we wrote all the letters of the alphabet on the board and asked if they recognized some of them. The result was that some students did in fact know some letters but no more than seven or eight and others knew two or three. This was an indication that it was going to be quite a challenging experience, for we would have had to start with very basic exercises to loosen up their hands by making horizontal, vertical, and diagonal lines and circles. This, of course, was primarily an exercise to be done at home, so we could use the classroom time to develop other activities.

In subsequent days, codifications were introduced to elicit themes. Because we knew all the students were familiar or directly involved with fishing activities, either currently or in the past, one codification represented a man fishing with rudimentary equipment. Just as we had anticipated, a lively discussion emerged. In it, we discussed quite a variety of themes related to fishing: the different methods used, the kinds of fish found in rivers, ponds, and sea, life at sea while fishing for long periods of time, and a comparison of the way fishing is done in this country both commercially and as a hobby. We not only learned a great deal about fishing but also found out how involved the students became once issues related to their lives were brought up. Everyone had something to say. The language they used was uniquely exquisite and unfamiliar to our ears. Their expressions, vocabulary, syntax, and the way they constructed their thoughts were a continuous delight to listen to but, most importantly, all those aspects of their way of expressing themselves were recorded for future references and class material. The curriculum was there. We did not have to make one, but guide it. They were making it. They were, we could say, without realizing it at first, co-investigators in the learning process.

The duration of discussions depends primarily on two factors: 1) how well the issue has been introduced; 2) how appealing the issue is to the students and their consequent interest and motivation to discuss it. In relation to the fishing example, the discussion developed almost throughout the entire class time. Now our role as teachers was to connect it with learning mechanical aspects of literacy. Because it is important to start with words that relate to a theme that appeals to the students, we did not bother studying the alphabet in the order known to everyone. Instead, we chose a key word; in this case, it was the word "*pesca* = *fishing*" which we proceeded to decode or break into syllables. Then we started to form every single syllable with the first consonant of the word "pesca" in combination with the vowels; and then the second one, but concentrating at this point mainly in the first one in order not to overwhelm the students.

On another day we would study the second consonant in combination with vowels as well. So far it was sufficient to become familiar with the different sounds of *p* with *a, e, i, o, u* and words that might result from the combination of the syllables. We also wrote on the board all the words related to fishing that the students used. The purpose was, first to show the participants how oral expression can be translated into written expression; second, to come back to those words at a proper moment when other letters found in them would have been introduced; and third, to use those words months later when students could read them and see by themselves how much they had progressed. The list of examples could be very extensive. It is important to note from the above that anything students might say about their lives and their interests could potentially become the themes and generative words to be used as a tool to develop their literacy skills and elicit discussions.

Finding topics and dialogues

As we have pointed out, the classroom was both the field of research and the center of learning. Hearing the students complain about their living conditions was an indication that we needed to develop class material around housing issues and tenants' rights. Likewise, hearing them complain about their working conditions was another indication that we needed to develop class material around worker's rights and discrimination.

Furthermore, we still had to deal with the issue of politics in the classroom, which is a very important element in the problem posing model. Given that students had had a bad experience in the past with discussing political issues in the classroom, the key was to expand the notion of politics and apply it to realms that were not often thought of as having a political dimension. In addition, in many circumstances, when we discussed political issues, the word *politics* was not even mentioned. Because students did not seem interested in discussing the politics of their country, we studied other possible ways to approach it. In the meantime, we worked on more immediate problems that involved politics, for instance, discrimination, workers' rights, legalization process, underpaid salaries, exploitation, tenant's rights, and so on. All these issues had a tremendous richness which could be explored in the classroom and often were intertwined, as we will see later.

The following example took place 8 months after we had started this class. At this point students had progressed considerably in their reading skills (with some difficulties, of course, but manageable). For this reason, the exercise was adequate for their level of reading and writing. In order to carry out many of our tasks, we tried to utilize the resources available in the area by connecting them with students' concerns and the mechanical aspects of literacy as well. With this rationale at the core of our praxis, we contacted an organization whose goal is to advocate and assist immigrant workers concerning their rights in the workplace, from getting the minimum wage to lawsuits in cases of poor working conditions. As a part of its goals, the organization translated a whole literature concerning workers' rights which was used in this particular situation.

First, the decision to do this lesson was based on hearing students complain that certain factories had not paid them for their labor or overtime. In this situation, students knew that something was not right, but could not react due to lack of knowledge of their rights and where to go for advocacy. Accordingly, we gave students a handout that explained workers' rights. This handout was divided into sections (Workplace Rights, Benefits and Compensation, Unions and Unemployment), so each day during one week we concentrated on one specific section.

Next, each section was divided into three components in the following order: reading, discussing, and writing. During the reading component students took about 40 minutes to read the material. In it, the organization explains its goal and then explains the rights workers have such as minimum wage, overtime regulations, working conditions, sick time. These readings were done both individually and collectively. For instance, because the language in the workers' rights handout was often technical and complicated, groups of three students concentrated on one specific section. Then, they discussed the content and attempted to understand it. After students in a given group had reached an agreement about the content of their respective section, they explained it to the rest of the class. Once the students finished reading this document, the class as a whole also dealt with the technical language and explained some unclear points. In this situation, either I or a student explained whatever needed to be clarified. Unanswered questions were addressed when representatives of the organization came to follow up on these issues.

The second component evolved around a discussion of the material previously read. While we were trying to understand the law, I asked the students if they had been in a situation where their rights had been violated. Not surprisingly, all of them had been discriminated against, exploited, or not paid at all. Given this situation, we proceeded to talk about their experiences and tried to figure out how knowledge of the law and of the existence of the organization could have helped to prevent such violations or counteracted them. In principle, the students were happy and enthusiastic to find out that they had certain rights, and especially to learn about them by themselves (by reading about their rights while they developed their literacy skills).

Without having directly discussed the political implications of this issue, it was obvious to them that it was a struggle of one class exploiting another and, not only that, but it is also a struggle between parts of the dominant Anglo society exploiting other racial groups. This situation is no different from the one that they experience in their native country where the oligarchy exploits the lower classes. They certainly know that. However, this

175

connection was automatically made by the students themselves. In Freire's terms, awareness of their current reality is essential for its transformation.

Our last component was writing, and in order to accomplish it, students were given an assignment in which they had to respond in writing to questions such as, *"In your own experience, when did you feel your rights had been violated, and how would the law protect you in such situations?"* In response to this question, students said the following:

> *"There were days when I got sick and I did not get pay for them."*
> *"I was pressured to work very hard for very little pay."*
> *"I did not get pay for overtime.",* etc.

When asked how we could solve those problems students responded:

> *"by consulting a lawyer"*
> *"by talking to someone who knows more about these things"*
> *"by consulting the organization in order to help us and clarify some of the laws that protect us."*

In this manner, all aspects such as their own experience, reading, and writing were emphasized to develop their mechanical skills, awareness of their own reality, and critical reflection upon it. A week after having read, discussed, and written about workers' rights, a workshop was presented by the organization previously mentioned. In the workshop, two presenters explained what we had read and then asked the students for specific examples to illustrate how the law could be applied. This was a success because having read the literature in advance, the students had thought about it, and therefore had many questions to ask. The presenters also provided a specific example of a lawsuit in progress for workers who had not been paid for several weeks and who had also been working under dangerous conditions at a factory of chemical products. I think that, after this activity, students became aware of other dimensions of working in this country which they would normally disregard or simply did not have access to due to the language barrier.

Moreover, it was interesting to find out from the students that although they knew they had been underpaid, some of them accepted it. The justification they provided was the fact that they are not U.S. citizens, and having a working permit did not seem to make a difference. Somehow they had this notion that their status (not being citizens) did not entitle them to seek equality in the workplace. If there is a lesson to learn from this unit, it was that we all deserve equal treatment in the workplace regardless of our status in this country, for there should not be hierarchies built around jobs based on race or nationality. To deny workplace equality to immigrants is to negate part of our humanity and, hence, the dichotomy between oppressors and oppressed gets perpetuated.

In this regard, dialogue was important because through it we found out what specific problems the students have had in the workplace. Once that information was acquired, our task was to find a way to make it a learning experience and also provide the guidance to work on the liberatory process, (i.e. bringing in the literature about workplace rights and discussing it with the students). Students certainly knew when something was not right at the workplace, which proves that often marginalized groups know their reality very well but do not know how to transform it. In addition, it was a process in which we all discovered how we might possibly transform an alienating situation, knowing the law is not always a guarantee of justice. For instance, presenters from the organization previously mentioned gave examples of collective action and organizing. They emphasized the importance of workers' involvement and organizing at the chemical factory by bringing to jurisprudence's attention the injustices and conditions they faced. In the end, solidarity among workers was a key element in making their voices heard.

Difficulties

Although most of the attempts to implement this approach using generative themes connected with literacy learning were successful, there were situations in which it did not happen as expected, but not always necessarily because the method itself has inadequacies. The problem stems from a series of factors that affect the classroom significantly and thus need to be taken into consideration. First, most students in our program worked long hours and consequently were exhausted by the end of the day. Our classes unfortunately suffered from being held in the evenings. The second factor involves more directly issues related to the approach. Students may not always want to be involved in discussions out of codifications and generative themes. For this reason, one must strive for a combination of activities to create a balance between discussions that lead to critical reflection and activities that lead to literacy acquisition. It is difficult and challenging to create this balance, but by no means impossible (see examples in *Finding Topics* and *Dialogues*).

In addition, the implementation of the participatory approach mainly requires teachers' creativity and students' participation. Initially, some of the difficulties we faced had to do with students' resistance to the approach. For example, students did not always feel that they were learning anything by discussing issues or themes. Second, because the approach strives for building a curriculum that evolves around students' issues, there were times when they did not feel comfortable enough to talk about certain aspects of their lives. Instead they preferred to concentrate heavily on developing their mechanical skills (i.e., working on syllabic structures without necessarily analyzing the word and its loaded meaning first). In other words, many times students wanted the teacher to deliver the information they needed in the banking model of teaching. We had the knowledge they wanted, and therefore they wanted us to deliver it. They wanted to learn how to write and read without going through the process of thinking why and how written language is related to issues of their every day life.

In terms of teachers' creativity, we had to deal with the fact that there are few Spanish literacy resources available to develop a curriculum. It is true that if we are to take students' issues and concerns to develop a curriculum, we could infer that we have enough resources. However, it requires a tremendous amount of effort to utilize students' issues creatively in developing the curriculum. Thus, every day becomes a challenging experience, which is positive to some extent, but it can also be overwhelming for both the teacher and the students. A given teacher does not always have all the solutions for all the problems that arise in literacy teaching; it is then important to have other resources available for the sake of serving students adequately.

Writing activities

While these themes were being explored and reading activities being developed, the literacy class also began to work on writing. Students' writing developed very slowly because students knew very few letters or none at the beginning of the program. The primary challenge at first was to develop very basic literacy skills such as how to loosen up their hands in order to be able to write letters. Students first had to do elemental exercises such as horizontal and vertical lines, and circles. At the same time, it was important to keep their motivation very high so the students could experience positive outcomes.

As classes progressed and only after having done very elemental exercises, the move to introducing the first letters was our next step. We gradually started to form small words with the letters known to the students. To expand the dimensions of the approach we found it appropriate, for instance, to talk about St. Valentine's Day in February. In Spanish it is also called the Day of Affection: *Día del cariño*. We discussed what this day meant for some people and the ways it is celebrated. Because this happened 2 weeks after we had started the program and students were not yet used to our approach, they seemed puzzled about why we were talking about this day. St. Valentine's Day was probably not enough justification for having this discussion, for they were there to learn technical skills instead. Later the word was written on the board and broken into syllables to encourage the students to form new words by combining the syllables:

Cariño

ca - ri - ño

ca-ce-ci-co-cu   ra-re-ri-ro-ru   ña-ñe-ñi-ño-ñi

cuco   ño ño

cara   rico   roca   cura   cero   coro   riña   caña   cuña

This is perhaps the part of literacy acquisition that is often omitted in participatory education discourse. Ideas and principles found in participatory education are quite inspiring and challenging. However, it is often emphasized to such degree that the technical aspects of literacy acquisition remain in the shadow. The point is that there is no way to actually acquire literacy without this activity of combining syllables to form new words and rewriting them repeatedly in order to also acquire a good command of penmanship. Lastly, we also have to talk about this component and not only about the wonderful discussions that illuminate critical reflection, for what happens before or after problem posing is part of the reality of acquiring literacy. Because critical reflection and mechanical aspects of literacy are both necessary to "become" literate and ideally enlightened, it is only by insisting on the importance of both that we begin to see results. For instance, as learners became familiar with more letters, our next step consisted of guiding the students to construct their own sentences.

In order to do an activity in which everyone could participate, we used cardboard cards of approximately 3" x 3" on which consonants and vowels were combined. In addition, there were cards with single consonants and vowels to be used when necessary. Then, students would brainstorm a thought to be constructed with the cards. The sentence would be formed on a felt board which would hold the cards. These were students' initial attempts to translate their thoughts into writing.

This activity was alternated with photographs which portrayed different classroom situations to motivate a discussion about learning. In some photographs, there were children and in others there were adults. Thus, the discussion evolved around learning in different stages of our lives and places. The following sentences were constructed as a result of this activity:

"Nunca es tarde para aprender." (It is never late to learn.)
"Todos podemos aprender si nos lo proponemos." (We all can learn if we have the initiative to do so.)
"La edad no debe impedirnos ir a la escuela." (Age should not stop us from going to school.)

This is only one example of the kind of activity that took place during the following 2 to 3 months. Simultaneously, we developed reading activities to complement their literacy learning. Students started by reading very short stories with illustrations on them. This exercise was done individually and collectively and followed by discussions. At the same time, we experienced a great amount of dialogue in the form of discussions around themes of interest to the students. Through dialogue, we came to know their interest and priorities, which ultimately led to the inclusion of the following activities.

As the group improved writing and reading skills, a new variety of techniques and strategies were introduced, for example, compositions around specific topics. Mother's Day was the first of many writing activities. Some of the students' first compositions illustrate how students' writing progressed:

En el día de la Madre	Translation: On Mother's Day
Madre mía en este día	Dear mother, in this day
me he sentido muy contento que al	I have felt very happy that
recordarte madre me siento	When I remember you I feel
muy orgulloso, madresita linda	very proud, wonderful dear mother
en este día te deseo lo más	in this day I wish you the
grande de mi vida,	greatest of my life,
madre soy	mother I am
el hijo por quien tu sufristes	the son for whom you suffered
para yo ser	so I could be
un hijo de tu corazón.	a son of your heart.

Carlos Morales, 13 de mayo de 1991

Carlos Morales literally did not know more than the vowels when he first came to our program. Unlike many other students who had some knowledge of some other letters and knew how to write a little bit, Carlos had to start from the beginning. He progressed very slowly. However, what worked to his advantage was the fact that everything he learned was new to him. This means that although he learned slowly, he learned well from the beginning, while students who had some reading and writing skills continued to make the same mistakes because what they knew was not necessarily correct. Carlos wrote very short compositions as we can see in the example, but his writings needed little correction. The conclusion is that sometimes it takes longer to teach people with limited literacy skills than to teach people who have no literacy skills since everything is new to them. It sometimes takes longer to unlearn something that we know improperly than to learn something that is new. Another student, Rosa Vargas, wrote about her experience of coming to the United States and leaving her children in El Salvador so she could try to support them:

> Yo Rosa, llegué a este lugar con sólo mi vestido. Amigas y amigos me ayudaron en la ropa y la comida porque yo no tenía dinero para comprar las cosas mías. Pero hoy le mando dinero a mis hijos que son: Reina, Magdalena, Carmen, y un niño varón que se llama Carlitos.
>
> Yo me dejé con mi marido. Vi crecer a todos mis hijos. Cuando m e vine dejé una niña de dos años. pero la cuida la niña más grande. Yo trabajo para mandarles todos lo que quieren, también me aflijo porque son cinco y por el momento no tengo trabajo.
>
> 29 de mayo de 1991

Translation:

> I, Rosa, came to this place only with one dress. Friends helped me at first with clothes and food because I did not have any money to buy those things myself. But, now I send money to my children, Reina, Magdalena, Carmen and a little boy whose name is Carlitos.
>
> I separated from my husband. I saw all my children grow up. When I left the littlest of my children was two years old, but the oldest looks after her. I work to send them whatever they want. I also worry because they are five children and at this moment I do not have a job.
>
> May 29, 1991

Letter writing

The inclusion of this segment is of vital importance, for it helps understand the impact that literacy had on the students. Originally all students in our program wanted to learn to write letters to their families and friends. Nevertheless, when we made our first attempts, students were insecure about their ability to achieve this long-wanted goal. Letter writing was our next step after students had written small compositions such as the one above. It was not until 5 months after the beginning of the program that we judged pertinent to start with this exercise. Their first hesitation had to do with feeling insecure about "actually writing a letter to someone." Another concern students had was that they still made too many errors and therefore no one would be able to read what they might write. They also experienced some fear about writing to someone for the first time. All this issues are perfectly understandable and were taken into account.

Around March of 1991 I met another Spanish Literacy teacher from New York City, with whom I discussed the possibility of doing a letter exchange exercise with her students.

180

Neither our students nor hers were ready for it when we first discussed this possibility, but 2 months later we talked again and decided that we would try it. She gave me a list of students' names and country of origin which I distributed among our students; each one picked one name to write to. The process was not easy at the beginning, for there was so much uncertainty among our students, yet they had enough enthusiasm to get started. We first had to compose a model letter on the board to show how they could write their own. During this activity every student contributed something he or she wanted to say. Once we did this, they started to write. The fact that they were going to write to students in New York city brought up two new issues. First, it would be hard to write to people they did not know at all. Second, it was timely and quite advantageous that they were going to write to people with whom they shared the same experience. The first was only a problem at the beginning, and the latter prevailed because, in fact, they did have so much to share with each other; they wrote back and forth exchanging their experiences and views of being illiterate, the reasons why they were illiterate and the effect that it had in their lives. To better illustrate this aspect, it is appropriate to show how some of our students at Harborside expressed this experience:

6 de Junio de 1991

Estimado amigo,

Es un placer saludarlo y mis deseos son que encuentre bien de salud y me alegro al saber que también otra persona como yo está tratando de resolver el problema de no saber leer pues yo soy también otro estudiante que estoy tratanto de aprender a leer y a escribir y estoy contento porque yo a veces pensaba que nunca iba a aprender a leer. Hoy me doy cuenta de que yo si podía aprender a leer pues tengo cinco años de estar en este país y yo nunca en mi vida había tenido el placer de escribir una carta aunque sea a mi mamá pues yo soy de El Salvador y tengo 32 años y mi nombre es Miguel Soto. Para mi ha sido gran placer el haber tenido la oportunidad de haberte escrito estas pocas palabras. Espero que me conteste que para mí va a ser gran placer poder compartir esta experiencia.

Atentamente,
Miguel Soto

Translation:

June 6, 1991

Dear friend:

It is a pleasure to send you my regards and I hope that you are O.K. I am happy to find out that there is another person like me who is trying to resolve the problem of not knowing how to read, for I am a student who is trying to learn how to read and write. I am also happy because sometimes I thought that I was never going to learn. Now, I realize that I could learn to read since I have been in this country for 5 years and never in my life I had had the pleasure to write a letter, not even to my mother in El Salvador where I come from. I am 32 years old and my name is Miguel Soto. It has been a great pleasure to have had the opportunity to write to you these few words. I hope that you answer me back since for me it will be a great pleasure to be able to share this experience.

Sincerely,
Miguel Soto

181

It is also important to keep in mind that the writing of this first letter took a week (9 hours of instruction) and the final letter was not sent until students had done one or two drafts in which corrections were made.

Successes: What could the students do outside the classroom?

To better understand the impact that literacy acquisition had on the students, we can look at the following aspects in addition to the actual gains in reading and writing proficiency: their attitudes and feelings, the things they could do with literacy outside the classroom, their contributions to the community, and the implications for their futures.

First, the most common attitude that students manifested was looking at themselves as more independent individuals. As students progressed in their learning, their confidence grew simultaneously. It is vital to note that not having to depend on others as much as they used to had a very positive impact on their lives. Being independent was manifested primarily through the things they could do now. For instance, many students felt very proud of being able to write letters to their families and relatives in their native countries. Others expressed great satisfaction at being able to read signs in Spanish in public places such as hospitals and the subway. Two students are part of an AA group in which they have responsibilities. One is the treasurer and the other the secretary. In both capacities they have to exercise what they learned in the literacy class. One of them has to register all the financial activities of the group, and other has to write the minutes of their meetings. In terms of other contributions to the community, as many students improved their literacy skills, they were able to help the lower level literacy students as well as relatives at home who could not attend classes.

Although our students had different goals and ideas about to what degree they wanted to improve their literacy skills, most of them felt that it was very important to move on to ESL classes. Many of them, in fact, are now attending ESL classes at Harborside. A few of them would like to go beyond ESL classes and continue their education; it is hard to tell how long it might take before these students reach their goals. However, what is most important is that they have discovered their potential and to what degree they want to transform their lives.

In sum, there is no doubt that dialogue is extremely important in order to know the students and their concerns. It is difficult to know to what extent teaching people how to write and read will liberate them from oppressive realities. However, learning how to write and read in itself increases self-esteem and independence not only in everyday life activities, but also to become fully responsible for one's reality, as Freire points out. For this to happen, discovering and awareness are important factors in the process. However we cannot assume that transformation will occur, at least in the way we, the teachers, define it. For, it is ultimately the students who have to decide what transformation means for them and how far they want to go toward achieving that goal.

Appendix B: Promoting Native Language Literacy at the HMSC

There were many facets to the process of promoting Creole instruction at the HMSC. The conversations often began at in-take when students said that they were worried about signing up for English class because they couldn't read and write; they were told that there was a class especially for them to help them work on their reading and writing and assured them that it would lead to English.

Another way of promoting Creole was incorporating dialogue about it into the content of classes: the teacher generally explained the rationale for Creole instruction during the first class sessions. One Intern framed it in terms of the education system in Haiti, saying that students in Haiti learn English only after they have already learned to read and write; they are accepted into English classes only after Grade 6 or 7. Students were reassured that it would lead them to English and were invited to try the Creole class before deciding whether to stay. If they were still reluctant, the teacher would suggest that they go to the ESL class and try it. Often, they would come back saying, "OK, I'm going to stay here for 3 months..."

Despite these initial explanations in terms of the pedagogical benefits of Creole literacy, at one point there seemed to be an undercurrent of discontent, connected to the broader issue of stigmatization of Creole. Jean-Marc Jean-Baptiste, the first Creole Master Teacher in the BCLTP, decided to address this concern through a general meeting of the students from all the literacy classes. When he invited students to voice their concerns, they said:

People who are already educated want the uneducated ones to learn Creole to hold them back. Learning Creole is something that only lower class people do - it's a way of keeping us ignorant. We already speak Creole so why do we need to learn it? We want to learn English as quickly as possible. In Haiti, people make fun of young people who learn to read and write in Creole; learning Creole is only for old people.

Students then took a vote; half opted for English instruction, a quarter wanted French, and a quarter wanted Creole. After the vote, they asked the teachers for their opinions. Jean-Marc told the group that he believes that you learn how to read and write faster in a language you already speak than in one you don't know; if you know how to read and write in your own language it is easier to learn the second language. Through this process of dialogue and negotiation, students decided that the classes should be set up as half Creole and half English. In reality, once the process of introducing ESL began, the amount of time varied: initially students wanted more time, but as they began to see the value of Creole literacy, the time for ESL diminished until students had a solid basis in literacy.

In a subsequent teacher-sharing session, we decided on three ways to follow up on this meeting. First, because the understanding of the rationale for Creole literacy was uneven among the group (some of the Interns themselves were uncomfortable discussing it with students because they weren't fully convinced of its value), we decided to invite Creole specialists from the Boston area in to facilitate a workshop for staff about the history of Creole, the rationale for Creole literacy, and the literacy campaigns in Haiti. Second, we decided to continue focusing literacy lessons on the sociopolitical context for learning or not learning Creole. Third, we decided to invite an outside speaker for a center-wide meeting to discuss Creole literacy in the context of the history and political situation in Haiti.

Shortly thereafter, the first of several project-sponsored Saturday Creole workshops was held at the HMSC; it was led by Haitian linguists and conducted in Creole. Because the Interns themselves had become literate in French, rather than Creole, the workshop provided a context to convince them of the value and legitimacy of Creole as a language, deepen their own understanding of the rules of Creole orthography, as well as the history of Creole linguistics and the issues/logistics of Creole literacy instruction in Haiti (the literacy campaigns). Several students also participated in the workshop.

In addition, a community member who had worked in Misyon Alfa (Haiti's mass literacy campaign conducted by the Catholic church) was invited to a meeting at the HMSC. He spoke about the literacy campaign, its approach to literacy instruction, the relationship between literacy and national development, and the rationale for learning to read and write in Creole. The entire student body at the Center was invited to attend the meeting (which was held during class time) so that there would be center-wide dialogue about Creole. The speaker linked illiteracy to political oppression, and presented the stigmatization of Creole as a tool used by the elite to maintain social stratification. He explained that by forcing the masses to learn to read and write in their second language and denying them education, the ruling classes had effectively silenced them and kept them from participating in the political and economic life of Haiti. He went on to explain how Misyon Alfa attempted to link education with social change through its approach of combining mechanical aspects of literacy acquisition with conscientization.

Students also spoke eloquently about their own experiences while becoming literate. Many gave moving testimony about both the realities of life without literacy and changes in their lives since becoming literate. A key theme was that of respect. One student said that the real problem of Haiti isn't literacy per se; it is people's lack of respect for each other. Illiterate people are made to feel stupid: they are teased and called "evening students" (because they go to school at night after work). She said that literacy doesn't make you able to think; you can think without literacy. For her, becoming literate meant a change both in how others viewed her and in how she viewed herself. Before she could read and write, people looked down on her; after she learned to read and write, her common-law husband had decided to marry her! Thus, the meeting went a long way toward taking the stigma off being illiterate, increasing the understanding between literacy and ESL students, making Creole literacy a center-wide concern, and situating it in a political context.

Several other factors contributed to the change in students' attitudes toward Creole. The general political situation in Haiti supported the process: the dialogue about "why Creole literacy" coincided with Aristide's election campaign in which respect for Creole was a central platform. In addition, teachers and Interns continued to focus on the issue as part of curriculum content. Students explored their own educational histories—why they hadn't had a chance to go to school and what being illiterate meant to them, as well as the broader question of why there is so much illiteracy in Haiti. Further, students began to see through practical experience how Creole could be a bridge to English as teachers introduced English for a few hours per week. By the end of the first 2 months of the project, students had stopped asking to be switched to ESL classes; by the end of the first 6 months, the waiting list for Creole classes had increased; students sometimes requested to stay in the classes even when they were ready to leave, and advanced ESL students began to ask to join the classes so they could learn to read and write in Creole.

Appendix C: Sample Training Workshops

This Appendix includes accounts of selected university-based training workshops that took place during the Bilingual Community Literacy Training Project (BCLTP). The workshops were held once a month on Saturday mornings for 3 hours. Both the objectives and the reflections in the following workshop descriptions were written retrospectively, based on minutes of staff meetings. Each session ended with a brief evaluation (which is not listed in every outline because it was routine). In addition, there was another evaluation discussion at each site during the week or two following the workshop. The reflections incorporate feedback from these evaluations. Please also note that we rotated facilitators for each activity within a session; hence, the term facilitator refers to different people.

Session I: Conceptual Framework

Objectives

The primary task during the first session is to set the tone for the trainings, and to present an introduction to the participatory approach. Our objectives were:

- to set a participatory tone, conveying to Interns that the training is as much theirs as ours
- to get to know each other: elicit from Interns their interest in the project, their backgrounds and preliminary perceptions of needs.
- to introduce a participatory approach, especially the idea of nonformal education and non-traditional student-teacher relations
- to set a direction for future trainings: giving a sense of what we hope to achieve and how we will proceed
- to model a concrete tool or activity that Interns can try with students

Overview of the session

1. **Welcome** in three languages; explanation of the agenda (10 min.)

2. **Introductory Activity** (45 min.)

   a. Everyone receives a piece of paper and is asked to fold it in four parts. In each square, they answer one of the following questions by writing something or drawing a picture about it:

   Who were you in your country?
   Who are you now?
   Who would you like to be?
   What would you like or expect from these trainings?

   b. We play a tape of Haitian music; everyone moves around in two concentric circles to the music. When the music stops, people in the inside circle pair up with the facing person in the outside circle; they then share what they have drawn or written.[1]

   c. The whole group reconvenes and each person introduces his or her partner to the others. The facilitator writes themes for each question.

---

[1]Thanks to Raul Añorve for inspiring this activity!

3. <u>Overview of the project; introduction of each site</u> (15 min.)

The project coordinator summarizes the wealth of Interns' backgrounds and strengths as presented in the previous activity and discusses the rationale for the project (to draw on their strengths in order to meet learners' needs). The notion of participatory training is introduced—that we don't want to just tell Interns what to do, but want to learn from each other and share what is happening at the different sites. Master Teachers each present a brief introduction to the sites.

4. <u>Sharing experiences and concerns in small group</u> (1 hr. with break)

a. Participants are divided into mixed site groups so they have a chance to talk to people from different sites. Each Intern has been asked to come prepared to share something concrete from his or her site: an activity or lesson that went well, a lesson they especially liked, a concern or a piece of student writing. Facilitators note issues, ideas, questions, and concerns. This activity is designed to allow participants from different sites to get to know a little about each others' sites and concerns, to begin to elicit Interns' concerns, and to establish an atmosphere of sharing.

b. Feedback to whole group: common concerns and issues are shared.

5. <u>Presentation on Freirean approach</u> (45 min.)

a. One of the Master Teachers presents background on the Freirean approach to situate our project in a broader context and show the relationship between literacy work in many "Third World" countries (like those that Interns come from) and literacy work in the U.S. The presentation focuses on:

•what Freire did in Brazil and why, including overheads of the codifications he used
•the relationship between conscientization and the mechanical aspects of literacy
•the steps in Freire's process of literacy instruction

b. The Coordinator facilitates discussion on why we're talking about an approach first and will investigate methods/techniques later. The dialogue includes these questions:

•What aspects of Freire's work do you think are relevant to work in the U.S. context? Which are not relevant? What specific principles can guide our work? (handouts)
•What themes for codification have you uncovered in your own work?
•Why did we organize the workshop the way we did, as a reflection of the approach (starting with participants' experiences, drawing issues from them, etc.)?
•How will the next several workshops will be set up?

7. <u>Evaluation</u> (15 min.)

Participants are invited to give feedback (in any language) on any reactions to the workshop, share ideas that they got from the workshop for something they might like to try with students, look for student issues that emerge in the classroom during the next month, read Hong Ngo's story "Reflections of a New Teacher" (the story of a Vietnamese woman's experiences in becoming an ESL teacher) and respond to it in terms of their own feelings and experiences.

Reflections

The most important point about the first session was that it initiated the process of uncovering themes and issues for subsequent exploration. Although some topics were identified by asking Interns directly what they would like to get from the trainings, the richest themes emerged from responses to structured activities and dialogue. Of course, this process of identifying issues mirrors what happens with adult learners: when asked directly what they want to do, they very often have a hard time identifying specific topics; however, when presented with catalyst or trigger activities, their concerns or needs emerge organically. The trick then is for the facilitator to listen for these themes and utilize them.

During the first workshop, two kinds of issues emerged: substantive issues about literacy acquisition and issues about the content/processes of the training. The substantive issues clustered around the question of the relation of the social context to literacy acquisition. One of the Interns said that he thought Hispanics don't feel they have to learn English because so many people in the U.S. speak Spanish. He felt that they are less motivated to learn English because they can get by without it. Implicit in his statement was the question: *What is the difference in the impact of the social context of literacy acquisition for Haitians and Hispanics?* However, when he used the word 'lazy' to describe his perception of the attitude of some Hispanics, he immediately generated heated reactions and a new issue was raised, the issue of *tensions between nationality groups.* Although we didn't pursue the discussion in the heat of the moment, we came back to this theme at the following workshop, using it to illustrate how "hot issues" can be identified. Once again, what happened in the workshop paralleled what happens in classes, and we tried to utilize this shared experience to illustrate a subsequent point.

A related question about the social context was "Is it possible for people who have two or three low-paying jobs to learn English?" In other words, *what is the effect of the conditions of people's lives on their ability to acquire English/literacy?* This was a question that recurred throughout the project, as we saw classes shrink and swell depending on what was happening in students' lives (see the section on implications). When we asked if people had uncovered any themes in their own work, one Intern mentioned that he had used pictures of the war in the Gulf because it was a timely issue; another Intern, however, said that you have to be careful with these pictures—students get upset because war pictures remind them of their own horrible situations. This raised the question about whether we should bring in loaded political themes and, if so, how. Finally, a question was raised about *how a Freirean approach could be implemented in North America,* where the political situation is so different from that in Latin American countries. Specifically, one of the Interns questioned the possibility of including a conscientization component in our work. Each of these questions about how literacy work is shaped by contextual factors laid the groundwork for future discussions.

Several training issues emerged in the evaluation which were to be key throughout the project. First, Interns said that they liked the chance to share ideas and exchange experiences with peers; they were especially interested to find that people from different backgrounds, working in different sites, had ideas similar to their own. Although Interns had been a little apprehensive, they felt that the atmosphere of the workshop was comfortable and they found that English was not a problem for them. Thus, *the value of providing time for sharing* was affirmed. Second, Interns said that wanted more time on the Freire presentation so that they could ask questions, and find ways to apply his work to their own classrooms; someone mentioned not having enough time to understand Freire. Implicit in these comments was the point that *it is important not to try to do too much and to allot time for dialogue.* The amount of discussion that was generated had surprised us. This tension between *being flexible so that unexpected issues can be explored* and *sticking to the topic so that we accomplish the objectives of the workshop* also mirrors a common classroom dilemma.

Finally, several Interns expressed the desire for more concrete links to classroom practice; they wanted to talk about what to do in the classroom. This tension between some Interns' desire for specific techniques and our resistance to prescriptions had to be negotiated throughout the project; in the section on training issues, we come back to this and explore its implications. Thus, in addition to presenting a conceptual framework, this workshop began our own process of participatory curriculum development as we found themes and issues to pursue in later trainings.

Session 2: Finding Learners' Issues

Objectives

We had ended the last session by discussing the relevance of Freire's notion of centering the curriculum on issues of importance in students' lives. In the intervening month, we asked Interns to look for issues in their work with students and bring them to share with the group. Our goal in this session was to address the questions, "What is an issue?" and "How do you find students' issues?" Objectives were:

- to link issues from the previous session to content of this session
- to explore the notion of student-generated themes
- to present a range of tools for finding student themes
- to incorporate and discuss Interns' observations/practice from the past month
- to practice finding themes by utilizing one tool
- to explore Interns' own learning experiences

Overview of the session

I. What is an issue? (introduction linking this workshop to the last one; 15 min.)

The facilitator reviews the discussion of the importance of basing the curriculum on issues that are important to learners. You know you've hit on a theme or issue when suddenly participants all start talking at once, can't stop talking about the topic and it relates to their social context. Three "hot issues" from last month's workshop were:

- The question of whether Spanish-speaking people need or want to learn English
- The question of whether the Freirean approach is relevant for the U.S.
- The question of whether we should talk about war, violence, and students' experiences in their home countries because these issues are too heavy.

II. How do you find issues?

a. Small group discussion (30 min.):Participants break into small groups (mixed sites) and share issues that they identified during the month. Two questions guide this discussion:

- What is an issue or theme that is important to your students?
- How did you identify this theme? How did the issue come up? What was your role in the process?

b. Whole group discussion (30 min.): The group reconvenes and two lists are made, one with learners' issues and the other with the ways participants found the issues; examples from our workshop were:

Student Issues		Ways of Finding Issues
finding an apartment or room	skin color	small group discussions
fishing	not having a husband	observations
work experience	wife not working	before/after class observations
difficulties finding work	motivation versus attendance	games
what students do at home	gender roles, men versus women	dialogue journals
what life used to be in their own country	lack of confidence	work on letters
child care		drawings, cartoons
use of the first language		pictures and photographs
		grammar exercises

c. Presentation on Ways of Finding Student Issues (30 min.): The Coordinator then summarizes what she sees on the two lists, noting that the main issues (in this case) seem revolve around:

- struggles of learning a new language/literacy
- classroom dynamics
- struggles of living in the U.S. (housing, work, etc.)
- life in the home country
- gender roles

She points out that Interns have identified two main ways of finding student issues:

-conscious listening: noting themes that arise spontaneously in heated or engaging discussions
-structured catalyst activities: activities that are designed to teach language/literacy while at the same time eliciting student experience and concerns

The coordinator then presents several other examples of catalyst activities using overheads and a handout. The group discusses examples from work at the sites.

III. Learning pictures activity: Using pictures to find issues (1 hour)

a. A set of photos that show various contexts for learning are spread out on a table. The photos are powerful images of people engaged in learning: a strict-looking teacher in front of rows of students, parents teaching kids to ride bikes, an old man carefully writing the alphabet, a circle of people studying, and so on. Each participant is asked to choose a picture that evokes a strong reaction , that reminds them of something, that they like or dislike, that makes them think about an experience in their own life. After they choose a picture, they are asked to write about it for 15 minutes in any language they choose.

b. Participants share what they have written (although they can choose whether to actually read it aloud or not) in groups of three.

c. Facilitators note themes that arise as people share their pictures; issues that arose in our workshop were:

- childhood memories
- participation and cooperation by students
- losing your children because of new
  country and language
- the fear of traditional teachers
- language barriers
- good teachers
- ways of learning

d. The facilitator asks how participants might use these pictures in their own classrooms in order to link the activity to teaching. Interns in our workshop said:
- They liked the activity because pictures can be used with any level, for literacy or ESL. If the pictures are powerful and related to students' own experiences they will evoke strong reactions - either discussion or writing.
- They can be used with open-ended questions or accompanied by *wh-* questions.

Reflections

This session was a prime example of the parallel between what we do in our workshop and what happens in the classroom. One of our main goals had been to link the workshops with Interns' practice. We attempted to do this by incorporating examples from our shared context of work (the issues we chose to illustrate the concept of *themes* were drawn from our previous workshop), by demonstrating specific techniques, activities and exercises for use in the classroom, and by modeling one activity to elicit issues by actually doing it together as a group.

Two seemingly conflicting responses to these attempts emerged in the evaluations. On the one hand, Interns said they appreciated the chance to share more with others. As someone put it, "I liked the fact that Interns had more to say this time." They appreciated the divergence of perspectives: "I learned how our opinions about pictures are so different and so similar sometimes even though we are from different countries." And they understood how the workshops were *showing* them a way of teaching: "I am learning by experience." On the other hand, when they were back at their centers, some of the Interns said that they were interested in talking more about the *mechanical problems in teaching literacy* and about specific teaching problems that come up in class. This surprised us for several reasons. First, we thought we had been specific in demonstrating concrete ideas for classroom use. Second, as we explained in the first session, we didn't want to start with mechanical questions, but rather with developing a way of thinking about teaching, listening, and responding to students' substantive/ experiential issues. Third, we didn't feel we could address the mechanical problems in our workshops because the three teaching contexts at the sites were so different (two were native language literacy in different languages and one was ESL).

Of course, the dilemmas we faced were similar to those that teachers face when students in a participatory classroom request traditional, skills-grammar-mechanical approaches to ESL and literacy instruction and when they are working in a multilevel class where learners have very different needs. We responded by trying to balance our own agenda with the request of participants by using the following strategies:

• set aside special workshop time for participants to talk about problems (mechanical or other)
• acknowledge that we can't meet everyone's needs in the monthly workshops
• model a process for addressing problems that can be used to deal both with teaching problems and with students' issues

In addition, we identified one "mechanical" problem that everyone encounters regardless of context, that we could address concretely, and that would open the door for deeper discussion of a meaning-centered view of literacy, namely, the issue of *corrections*. This issue was timely because one of the Master Teachers had noted that an Intern was correcting learners' errors for them (erasing incorrect writing and rewriting it). We discussed posing the issue of corrections as a universal teaching problem and drawing out a range of alternative strategies (including our own) for handling them. In this way we hoped again to model a process, the process of problem-posing.

Thus, this workshop was key in highlighting an issue that turned out to be central throughout the life of the project: the issue of negotiating our own agenda with Interns' desire for classroom techniques and mechanical solutions. As will be seen, both our thinking and their thinking evolved over time; by the end of the project, we had new insights about how and when to incorporate techniques, and they had significantly changed their conceptions about the role of mechanical aspects in literacy instruction.

Session 3: The Language Experience Approach

Objectives

This session proceeds with the next step of participatory curriculum development, moving on to the question, "What do you do with an issue after you've found it?" In this stage, issues are explored further through a variety of tools which extend literacy and language proficiency. This session focuses on one of these tools, the Language Experience Approach (LEA), and responds to the request to address mechanical problems of literacy as well. The objectives were:

- to demonstrate one tool (LEA) for exploring a theme through literacy work
- to address one mechanical teaching problem (handling corrections) in a problem-posing format
- to provide space to address other problems of practice

Overview of the session

1. **Introduction** (linking this workshop to the last one; 15 min.)

The facilitator reviews what happened at the last workshop, summarizing the main themes from students' lives and the tools for finding issues. She introduces the next stage of the curriculum development process which addresses the question, "What do you do with students' issues once you find them?" and explains that we will be exploring this question in the next several sessions.

2. **What do you do with issues in class?** (small group activity; 30 min.)

Participants break into mixed site groups to share issues that they have uncovered, how they found them, and what they did with them. They choose one student story that they will report back to the whole group.

3. **The Language Experience Approach (LEA)** (1 hr., 15 min.)

a. Group feedback: The groups reconvene and each one reports back. The facilitator writes one of the stories using the LEA approach as it is being told. (This section of the workshop did not proceed according to plan for us; what actually happened is described in the reflections.)

b. Presentation on LEA: The facilitator presents LEA as one way of dealing with an issue. She starts by explaining/defining the term and presenting real examples from classes at the sites. The participating teachers who generated the stories describe the process (where the story came from, how it was written, what the class did with it afterwards). Responses to the following questions are elicited from the group.

- *Why do LEA?*
    It's a way to make a discussion legitimate by extending it to language/literacy work.
    It links oral language with the written symbol.
    It's easier for students to read because it's their own words.
    It's a way to reverse roles in the classroom.
    It starts with meaning and connects mechanical work to it.
    It stimulates participation.
    It ensures that content is relevant.
    It helps in finding what students need to work on.
    It allows the teacher to stall for time if he or she doesn't know how to address a "hot" issue.

•*How do we do LEA?*
The emphasis is on being a good listener, writing what students say, and going through various stages of reading the story. Again, examples are presented in typed format.
•*What do we do with LEA stories once they have been generated?*
The facilitator asks the group how they would follow up on one of the sample stories, eliciting a range of responses and emphasizing that in a participatory approach, the group should be sure to come back to the issue that prompted the story, rather than using the exercises as a pretext for grammar/skills work.

•*What are some questions or debates about LEA?*
The facilitator asks the group if they would write the LEA story in the students' exact words (even with errors) or correct them. The group discusses various strategies. The facilitator summarizes the debate about this issue in the ESL field. The various factors influencing the choice of strategies are discussed.

4. <u>Handling corrections</u> (30 min.)

The facilitator presents a real piece of student writing with many errors of spelling and grammar. He asks participants how they might respond to this piece of writing: their strategies are listed on newsprint. In our session, responses included:

- teacher corrects for student
- it depends on level, student, context, purpose and the audience
- whole class correction
- make students comfortable with making mistakes
- don't focus on making corrections; focus on meaning and respond to meaning
- through response in which teacher models correct forms
- find problem areas and teach those later

5. <u>Problems or questions about practice</u> (15 min.)

The facilitator asks if anyone has a pressing teaching problem that he or she would like to address to the group. In our session, a spelling problem in Spanish and a related problem in Creole (regarding confusion between *j* and *g*) were discussed.

Reflections

Perhaps the most significant aspect of this session was that it did not go as planned. The first deviation from our expectations occurred in the small group discussions. Instead of talking about what to do with students' issues, many of the participants discussed the content of the issues themselves—the students' problems finding jobs, their socioeconomic difficulties, and so on. Many of the participants expressed that they are struggling with these issues and sometimes feel powerless to do anything because the problems seem overwhelming.

When it came time to report back a story from each group and demonstrate the language experience approach, the accounts of the small group discussions were so powerful that it seemed inappropriate to write the stories: trying to write the participants' exact words was blocking the discussion. The LEA exercise felt like a mechanical response to a substantive issue. Thus, again, we deviated from the plan in that the facilitator decided to write the main points of the discussion on newsprint (rather than writing the stories). She then asked participants to talk about how they respond to the enormous issues that students are facing. The group came up with the following strategies:

- trying to help students directly (e.g., refer them to agencies, help them fill out forms, etc.)
- discussing the reasons for the problems; seeing how deeply learners can think about the issues; using *why* questions to get at the social roots of the problem
- posing problem back to students so they can discuss possible strategies and learners can come up with their own solutions; letting students help each other
- work with the problem by building vocabulary, doing exercises about applying for jobs
- connect issue with reading and writing
- invite in outside resources

Of course, the interesting thing about how this workshop developed is that, again, it mirrors what happens in class: if you try to respond to a loaded issue with a mechanical exercise, it may feel inappropriate. Having to abandon the plan and let the lesson go in its own direction is probably more the norm than the exception. Thus, in the workshop itself, we stopped to reflect on what was happening: the facilitator explained what we had planned to do, why we changed the plan, and how this is like what happens in teaching.

A second point about this workshop is that it modeled problem-posing in dealing with Interns' issues. At three points during the session, the facilitator posed a teaching issue back to the group for dialogue (in discussing how to respond to loaded issues, how to write students' language, and how to respond to errors). In each case, the facilitator elicited strategies and wrote down the range of options that were mentioned. Project staff participated in this process, contributing their ideas alongside those of Interns. Thus, rather than telling participants what to do, a tone of jointly constructing alternatives was set. This process sent the message that there's no single way that will fit all circumstances; each teacher has to assess the context, examine the purposes, and base decisions on a range of factors.

Finally, because the session explicitly included sections on mechanical problems, it represented an attempt to model a negotiated curriculum that addressed participants' concerns. However, back at the sites, one of the Interns said she still felt that the workshops were divorced from what happens in class and that there should be more focus on methods and techniques. She said that the process of the workshops and the approach to education is too informal. She also said, "I don't think we can solve the problems of the world. Why do we talk so much about unemployment —this is not a jobs agency." Her comments caused a strong reaction from other Interns, one of whom said, "So what happens to *thinking* if you present worksheets and follow formal methods?" Another said that some of the students had come to the program because the teaching was too formal at other sites. At another site, a similar discussion took place: when one Intern said she had expected more formal presentation of methods, another responded that the purpose of the workshops was not just to present one way to do things, but to provide a place to share ideas and debate. In retrospect, what these discussions represent is the Interns taking on the debate about formal versus informal education themselves, indicating that some Interns had internalized the participatory approach to the extent that they were able to defend it and argue for it.

193

Session 4: Making and Using Codes

Objectives

Continuing with the question of what to you do with an issue once you find it, this session focuses on developing problem-posing codes. Where the previous workshop had implemented a problem-posing process in addressing Interns' teaching issues, this session makes that process explicit and extends its application to learners' issues. It models the process of problem-posing by applying it to a recurring Intern issue—the advantages/disadvantages of nonformal teaching approaches, thus continuing to explore participants' concerns while providing a tool for classroom use. The objectives were:

- to model the process of using codes to explore an Intern issue
- to further explore the issue of formal versus nonformal approaches to education
- to demonstrate and practice developing codes and dialogue questions around student issues

Overview of the session

I. Problem-posing skit

a. _Presentation of skit_ (5 min.): Two Master Teachers act out the following conversation. One teacher voices many of the concerns that Interns had expressed (about focusing on skills, grammar, etc.) rather than social problems; the other teacher utilizes student issues to develop literacy work.

Ana: How was your week? What did you do?

Byron: Oh, the usual thing, we did the next chapter in the book.

Ana: How did it go? What did you do with it?

B: They read the story and did the exercises.

A: Did they like it?

B: Oh, I don't know. Some of them were lost and some liked it, but they still don't remember the past tense. What about you?

A: I started by asking about their weekends. I was trying to review the past tense and to see what they were thinking about.

B: Did they use the past tense?

A: Some of them did but what we ended up talking about was their worries about their kids playing outside.

B: But what was the lesson?

A: That was the lesson! They talked about it for the whole class.

B: The whole class? My students would never do that. They want the teacher to come with a work sheet or book. You can't solve all their problems. This is supposed to be a language class, not a welfare office.

A: Well, they came up with a lot of ideas and we wrote them up for next time. They always seem more interested when we talk about their lives.

B: How are they going to learn to read and write that way?

---

b. <u>Whole group dialogue</u> (30 min.): The facilitator guides dialogue through the five-step questioning process outlined by Wallerstein (1983) to explore the issues represented by the code. The dialogue moves through the following general types of question:

- What happened in this skit? What did you see?
- What was the problem here?
- Does this seem familiar? Have you experienced anything similar?
- Where do these perspectives come from? Why do some people prefer one/the other?
- What can be done about this conflict in perspectives?

III. Presentation about developing codes and dialogue questions (30 min.)

a. <u>Introduction to problem-posing codes</u>: The presenter reflects on what had just happened, noting that the code was developed in response to concerns we had heard: the issue of traditional versus participatory approaches applies as much to our own workshops as to work with students. She makes the five steps to the questioning process explicit as well. Problem-posing codes are defined as a tool for exploring learners' issues while developing language/literacy.

b. <u>Examples of codes</u>: The presenter presents several additional examples of codes that have either been developed in this project or for students similar to those in our classes. Some of the examples evoke heated discussion of the issue presented in the code, while others fall flat.

c. <u>Guidelines for developing codes and dialogue questions</u>: Based on the reactions to the previous examples, the group then discusses what makes a code work (i.e., it evokes heated response, dialogue, and social analysis). The presenter then generalizes about the characteristics of a "good" code and explains the rationale for the five steps of the dialogue process.

d. <u>Language/literacy focus</u>: The presenter asks if participants think this kind of activity "counts" as language/literacy work and, if so, how. She asks participants to discuss how they might incorporate a specific focus on "skills."

III. Developing codes and dialogue questions activity

a. <u>Making codes and questions</u> (45 min.): Participants break into small groups with others from the same site. They are given handouts with guidelines for developing codes and dialogue questions, newsprint, and markers. Each group identifies an issue that has come up with students at their site and develops a code and dialogue questions based on this issue. They write the code and questions on the newsprint.

b. <u>Presentation of codes</u> (45 min.): Each group acts out its code, and someone in it guides discussion using the dialogue questions. The newsprint is put up; the group provides feedback and reflects on the process.

The starting code about traditional versus nonformal teaching immediately triggered an animated response among participants. Although we had (perhaps naively) anticipated that the discussion would focus on which approach is more effective, they talked about students' expectations: they said that students often expect a traditional teacher who determines what needs to be taught; thus, it is important to combine aspects of both approaches, drawing on students' issues but at the same time including traditional methods to make them feel that it is "real" teaching. In addition, participants again raised the issue of context, arguing that the extent to which one's approach is traditional versus participatory depends on factors like the content of the class, the atmosphere, and the level. In this discussion, some Interns felt that the kind of conversation elicited in a participatory approach is appropriate for ESL class (because students need to develop speaking skills), but less important in first language literacy class. They also felt that higher levels expect more traditional teaching. Finally, they felt that the approach may vary depending on the mood of the class on a given day.

This led to a discussion of the function of a predetermined curriculum. One of the Interns said that it is difficult to implement a participatory approach as a new teacher because it requires so much thinking on your feet: she felt that new teachers need a minimum curriculum at the beginning which they can refer to. However, even the best planned lesson can fall flat unexpectedly: sometimes you have to change what you are doing mid-stream because something comes up or because students don't understand it. The coordinator then introduced the concept of the *emergent curriculum*, framing its goals in terms of trying to *uncover student needs* rather than only trying to *cover the curriculum*.

Finally, we ended this section by discussing why we had introduced this code: in addition to being an issue for teachers in the classroom, it is an issue in our own training. We talked about our own sense in the core group that Interns were expecting a more traditional approach to teacher training in which they would be told what to do and given prescriptions for techniques. We made explicit our own philosophy of training—that we hoped to model a participatory approach in the workshops.

In the next part of the workshop, when characteristics and examples of codes were presented, the first example of a code immediately evoked heated discussion. It was a code about the dynamics of language use and prompted people to talk about how intimidated they feel when someone speaks better English than they do. Another code about whether to learn Creole triggered responses primarily from the Haitian participants. We discussed why the codes elicited differential responses, noting that codes need to reflect familiar problems of the particular group of learners.

The final segment of the workshop focused on site-based groups developing their own codes. The Jackson-Mann (mixed ESL) group developed a code about using the first language in the ESL classroom. The Haitian Multi-Service Center group developed a code about students being too distracted by their worries about employment (no job, no money) to pay attention in class. The East Boston group developed a code about whether students feel ready to begin learning English, with some students wanting to get on with it while others want to continue with Spanish literacy. There were two notable points about the development of these codes: first, everyone felt that it was easy to agree on a problem or theme for the codes—each of the codes summarized the state of the classes at that site; second, each of the codes themselves triggered an outpouring of suggestions for "solutions" to the problem from participants from other sites, as well as a sharing of related experiences. While the Interns' initial response was to try to find the "correct" way of handling each issue, the facilitator proposed doing the code in class to work out alternatives or strategies with students.

In summary, the workshop affirmed the power of codes as a process to generate dialogue and creative thinking. In each of the situations where a code was presented, the Interns responded as though the issue were their own and jumped into the discussion. The challenge in this workshop was to get Interns to step back, think of the codes as teaching tools, and consider how they might be used with students. There are two further points that Interns made: the first is that we need to combine traditional and participatory approaches (rather than trying to focus exclusively on learner-driven curriculum) in order to meet learners' expectations in certain contexts; the second is that a certain degree of predetermined structure is necessary, not just for learners, but for the Interns, particularly as they begin their teaching, in order to give them a sense of security and direction.

Session 5: Socio-drama

Objectives

This session presents an additional tool for developing language and literacy while exploring student issues. It builds on the codes presented at the previous workshop and extends them to a range of theater applications in literacy education. In addition, because an outside presenter from another participatory literacy education program facilitated the workshop, Interns were able to see our own project as part of a larger participatory literacy education initiative. Objectives were:

- to reflect on Interns' practice using codes with their students
- to extend the applications of the code development process of the previous workshop
- to explore the rationale and processes of using theater techniques in literacy education
- to practice theater exercises which can be used with learners
- to hear about a related participatory literacy education project in New York

Overview of the session

1. Codes developed at sites (30 min.)

After a brief introduction of new participants and the presenter, sites present codes that they have developed since the previous workshop, explain why they developed them and how they followed up on it in class. In this case, two codes were presented, one about the use of the first language in ESL class and one about a woman who goes to the doctor with a back problem, and is given Tylenol and a bill for $80.

2. Uses of theater in literacy education (1 hr.)

Klaudia Rivera from El Barrio Popular Education Program in NYC presented this segment of the workshop. Her views of theater education are based on the work of Agosto Boal whose work emphasizes making theater a vehicle for popularizing culture, rather than entertaining the elite.

a. Rationale for using theater in literacy education: Klaudia said that there are many reasons for using theater in literacy education. It opens many possibilities and allows you to:

- create a special space in the classroom
- become somebody else
- convey a message quickly
- experiment with reality, to show reality in a different way and to imagine new possibilities

b. The process of using theater: Klaudia said that the process of using theater to address student issues is even more important than the actual performance (unlike in traditional theater where the ultimate goal is a polished performance). The process, like a lesson, is not static. It includes:

- finding an issue (from the community, school, etc.)
- making a code or skit with students: this is different from what was presented at the last workshop because *students are involved in making the code*
- using literacy: other students take notes as the skit is developing; at first they may write words, then sentences, and finally a script. They can take notes about what is good, what relates to their experience, and so on.
- doing social analysis: there is a constant process of revision and construction with acting and analysis woven together. As students are acting, if someone else says they had a similar

experience, Klaudia says, "Show it to me." Students all participate in showing their experiences related to a theme until the group finds what is common, the aspects that make it a general experience. This becomes a form of analysis: you try to discover through the process what is systematic in people's experiences. The teacher asks questions like, "Is the doctor personally like this or are doctors in general like this?" As participants review the skit, the teacher asks students to find places where the actors are acting in ways that impose systematic constraints on them. As people recognize the tools or strategies that limit them, they can begin to challenge them.

- **developing strategies**: Klaudia said that recognizing how the system imposes its strategies on you isn't enough; you have to have your own strategies. Usually, when you get home from the doctor, you think, "I should have done this.. .or said that...." Situations often repeat themselves. Theater allows you the space to rehearse strategies for doing things differently. Here it is important to remember that there are no right endings. Students should be invited to act out alternative strategies. As people make suggestions for how to respond to the doctor, the teacher says, "Show me." After students act out their strategies, she asks, "Would this really happen?" As students share stories and strategies, they see that problems they have internalized as their personal problems are general.

3. Demonstration of theater exercises for classroom use (1 hr.)

a. Concentration exercise: Everyone stands in a circle and the leader starts a clapping pattern, asking everyone to pass it around; each one does the same exercise with the next person (the purpose is to relax people and get them to concentrate).

b. Body images: Klaudia said that there are ways to form images other than pictures. She divided the group in two and asked each group to think of two words that had social meaning for them. One group then acted out the word in a static image or pose. The other group then moved the people around to create a group image. By chance both groups chose the word homelessness. Klaudia asked each group to find a pose for this word. Then the subgroups looked around to see how others had made this image. We talked about this as a way to explore stereotypes. Another word was discrimination. After one group had made the images, Klaudia asked the others to choose an image that reminded them of something in their own experience. This could become a catalyst for individual writing or for developing a group play.

c. Classroom uses: Klaudia elicited ways the exercises could be used in class. Ideas were:

- Divide the class in half; one half acts out a socially important word and the others guess what their image represents. They write about what they see and how it relates to their lives.
- Use these exercises when students are tired.
- Use these exercises when students are having a hard time concentrating because they're worried; ask students to choose a word that represents something they're worried about and act it out. They can go on to write key words, a short play, and so on, depending on their level.

5. El Barrio Popular Education Program (25 min.)

Several points in Klaudia's description of the El Barrio Program were particularly relevant for us:
- The classes are based on students' experiences; student writings are published in a yearly magazine which becomes a kind of evaluation tool.
- The curriculum is connected to the community. Students do research and writing about issues in their community.
- The eventual goal of the program is complete community control. Students participate in the board and get leadership training.

Reflections

This workshop was characterized by an increasingly active and critical role on the part of the Interns. The first indication of this growing participation by Interns was the fact that they began the session by presenting skits that they had developed as a result of the previous training workshop. Two of the sites had identified themes from within their own learner groups, written codes according to the guidelines we had presented, tried them with their students, and come to our session prepared to share them with the group. By beginning with their skits and incorporating something they had developed into the training, we were able to create an explicit link between the Interns' practice and the Saturday sessions.

The second indication of the growing critical awareness on the part of Interns was reflected in the questions that they posed to the outside presenter. Rather than accepting Klaudia's presentation unquestioningly, they engaged in a lively and active discussion, bringing up their hesitations and concerns about the approach she was presenting. For example, when Klaudia suggested involving students in making a code about their own problem (rather than just making a code for them based on what the teacher has observed), one of the Interns asked, "What if the students don't want to show or talk about an issue because it may hurt someone?" Klaudia responded by explaining how to decide which issues may be suitable for theater work: in some cases, you know an issue is probably safe if it comes up in the context of a group discussion; in other cases, an issue may arise in a personal, one-to-one conversation and you know it is actually a group issue, but rather than presenting it directly, you may deal with it from an outside position, bringing in a stimulus from outside the class. Another example of a critical question occurred when Klaudia suggested that some learners should record the language and the action while others are acting; someone asked how this can be done quickly if the participants either don't speak the same language or are limited in their writing ability. Klaudia responded that for the purposes of this exercise, people can document what is happening in their own language, writing it any way they hear it or can represent it.

Another important aspect of this session was the fact that it situated our project in a larger context and showed participants that other programs are approaching their work in a similar manner. Because the El Barrio project has a much longer history, and is more established in pursing a participatory approach, it gave participants a sense of the potential of the work we are doing. In addition, Klaudia invited Interns to participate in a meeting of community-based educators in NYC later in the summer, thus creating a concrete link between our project and others. This connection to something beyond our particular programs and city added a certain legitimacy to the approach, showing that although the participatory and native language literacy orientation is not "mainstream," it is gaining increasing acceptance.

Participants' active engagement with the workshop continued after the session was over, as evidenced by what they did in their classrooms and what they said in their evaluations. One Intern asked to have a copy of the Boal book to read; several others followed up with theater exercises in their classes. One of the new Interns at the Haitian Center, for example, used the exercises in class when she noticed that students were particularly down—worried about finding work, and so on. She started with the warm-up exercises as a way to loosen people up, get them motivated and less distracted by their worries. Then she had the class divide into two groups and explained that the exercise was a way to help them get started with a dialogue/story (they were having trouble deciding on what they wanted to write about). Each group chose a word that had social meaning for them; the words they chose were *pov* (poor) and *maladi* (illness). One group acted while the other reacted. Then she wrote sentences on the board based on what they had seen and described. Many of the Interns commented on how much they liked the workshop because it was active; this comment seemed to implicitly challenge the view that training is "good" when it involves transmission of information.

A Party: Between Sessions 5 and 6, we had a party in which everyone brought food and music from their home countries. Many of the Interns commented on the fact that they appreciated this chance to get to know each other outside the context of work. Parties go a long way toward consolidating groups!

Session 6: The Photostory

Objectives

In this session, we invited a literacy educator from the Boston area, Cathy Walsh, to explore how popular education techniques which had been developed in Latin American could be applied in North America. The specific focus of this workshop was a model of learner-generated literacy materials (the photostory) that addresses issues of the social context. The objectives of this session were:

- to demonstrate processes for connecting social analysis to literacy development
- to show how one learner-generated materials project developed from beginning to end
- to model additional tools for participatory curriculum development (problem-posing trees, photo-stories, and mapping)
- to continue to connect the work of the project to a broader international context

Overview of the session

1. **Introduction** of the context and rationale for the workshop (20 min.)

The focus of the workshop is a project in an urban high school involving students from Puerto Rico, Haiti, and Central America with limited first language literacy and schooling. Cathy began by arguing that popular education techniques developed in Latin America are particularly suitable for this group of students because the traditional approach only makes them feel that they don't know anything themselves, whereas a participatory approach:

- uses learners' knowledge
- builds upon their collective concerns
- actively engages learners in the processes of developing their own knowledge and skill
- situates learners in what they are learning so that they have a reason to develop their literacy
- promotes dialogue as students learn from each other by listening
- leads to action and an opportunity to change the situation in their community.

2. **Generating photostories** (step-by-step description of the process; 1 hr., 30 min.):

a. Photographs as codes: One technique for starting group photostories is to show a photograph on an overhead projector. This process helps everyone to focus on one thing. Cathy demonstrated with a photo of a person in a doorway. This photo, when shown to the high school students, was accompanied by dialogue about what they saw, why the person was there, how he felt, whether there was a problem, and whether they had ever felt the way they thought he felt. The students then brainstorm what the picture makes them think about and the teacher writes down key words while students are talking. These become initial words for literacy work.

b. Problem-posing trees: Because students may have trouble with an abstract discussion of the issues that they identify during the brainstorming session, Cathy draws a picture of a tree to symbolize the problem under consideration. This symbol takes the focus off the purely linguistic level and shifts the focus to social analysis. In the tree image, the trunk of the tree represents the problem, the roots represent the causes, the branches and leaves represent the results or effects of the problem and a watering can represents possible solutions or strategies for addressing it. Participants can then draw symbols to represent their view of each aspect of the problem (if they are not yet able to write words). The following diagram represents the way workshop participants analyzed the problem which emerged from the photo code:

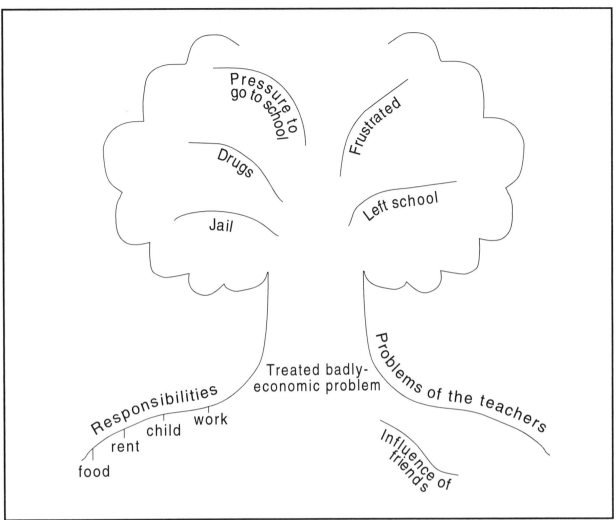

Problem-posing tree developed by workshop participants

Cathy pointed out that if you focus only on the cause of problems, students may feel fatalistic while if you focus on things to change, they might feel more positive. She says that for a tree to grow and bear fruit, it needs nourishment; she uses the watering can to frame questions like, "What will we put in the soil to change the roots? What can we do to confront discrimination?" Cathy suggests using a tree each time you start a new theme to frame analysis and elicit participants' views.

c. Generating a story: Once an issue has been identified and analyzed, the group works together to generate a story using the original picture as a catalyst. The advantage of using a photo is that students don't have to talk about themselves but can project their issues and concerns onto the person in the picture. The students give the person in the picture a name (in this case Julian) and talk about him without having to expose themselves. They discuss the treatment he receives in school, and his economic problems, the roots of the problem (in this case, responsibilities for his work, child, rent and food, the influence of his friends, problems with teachers, suspensions, lack of respect, tardiness). They identify effects such as drugs, jail, a court which obliged him to go back to school, and leaving home. The students in Cathy's group wanted Julian to go back to school and went on to generate reasons for him to come back.

d. <u>Drawing your way into literacy</u>: When Cathy suggested writing Julian's story, they initially said, "We don't know how to read and write—we can't do this." To get students into the process of writing a story, Cathy told them to think of three ideas related to the story and draw pictures representing those ideas. She then told them to write about the drawings, helping each other in small groups. The students put their writings on the wall and discussed them in a large group. They expanded on ideas of each small group and continued the dialogue, bringing in their own stories. It took Cathy's group eight 1 hour sessions to develop a story in this way.

e. <u>Putting the photostory together</u>: As the students develop the story, they take on different roles and responsibilities. Someone acts as director, recording which are the strongest pictures. Someone takes notes about the pictures, and some take photos based on the notes. After the pictures are taken, the story goes through another revision process. New issues may emerge during the process. In Julian's case, once the story had him deciding to go back to school, the question of what would happen when he went back arose. This led students to focus on their lives in schools, and on the rules that seemed to push them out. They discussed where school rules come from, who wrote them, and decided to rewrite three of the rules.

f. <u>Producing the photostory</u>: If students decide they want to publish their story (make it public), they face issues of editing, typing, lay-out, and so on. The decision-making process in Cathy's group was in the students' hands: they formed an editorial board, learned how to do word processing, made decisions about editing, etc. The responsibility for production was theirs.

g. <u>Action</u>: Ideally, the function of the process goes beyond literacy work to address the issue which gave rise to the story. In the case of Cathy's project, students organized a book party to which they invited family, friends, and school administration, resulting in some changes in the rules and a new respect for the learners.

3. **Mapping** (30 min.)

a. <u>Rationale</u>: To extend our discussion of linking literacy work to social analysis, Cathy introduced the technique of mapping which is used in Latin America. Mapping is:

- a strategy for identifying and documenting issues
- a way to record and facilitate discussion and dialogue
- a way to think in visual rather than verbal form
- a way to situate and analyze aspects of participants' lives in a broader context
- a way to connect individual or group issues to social institutions
- a way to facilitate critical thinking

b. <u>Process</u>: The mapping process involves a three-step process: 1)drawing important issues in participants' lives, asking them what life is like for them (usually relating to church, community, employment); 2) connecting the issue to institutions (drawing surrounding institutions that affect the problem area, and asking questions like "Why is the factory closed?"); and 3) looking at broader social factors (what are the power structures that shape the experiences of their lives?).

c. <u>Practice</u>: Participants look at sample mapping exercises and then break into groups to do their own mapping exercises related to three issues that they face (in this case as literacy workers). In our session, the issues were: learners' attitudes toward teachers/Interns based on their status, language background, race/ethnicity; learners' preoccupations with social problems that impede learning; barriers to implementing a participatory approach, such as students' attitudes toward assessment.

As in the previous session, participants immediately jumped into the exercises, bringing their own experiences and analyses to the theme that Cathy's students had identified. The duality of their roles as both immigrants and teachers enabled them to relate to the substance of the issue (in this case, discrimination that language minority students often face in schooling) and to the teaching dynamics of utilizing this approach. Thus, for example, the tree exercise prompted one of the Interns to talk about how she had experienced the high school students' issue herself in her first class at community college (when a teacher told her she would not pass the class just because English wasn't her first language). Interns also became very involved in discussion of the analysis of root causes of the students' dropping out of school; one of them posed the questions, "Who is responsible for making people not get an education?" and "Why doesn't the government want some people to get ahead?" This brought up a discussion of discrimination and its functions.

In terms of teaching issues, Interns also responded with their own understandings of the realities of classroom life, sometimes challenging the presenter with very specific questions about implementation. For example, one Intern asked whether Cathy introduces the letters of the alphabet before beginning the problem-posing trees with initial literacy students. Another Intern asked, "How you do these trees in an ESL class where some students expect a traditional grammar-based approach?" Another asked, "What if students are bored with social analysis and want mechanical exercises? How do you change their attitudes?" And one Intern told the story of his own ESL teacher meeting with great resistance when she asked students to bring pictures to class. Just the fact that the Interns felt confident enough to ask these questions of an "outside expert" revealed a change in their view of themselves and their knowledge. Cathy responded with specific examples from her own practice (e.g., "I tell them that this helps me create what we will do in class. I need to know what you think. I need to learn. We will do grammar, reading and writing in order to make this relevant to you. This is my form of taking notes. This is what I need."). With this kind of sharing, the tone of the workshop was one of dialogue between knowledgeable peers rather than one of an expert telling novices what to do.

In the final segment of the workshop, when Cathy asked participants to map specific issues from their own practice at the sites, they were immediately able to pinpoint issues; for example, Interns from one site drew a picture of registration day at the site, with most of the students signing up for the North American teacher's class and few signing up for the classes of the Hispanic teachers. Another site drew a student who was lost in thought about money, Haiti, and the White House. Although we didn't have time to fully explore this tool, the fact that it was relatively easy to pinpoint these issues revealed how reflective the Interns had become about their practice. In addition, it helped us to identify some training issues and laid the groundwork for the following session in which we applied the problem-posing process to teaching issues in a more systematic way.

The evaluation of the workshop at the sites revealed several points about the Interns' development as well as revealing a training issue. First of all, the Interns' growing sense of confidence was confirmed by the fact that they openly acknowledged that they really didn't understand the mapping exercise (because of time constraints). Secondly, the Interns exhibited a new level of comfort with evaluating in a critical and two-sided way (rather than feeling they had to give only positive feedback): on the one hand, some questioned the feasibility of doing the tree exercise with beginning literacy students (saying that students might not have the skills to do it or be too "lazy" to think critically); on the other, there was a very positive reaction to the photostory idea. The training issue that was raised for us concerned the relationship between the workshops and implementation of the ideas in the classrooms: the heated discussion about the purposes and value of doing problem-posing trees in the on-site evaluations indicated to us that *on-site follow-up is key in making the transition from the training to implementation.* It allowed Interns to ask questions, express doubts, and through the process of explaining their understandings to each other, take ownership of the ideas. They were able to internalize what they had learned and think about ways of applying it in their own work as they explained it to each other. In terms of actual implementation, the process was uneven: all of the sites decided to use photos and transparencies as tools for catalyzing discussion. The workshop inspired one Intern to embark on a photostory project with her students.

Session 9: Where We've Been, Where We're Going

This session will be presented in a different format because its structure differed from that of other workshops. We had invited an outside presenter to talk about literacy campaigns in Latin America as a response to earlier requests. However, the night before the session, the presenter had to cancel for personal reasons. We decided on the spur-of-the-moment to use the occasion to report back and reflect on the New York City Conference, as well as assess past and future directions. The session was thus divided into three parts. First, people who had been to the New York conference shared what they had learned and their reactions with people who had not been able to attend. Second, we talked about what people did and didn't like about the trainings to date. Third, we generated a list of topics for future workshops.

During the part when people shared reactions to the conference, Interns spoke with ease and confidence about the sessions they had attended; there was a genuine sense of exchange. Everyone had an experience that they had something to say about. They were, as Ana said later in the evaluation, being themselves and sharing feelings, owning what they had to say. During this discussion, Elsa asked if people had felt uncomfortable about the fact that there had been so much focus on the political nature of literacy work. This triggered a heated discussion, with some people arguing that politics had no place in the classroom, others arguing that literacy is always inherently political, and still others asking for clarification, definitions, or taking a middle position.

During the evaluation of past sessions, people said that they liked both the sessions we did ourselves and the ones when outside presenters were invited. Some people said again that we should provide more concrete teaching techniques and skills work. There was also a sense that the terminology and readings were at times too technical/difficult to understand; the way things are worded is not always accessible.

Reflections

After the workshop, Julio said that this session supported his belief that formality isn't always the best approach. The fact that we didn't plan the workshop (or that our plan fell through) turned out to be a good thing: it was one of the best workshops we had had. He said that in Haitian culture, when there is a discussion, the way one shows knowledge is by making a statement with a challenge or disagreement at the end of it; in meetings, people take the opportunity to challenge ideas, so that discussions are more self-generating, less preplanned. The Anglo idea of preparing everything carefully may not work in Haitian society. Thus, this session seemed to him to be more culturally congruent than some that were so carefully scheduled in terms of sequences of activities.

The section on planning future workshops highlighted some interesting contradictions: in terms of workshop process, on the one hand, everyone participated eagerly and said it was one of the best sessions we had had. Yet, when it came time to think about future sessions, they said they wanted outside experts to come in. In some ways, this is exactly what happens in class: students may say they want the teacher to tell them what to do and to teach traditional grammar lessons, but often the lessons they like best and are most engaged in are the ones that center on a student issues and are least 'traditional' in format; yet, even after they see this, they still ask for grammar the next time.

In terms of workshop content, a similar contradiction arose. People were most engaged in the discussion about politics and said they wanted to explore this issue more; yet, most of the other sessions that were suggested were of a more teaching methods/strategies nature (e.g., learning games and techniques for making the transition from Native Language Literacy to ESL). In our staff discussions after the session, we traced this problem (the concern with methods training) in part to the title of our project: because the project is called a *training* project, participants bring a training schema to it, expecting that they will learn specific skills and techniques. For the remaining workshops, the project staff tried to address these contradictions by continuing to create structures that integrated substantive presentations in a participatory format and by including content about teaching techniques as well as loaded pedagogical issues.

Session 10: What Does Politics Have to Do with Literacy?

Objectives

As a result of the discussion at the previous session, it was clear that some participants resisted the Freirean notion of linking literacy work with socio-political analysis and change. This resistance was based in part on their notion of equating politics with wars, political parties, racism, etc. and their feeling that these "heavy" issues had no place in the literacy classroom. Objectives were:

- to allow participants to make explicit their views about and resistances to politics in the classroom
- to demystify the term *politics*
- to examine how political relationships are manifested in day-to-day experiences
- to show how politics enters into literacy teaching whether we recognize it or not
- to demonstrate concrete ways of integrating political analysis into literacy teaching.

Overview of the session

1. Introductions - icebreaker (20 min.)

Each participant shares two things about him or herself that others in the group don't know.

2. Nightmare skits (45 min.)

a. Introduction of workshop: The facilitator explains why we've chosen to do this workshop. Freire and others stressed at the conference that education is never neutral and that everything you do in the classroom is political. Because not everyone is comfortable with this notion, the purpose of the workshop is to explore it further, to look at how we view politics, and how it relates to literacy work.

b. Small group discussion of fears: In three small groups, participants discuss their worst nightmares, fears, and experiences about bringing politics into the classroom.

c. Making skits: Each group creates and presents a 2-minute skit depicting a nightmare of bringing politics into the classroom.

d. Whole group discussion: After each skit, the facilitator asks, "What is this nightmare?" (naming the fear) and "How is politics represented or defined in this skit?" She then asks, "What else counts as politics? What else could be called political?" The group considers alternatives.

3. The banana exercise - What counts as politics? (30 min.)

The facilitator brings in a banana. She asks, "Who thinks that this banana represents a political issue?" She then goes on with the following kinds of questions:

- Where does the banana come from?
- Who grew it? How was it produced?
- What does the sticker on it symbolize?
- How did it get here?
- Who benefits the most from it?
- How does the banana relate to your experience?

After the discussion of political and economic relationships represented by the banana, the group comes back to the question of defining what is political. The notion that political relationships are embedded in everyday, taken-for-granted objects and experiences is explored.

4. Examining political aspects of literacy materials (45 min.)

Two examples of ESL literacy materials from published texts are projected on the overhead. One shows a seemingly cheerful worker who fixes TVs without complaining because she needs the money for her rent. It appears to be a rather straightforward lesson with no obvious issue raised. The other shows a refugee being interviewed for a job in a hospital kitchen; although he was a college math teacher, he is offered a job washing dishes. It poses the problem of underemployment quite directly. The facilitator asks the following questions:

- What do you see here?
- Do you see any political aspects implicit in either of these?
- What message do you think each sends?
- What is the view of the learner in each?
- What is the view of work and the worker's role?
- How do you think students would react to each?
- What might you do/how would you follow up on each of these in class?

The discussion draws out the fact that there may be an underlying political message in even the most neutral-seeming materials. Although wrapped in a nice story, the TV example seems to imply that the worker has to be quiet even though she is overworked and underpaid because otherwise she will lose her job. In the other story, the discussion questions invite learners to look at the story critically, relate it to their own experience and explore alternatives. Often the political dimension is implicit in the ways learners are viewed, the choices offered them, or the roles projected onto them. Even when we think lessons are nonpolitical, they contain hidden messages about how students relate to their social context (in this case, work) and what they can do about it. Thus, whether or not we recognize it, we are always making choices about politics in terms of what we teach and how we teach it.

5. Connecting politics with teaching literacy: a video example (30 min.)

An example from the video series Workplays (SMU Labor Education Center) is shown. The clip is of an Asian man who is laid off even though he has seniority over a North American man. The group views the video and discusses how the tape might be used in an ESL/literacy class with previewing, predicting, listening exercises, vocabulary work, presentation of legal information, reading exercises, and so on. The group discusses the power of using a real story (as presented in the video) as opposed to just introducing an abstract political concept like discrimination.

6. What next? Classroom applications (30 min.)

The facilitator asks the group to brainstorm about what they have gotten out of the workshop that they might use in the classroom. Participants share any new understandings they have gotten from the workshop.

The icebreaker, although simple, was powerful because it gave people the chance to share something from a part of their lives that group members didn't know about: for example, someone talked about being separated from her husband and someone else talked about being afraid to speak out because of fear of being judged.

The nightmare skits confirmed the core staff's perception that Interns were defining politics as relating to "heavy" and global issues. In one skit, learners are talking among themselves about losing their relatives in war; the teacher comes in and tells them to think about why they are all in the U.S. and can't go home. The students become silent; when the teacher asks why, they say they don't want to talk about it. The second skit was about Martin Luther King; when the learners in the skit react to a reading, a disagreement erupts: one student says there is still discrimination in the world and the other says there is no problem. The teachers changes the subject to food. The third skit, like the first, raises the question of the learners' situations in their home country. In this case, one teacher reads a poem about El Salvador and another, who is not Salvadoran, complains that the content is not appropriate. The teachers start to argue, the first one saying that the second doesn't know anything about the situation in El Salvador. In each case, politics was defined as addressing global issues that are extremely loaded and was brought into the classroom in a direct and explicit way by the teacher; the teacher seemed to be imposing his or her agenda and students were resisting it. In discussion, Interns said that students don't want to talk about politics because it reminds them of their horrible experiences at home (war, killing, losing relatives, fighting); they expressed fear about introducing anything political because it may lead to a fight among students. However, through discussion, participants came to an understanding that the discomfort may arise, first, from the way they have been defining politics and, second, from the way it was introduced by the teachers in the skits.

The banana exercise followed nicely from the second skit, in which the teacher shifted to food as a "neutral" topic. After going through the discussion questions about the banana (which elicited the notion of the power relations and multinational politics involved in the production, marketing, exporting, and consumption of food), we talked about two ways of dealing with *banana* in a literacy classroom: traditionally, the word would be introduced, broken into syllables or syllable families, and used in sentences. In the second way, the presentation of the word would be contextualized in discussion linking it to learners' lives (using questions like those we went through together). The exercise showed an alternative both to a traditional mechanical lesson and to an explicitly political one.

The discussion of the two sets of materials demonstrated the effectiveness of bringing the social context into the classroom in a problem-posing way. Although the first lesson elicited little reaction, the second one (with the college teacher being interviewed for a dishwashing job) evoked immediate and animated response: it represented precisely the situation of several of the Interns who had higher education in their homelands and were working in factories or hotels here. As such, it demonstrated how this approach to bringing day-to-day politics into the classroom can trigger communication, generating both language use and critical thinking. The video excerpt evoked the same kind of energetic response. Discussion centered around discrimination against Haitian refugees by the INS, political asylum, the differences in the ways that Haitians and Hispanics are discriminated against. In both cases, participants felt that their own stories were represented by the codes in the lessons. In reflecting on the video, we noted that the force of the response came from the fact that the issue had been introduced through a story that participants could relate to rather than by the teacher introducing a general political concept (like "Discrimination" with a capital D!).

In the evaluation, Interns said that they felt clearer about the concept of politics and somewhat relieved to find that it can be seen more broadly than as just focusing on heavy issues. They liked the banana exercise because it illustrated the point about the politics in daily life so concretely and helped them to see how we take everyday things for granted without thinking about what's behind them. One criticism the staff had in the post-workshop evaluation was that, while talking about not imposing our views on students and allowing them to come to their own conclusions, the coordinator (me!) did not leave enough time for participants to come to their own conclusions and offered interpretations too quickly. Workshop leaders, like teachers, need to learn to wait for participants to figure things out for themselves!

Session 11: Working with Transitional and Beginning ESL Students

Objectives

The motivation for this workshop came from the fact that many of the students who had begun native language literacy during the past year were now making the transition to ESL and that several of the Interns were now teaching beginning ESL independently. The objectives of the session were:

- to identify difficulties Interns were experiencing working with these levels
- to develop a framework and guiding principles for teaching these levels
- to demonstrate a range of techniques for working with these levels
- to demonstrate a process for integrating topics, activities, and skills work
- to integrate mechanical aspects of teaching with creative aspects

Overview of the session

1. **Conference planning** (45 min.)

   The Project was invited to make a presentation at a state-wide ESL educators conference. We spent the first part of this workshop planning our presentation (which was similar to the one in NYC).

2. **Problem identification** (15 min.)

   Participants brainstorm a list of problems encountered in teaching transitional ESL or beginning ESL. In this session, the list included:

   - how to explain a new word
   - many first languages in the same class
   - how to keep students involved, interested
   - how to balance repetition with new information
   - how to get people talking
   - how to deal with students who are expecting a White, Anglo teacher

3. **A framework and guiding principles: video and discussion** (30 min.)

   In this section, a video, "The ABC's of ESL: Developing Literacy" (Teacher To Teacher series, New Readers' Press) is presented. The video focuses on teaching colors to a beginning ESL literacy class.

   a. Brainstorming: Before viewing the video, the group brainstorms as many activities as they can for teaching colors to a beginning ESL/literacy class.

   b. Viewing of video: As participants view the video, they note each technique and activity that the teacher uses to present colors.

   c. Responding to the video: First, participants give their gut reactions to the video, responding to the questions, "How do you think your students would react to this class?" and "What did you like/not like about this video?" Then the group analyzes exactly what the teacher did, listing techniques and activities. They go on to discuss, "What else could you do to teach colors?" and "How is this similar to/different from what you do?", comparing the list generated before viewing the video to what the teacher in the video did.

d. <u>Generalizing to guiding principles</u>: From the discussion of the video and participants' experiences, general guidelines for working with transitional/beginning ESL classes are generated; our group came up with the following guidelines:

- involve students in choosing the topic
- start with what they already know: letters, words, L1 literacy, experiences
- elicit their experiences, stories, ideas (using any means possible: drawing, L1, etc.)
- use the classroom environment (pictures, objects, space, etc.)
- encourage students to work together and help each other
- use nonlinguistic, visual support: photos, pictures, charts, time lines, drawing...
- involve learners actively: movement, physical activity, mime, games
- combine several activities for the same topic
- combine speaking, listening, reading, writing
- provide some structure (chart, model sentences, etc.) but let student provide content
- make sure English work is meaningful and in context; don't present isolated words unrelated to the topic

4. **Presentation on techniques** (45 min.)

Each of the Master Teachers and the Curriculum Specialist gives an example (with handouts) of his or her work with transitional/beginning ESL students, including:

- a technique for identifying a topic and developing activities related to it
- techniques for eliciting and exploring student ideas once a topic has been chosen
  - -pictures
  - -clustering
  - -charts
- time lines: a technique for learning about students' backgrounds, helping them get to know each other and develop language from content related to their lives
- techniques for following up with ESL vocabulary and grammar once a topic has been chosen and explored:
  - -using the native language as a bridge to ESL vocabulary
  - -language experience stories
  - -*wh-* questions
  - -flash cards
  - -copying and matching exercises
  - -cloze exercises

5. **Lesson planning** (30 min.)

Participants work in small groups with others from their site to design activities to identify a topic, elicit student ideas, explore the topic, and follow up on it with vocabulary/grammar exercises. Because the other segments of this session took longer than expected, we did not get to this segment; however, a workshop that did not include the 45-minute conference preparation could include this activity.

Reflections

The video was used to trigger reaction: it served as a kind of mirror for reflecting on the Interns' own practice. It confirmed how much they already know and the strength of their critical framework. In the discussion, Interns noted that many of the activities that the teacher in the video did were similar to those they had mentioned in the previewing brainstorming or already do in their classes. They did get new ideas about using physical activities and puzzles to encourage students to work together. One Intern especially liked the variety of activities that were combined. However, they also criticized several aspects of what they saw: one Intern said that her students wouldn't want to spend 2 hours working on colors; another said that his students might find the games and teaching style too childish. A key point in the discussion revolved around the fact that the teacher didn't do much to draw out the students' experiences; at the end of the video we didn't know anything about the students (except how to say *rainbow* in different languages). Several Interns also mentioned that these techniques might not work for everyone: in reality, each group is different and it is up to the teacher to try things out and evaluate them.

Most importantly, the video demystified the notion that "experts" have all the answers or that there is a particular set of techniques that should be used for this level. It made Interns realize how much they already know, and that, in fact, they may be more in touch with students than "professional" literacy educators. The fact that they stressed the need for teachers to experiment and evaluate for themselves indicated movement away from the stance of mechanically applying a standard set of techniques and toward inquiry-oriented practice. From the perspective of the core group, the video seemed a particularly effective tool for eliciting discussion because it was concrete, external, and visual. Because the presentation came from outside our group and was not live, everyone felt especially comfortable about being critical. They also liked seeing how a "real" ESL teacher worked and were amazed at what this caused them to realize about their own work.

The presentation of techniques by the Master Teachers and Curriculum Specialist was especially well-received because it was very concrete. Interns particularly appreciated the many handouts. The combination of a broad conceptual framework and very down-to-earth activities was useful. It is also important to note that the Interns did not approach the handouts with the view "I can use this in my class..." but rather, "This gives me an idea for something I can develop in my class..." In other words, Interns saw both the relevance of particular activities and the importance of adapting them to fit their own situations. Taken together, the reactions to the video and the presentation indicated a significant shift in Interns' attitudes: although they appreciated the new information, they no longer wanted someone to tell them what to do. Rather, they saw the techniques as resources to draw on in developing their own curriculum.

Finally, of course, the issue of trying to do too much in a single workshop was particularly evident: in our attempt to address the Interns' demand for practical classroom techniques, we probably tried to pack in too much, so that we didn't have time for the segment bridging the workshop back to practice. Nevertheless, the Interns who had previously been most concerned with mechanical aspects of teaching felt that this was the best workshop so far because it addressed the needs of low-level students, it included a great deal that could be directly adapted for the classroom, and it was relevant not just to ESL, but to L1 literacy as well.

In our post-workshop staff evaluation, this feedback from the Interns prompted Byron to ask whether we need to rethink the way we approach the sequence of trainings. We had started by presenting a rationale and broad overview of the participatory (nontraditional) approach, but he wondered if it might not have been better to start with presenting the more traditional approach first, allowing Interns to try out more mechanical techniques before introducing alternatives. He said that they may need to see in practice how the traditional methods work before they can understand their limitations and embrace alternatives. Of course, the dilemma is, do we want to train people to do something that we feel is less effective or start right out with the approach that we support?

Session 12: Games for Native Language Literacy and ESL

Objectives

At the previous workshop, one of the Interns had given the group a packet of teaching games. The core group then invited him to prepare this workshop with the Curriculum Specialist. Objectives were:

- to develop Intern leadership in designing and conducting a workshop
- to demonstrate a range of games which participants can use in their classes
- to elicit other games that participants have used
- to have fun!

Overview of the Session

1. Demonstration of games (2 hr.)

For each game, there are 5 minutes of explanation, 5 to 10 minutes for playing the game, and 5 to 10 minutes for discussion. Discussion addresses what participants find useful/dislike about the game, how they might adapt it to teach their group and what variations might be developed to teach different content. Games (with handouts describing the purpose, materials, preparation, and procedure for each game) included:

- Pictionary (to review vocabulary)
- Do what it says (a board game with index cards that can be used to teach vocab, verbs, etc.)
- Bingo (to review math, vocab, grammar, etc.)
- Guess what I'm thinking (to review question formation)
- Alphabet game (to review alphabetical order)
- Paper bag game (vocab and question formation)
- Category game (vocab and question formation)

2. Sharing games (30 min.)

During this time, anyone in the group can share a game (by teaching it to others or describing it) with the whole group. In our session, games included a word search, a mime game for teaching daily routines, a telephone game, and a guessing game.

Reflections

Everyone reacted positively to this workshop because it was active, practical, and not too cerebral. Of course, the most significant aspect of this workshop was the fact that it was led by one of the Interns. Discussion after each game revealed a balance of concern with the logistics of each game (how you introduce it and adapt it for various levels/content areas, etc.) and concern with linking it to a meaningful context. The Intern presenter stressed the importance of linking a game to preceding work: for example, a word game might be introduced after work on a story, using key words from the story. He emphasized the need to have a context, saying that if you present words without preparation, students will be lost. For example, in the category game, one group names a category, brainstorms a list of ideas associated with that category, and erases the name of the category; the other group looks at the list and tries to guess the category. This game is a way to bring out concerns from people's daily lives; the categories that small groups chose were: unemployment, money, and Paulo Freire; the brainstorming served as a humorous review of concepts we had been struggling with (conscientization, politics, education, and so on).

Session 14: Assessing Student Progress

Objectives

As the end of the project was drawing near and we were thinking about the impact of our work, we decided to focus on tools for assessing student progress. Objectives were:

- to identify the range of ways of doing assessment already in use in the project
- to evaluate these existing tools (advantages, limitations)
- to present a framework for alternative evaluation in order to broaden the range of tools
- to demonstrate several alternative tools
- to evaluate these tools in terms of participants' teaching contexts
- to develop a plan for implementing some alternative tools

Overview of the Session

1. What do you already do to evaluate progress? (30 min.)

The coordinator presents the context of this workshop: As we think about reporting about the impact of this project, what would you say about progress students have made? What can they do now that they couldn't do before? How do you know? Participants discuss these questions in site-based small groups, listing responses on newsprint:

WHAT PROGRESS?	HOW DO YOU KNOW? Assessment Tools

2. What is the range of tools used in the project? What do you like/dislike about each? (15 min.)

Small groups report back to the whole group; a "master list" of tools used in the project is generated. The tools are grouped in two categories—formal and informal tools. Two charts are made to evaluate the advantages of formal and informal assessment.

Formal Assessment		Informal Assessment	
advantages	disadvantages	advantages	disadvantages

3. <u>Presentation - What are some alternatives?</u> (with handouts; 30 min.)

a. <u>Summary of critiques</u>: The coordinator summarizes the advantages and disadvantages of formal assessment tools (like tests) from the lists generated by the group; she then does the same for informal tools. This discussion is then linked to the debate within the field of adult education; the Interns' critiques are similar to many of the critiques from researchers. The challenge is to combine the good features of both kinds of assessment, developing a systematic assessment framework that includes better documentation of informal assessment as well as some formal assessment.

b. <u>Rationale and principles of alternative assessment</u>: The coordinator gives an overview of where the field has come in terms of alternative assessment. She stresses that assessment should be program-based and learner-centered; it should help students reach their own goals, build on their strengths, and not just look for weaknesses; it should be connected to learning, rather than separate from it; it should not depend on a single tool or procedure (like a test) but include many kinds of feedback.

c. <u>Organizing assessment</u>: The facilitator presents a general framework for categorizing assessment tools (tools that are used BEFORE, DURING, and AFTER an instructional cycle). She presents examples of start-up tools, tools for ongoing use, and end-of-cycle tools.

4. <u>Evaluating alternative assessment tools</u> (30 min.)[2]

Participants divide into three groups and are given a packet of start-up tools, ongoing tools, and end-of-cycle tools, respectively (one packet per group). Each packet contains at least five examples ranging from more formal (e.g., BEST Test items) to more informal (inventories, observation checklists). They evaluate the tools in their packet using the following guiding questions:

- What is this tool? What does it assess?
- How should it be used?
- What do you like or dislike about it?
- Could you imagine using it with your students? Why/why not?
- How might you change it to make it more useful?
- What else do you use to assess the same thing?

5. <u>Sharing tools</u> (30 min.)

The whole group reconvenes and each group presents one or two of the tools it likes best from the packet. They explain what it might be used for, why they like it, and how it can be adapted.

6. <u>Action plans</u> (30 min.)

Participants go back to small groups with others from their own site and select something from the workshop that they would like to pursue at their sites. Discussion guidelines are

- Of all the tools and procedures we discussed today, which ones did you especially like?
- Which seemed most useful for your students?
- Discuss the steps you may take to adapt these tools for use at your site.

---

[2]Thanks to Loren McGrail for inspiring this exercise.

Reflections

Ironically, it was in this last workshop that we were able to most successfully deal with many of the training issues we had struggled with throughout the life of the project: the workshop fit nicely with the model of 1) starting with participants' experiences; 2) analyzing that experience by looking for patterns and making generalizations; 3) presenting new information in a theoretical framework; 4) exploring specific classroom activities in-depth and practicing new skills; 5) reconvening for further reflection; and 5) developing an action plan to link the workshop to practice. It combined a very practical, methodological orientation with broader, social-contextual analysis; there was a balance between eliciting, presenting, and engaging in hands-on activities. The logistics were smooth in terms of not packing in too much, yet allowing for a range of participant structures and activities.

The idea of starting with the questions, "What can your students do now that they couldn't do before?" and "How do you know?" was effective in eliciting both the formal and informal ways of assessing students. If the question had been "How do you assess students?" the responses would probably have focused mainly on the formal tools. As it was, Interns mentioned both formal tools such as spelling tests, dictations, and so on, and informal tools such as student self-reports of literacy use outside of class, and observation of classroom behavior. Their discussion of the advantages and disadvantages of each mirrored the current debate about assessment in the field. They felt that informal tools yielded more accurate, varied, and realistic data as well as being more congruent with the pedagogical approach, but that their processes and format for collecting this data were not yet systematic.

In critiquing the tools, Interns mentioned that many of the tools were similar to what they already do in a rudimentary way, but much more explicit in terms of analysis of data. For example, they collect student writings in a portfolio but don't have a checklist for periodically analyzing the writings according to specified criteria. They especially liked assessment tools that include pictures, nonverbal formats, charts, and checklists because of their simplicity and because they allow for student self-evaluation. They disliked the more formal tools like the BEST test because the scoring was unclear and subjective, it was too difficult for beginning students, patronizing toward testers, and might make students feel bad; in general, they felt it was contrived and unrealistic. They also felt that some of the examples of alternative tools were too long and cumbersome for use with many students; they stressed the fact that teachers don't often have time for extensive written documentation. Overall, they seemed to like many of the formats of the tools they reviewed but wanted to adapt the content to fit the particular needs of their own groups. The specific formats they mentioned pursuing at the sites were: open-ended question format with space for anecdotal information, pictures, checklists, portfolios with checklists, and modified writing samples. They also mentioned utilizing these site-specific tools on a periodic basis (e.g., once a month) to get data more regularly.

The workshop ended with an air of excitement and energy; everyone felt they had gotten something out of it that they wanted to try at their sites. They commented that the workshop had helped them to visualize what they had been doing all along, and to imagine how to make it into a more coherent system. They came away wanting to spend more time at the sites developing something for future use. Of course, the biggest contradiction of this session was the fact that it came toward the end of the project. In retrospect, participants wished that this session had been earlier, so that they could have developed better systems for documenting student progress all along the way. At the same time, however, it was clear that they couldn't have made as much sense of this workshop and known how to interact with the tools critically without the base of experience developed through practice. It was through the process of reflecting back on practice and accumulated progress that they were able to determine which tools might be useful and how to adapt them.

References

The ABC's of ESL: Developing Literacy. 1988. Video in *Teacher To Teacher* series. Syracuse, NY: New Readers' Press.

Arnold, R., B. Burke, C. James, D. Martin and B. Thomas. 1991. *Education for a change.* Toronto: Between the Lines Press and Doris Marshall Institute for Education and Action.

Auerbach, E. 1992. *Making meaning, making change: Participatory curriculum development for adult ESL literacy.* Washington, DC, and McHenry, IL: Center for Applied Linguistics and Delta Systems.

Barndt, D. 1986. *English at work: A tool kit for teachers.* No. York, Ontario: Core Foundation.

Barndt, D. 1987. *Themes and tools for ESL: How to choose them and use them.* Toronto: Ministry of Citizenship, Province of Ontario.

Candlin, C. 1984. Syllabus design as critical process. In C. Brumfit (Ed.), *General English syllabus design.* Oxford: Pergamon Press, 29-46.

Cardenal, F. 1990. Special presentation, Literacy 2000. In *Literacy 2000, conference summary.* New Westminster, BC: Douglas College, 412-448.

Carrell, P. and J. Eisterhold. 1983. Schema theory and ESL reading pedagogy. *TESOL Quarterly,* 17(4), 553-573.

Collingham, M. 1988. Making use of students' linguistic resources. In S. Nicholls and E. Hoadley-Maidment (Eds.), *Current issues in teaching English as a second language to adults.* London: Edward Arnold, 81-85.

Cummins, J. 1981. The role of primary language development in promoting educational success for language minority students. In California State University, *Schooling and language minority students: A theoretical framework.* Los Angeles: California State Department of Education, 3-49.

D'Annunzio, A. 1991. Using bilingual tutors and non-directive approaches in ESL: A follow-up report. *Connections: A Journal of Adult Literacy,* 4, 51-52.

Freire, P. 1970. *Pedagogy of the oppressed.* New York: Seabury Press.

Freire, P. and D. Macedo. 1987. *Literacy: Reading the word and the world.* So. Hadley, MA: Bergin & Garvey.

Garcia, E. 1991. *Education of linguistically and culturally diverse students: Effective instructional practices.* Santa Cruz: National Center for Research on Cultural Diversity and Second Language Learning.

Gee, J. 1990. *Social linguistics and literacies: Ideology in discourses.* London: The Falmer Press.

Gephard, J. 1990. Interaction in a teaching practicum. In J. Richards and D. Nunan (Eds.), *Second language teacher education.* Cambridge: Cambridge University Press, 118-131.

Gillespie, M. and E. Ballering. 1992. *Adult native language literacy: A synthesis and plan for research and action* (draft). Washington, DC: The Center for Applied Linguistics.

Heath, S. 1983. *Ways with words.* Cambridge: Cambridge University Press.

Hemmindinger, A. 1987. *Two models for using problem-posing and cultural sharing in teaching the Hmong English as a second language and first language literacy.* Unpublished master's thesis, St. Francis Xavier University, Antigonish, Nova Scotia.

Hooper, R. 1992. Breaking the waiting list logjam: Training peer tutors for ESL. *All Write News* (Adult Literacy Resource Institute, Boston), 8(6), 1-4.

Hornberger, N. H. and J. Hardman. (1994). Literacy as cultural practice and cognitive skill: Biliteracy in a Cambodian adult ESL class and a Puerto Rican GED Program. In D. Spener (Ed.), *Adult biliteracy in the United States.* Washington, DC: Center for Applied Linguistics and Delta Systems.

Kazemek, F. 1988. Necessary changes: Professional involvement in adult literacy programs. *Harvard Educational Review,* 58(4), 464-487.

Klassen, C. 1991. Bilingual written language use by low-education Latin American newcomers. In D. Barton and R. Ivanic (Eds.), *Writing in the community.* Written Communication Annual (6). London: Sage, 38-57.

Knowles, M. 1984. *Andragogy in action.* San Francisco: Jossey-Bass.

Lytle, S. 1991. *Living literacy: Rethinking development in adulthood.* Unpublished manuscript, Philadelphia: University of Pennsylvania, Graduate School of Education.

Modiano, N. 1968. National or mother tongue in beginning reading: A comparative study. *Research in the Teaching of English,* 2, 32-43.

Nash, A., A. Cason, M. Rhum, L. McGrail and R. Gomez-Sanford. 1992. *Talking shop: A curriculum sourcebook for participatory adult ESL.* Washington, DC, and McHenry, IL: Center for Applied Linguistics and Delta Systems.

Ndaba, E. 1990. *I told myself I'm going to learn.* Johannesburg, South Africa: English Literacy Project.

Need I say more: A literary magazine of adult student writings. Boston, MA: Adult Literacy Resource Institute.

Nunan, D. 1988. *The learner-centred curriculum.* Cambridge: Cambridge University Press.

Phillipson, R. 1992. *Linguistic imperialism.* Oxford: Oxford University Press.

Reder, S. 1987. Comparative aspects of functional literacy development: Three ethnic American communities. In D. Wagner (Ed.), *The future of literacy in a changing world.* New York: Pergamon, 250-270.

Rivera, K. 1988. Not "either/or" but "and": Literacy for non-English speakers. *Focus on Basics,* 1(3/4), Spring/Summer, 1-3.

Rivera, K. 1990. *Developing native language literacy in language minority adult learners.* ERIC Digest, National Clearinghouse on Literacy Education, Center for Applied Linguistics.

Robson, B. 1982. Hmong literacy, formal education and their effects on performance in an ESL class. In B. Downing and O. Douglas (Eds.), *The Hmong in the West.* Minneapolis: Center for Urban and Regional Affairs, University of Minnesota.

Street, B. 1984. *Literacy in theory and practice.* Cambridge: Cambridge University Press.

Strei, G. 1992. Advantages of native language literacy programs: Pilot project. *TESOL Refugee Concerns Newsletter,* 7.

Tannen, D. 1982. *Spoken and written language.* Norwood, NJ: Ablex.

Taylor, D. and C. Dorsey-Gaines. 1988. *Growing up literate: Learning from inner-city families.* Portsmouth, NH: Heinemann.

Thonis, E. 1990. Who should teach language minority students? *Reading Today,* June/July, 19.

Vargas, A. 1986. *Illiteracy in the Hispanic community.* Report of the National Council of La Raza. Washington, DC: National Council of La Raza.

Voices: New writers for new readers. Surrey, BC: Invergarry Learning Centre.

Wallerstein, N. 1983. *Language and culture in conflict: Problem-posing in the ESL classroom.* Reading, MA: Addison-Wesley.

Wiley, T. G. 1990-1991. Disembedding Chicano literacy. *School of Education Journal,* 8(1), California State University, Long Beach, 49-54.

Resources for Training

Arnold, R., D. Barndt, and B. Burke. 1985. *A new weave: Popular education in Canada and Central America.* Toronto: CUSO Development Education and Ontario Institute for Studies in Education.

Arnold, R., B. Burke, C. James, D. Martin and B. Thomas. 1991. *Education for a change.* Toronto: Between the Lines Press and Doris Marshall Institute for Education and Action.

Association for Community-Based Education (ACBE). 1988. *Literacy for empowerment.* Washington, DC: ACBE.

Auerbach, E. 1992. *Making meaning, making change: Participatory curriculum development for adult ESL literacy.* Washington, DC, and McHenry, IL: Center for Applied Linguistics and Delta Systems.

Barndt, D. 1986. *English at work: A tool kit for teachers.* No. York, Ontario: Core Foundation.

Barndt, D. 1987. *Themes and tools for ESL: How to choose them and use them.* Toronto: Ministry of Citizenship, Province of Ontario.

Barndt, D. (no date). *Just getting there: Creating visual tools for collective analysis.* Toronto: Participatory Research Group.

Gillespie, M. 1990. *Many literacies: Modules for training adult beginning readers and tutors.* Amherst, MA: Center for International Education.

Goute Sèl. No date. (Haitian Creole literacy text - no bibliographic information available).

Group leader's notes: A guide for literacy teachers. 1988. Department of Adult Education and Extra-Mural Studies, University of Cape Town, Claremont, South Africa: David Philip, Publisher Ltd.

Hewitt, Lee et al. (no date). *Teachers' stories: Expanding the boundaries with the participatory approach.* Boston, MA: SABES.

Hope, A. and S. Timmel. 1988. *Training for transformation.* Giveru, Zimbabwe: Mambo Press.

Literacy promoter's handbook. 1987. SWAPO Literacy Campaign. London: Namibia Refugee Project.

Lytle, S. 1992. Staff development through practitioner research. *Connections.* National Center on Adult Literacy (NCAL) Newsletter. Philadelphia: University of Pennsylvania, 2.

Marshall, J. (no date). *Training for empowerment.* Toronto: International Council for Adult Education.

Nash, A., A. Cason, M. Rhum, L. McGrail and R. Gomez-Sanford. 1992. *Talking shop: A curriculum sourcebook for participatory adult ESL.* Washington, DC, and McHenry, IL: Center for Applied Linguistics and Delta Systems.

Study of ABE/ESL instructor training approaches. 1992. U.S. Department of Education. Washington, DC: Pelavin Associates, Inc.

Vella, J. 1989. *Learning to teach: Training of trainers for community development.* Washington, DC and Westport, CT: OEF International and Save the Children Federation.

Voices: New writers for new readers. Surrey, BC: Invergarry Learning Centre.

Wedepohl, L. 1988. *Learning from a literacy project.* Department of Adult Education and Extra-Mural Studies, University of Cape Town, Claremont, South Africa: David Philip, Publisher Ltd.

Witthaus, G. 1992. *A handbook for literacy teachers: Methods for teaching English literacy to adults.* Johannesburg, SA: English Literacy Project.